PRELUDE:
What If?

What if you were a Master Creator?

What if you were so good at creating, you could create anything you wanted from seemingly nothing at all?

What if you were so good at creation that you were famous for it?

What if you were so good at creation, creating started becoming dull? Although you had the admiration of world after world (some of which you helped create), you began to miss the challenge you felt earlier in your creative career.

What if you had a chance to relive the thrill of victory and the agony of defeat you so enjoyed at some former time and place?

So, Master Creator that you are, you created a button marked "Greater Challenge."

You considered all that might be contained in the concept of "Greater Challenge," decided "Greater Challenge" would probably provide some of the excitement and satisfaction you missed from your apprentice days, took a deep breath, pushed the button . . .

. . . and found yourself where you are right now, feeling what you're feeling now, thinking what you're thinking now, with everything in your life precisely the way it is now, reading this book.

Men are born to succeed,
not to fail.

HENRY DAVID THOREAU

DO IT!
Let's Get Off Our Buts

Peter McWilliams

This book is available on unabridged
audio-cassette tapes, read by the author.

Prelude Press

8159 Santa Monica Boulevard
Los Angeles, California 90046

1-800-LIFE-101

ISBN: 0-931580-63-3

Editor: Jean Sedillos
Desktop publishing: Carol Taylor & Todd Charleville
Production: Paurvi Trivedi

*I might repeat to myself,
slowly and soothingly,
a list of quotations beautiful
from minds profound—
if I can remember
any of the damn things.*

Dorothy Parker

Contents

PART TWO
BUILT FOR SUCCESS
(programmed for failure, perhaps, but)
BUILT FOR SUCCESS

PART FOUR
BECOMING PASSIONATE ABOUT YOUR DREAM

PART FIVE

PART SIX

APPENDIX
SELECTIONS FROM OTHER BOOKS
BY PETER McWILLIAMS

*Regret for the things we did
can be tempered by time;
it is regret
for the things we did not do
that is inconsolable.*

Sydney J. Harris

DO IT!
Let's Get Off Our Buts

*Properly, we should
read for power.
Man reading should be
man intensely alive.
The book should be
a ball of light
in one's hand.*

EZRA POUND

INTRODUCTION:
How Do You Do?

We all have a dream, a heart's desire. Most have more than one. Some of us have an entire entourage. This is a book of practical suggestions for discovering (or rediscovering) those dreams, choosing which ones to pursue, and achieving them.

There's a lot of good news about our dreams:

- By pursuing any *one* of our dreams, we can find fulfillment. We don't need to pursue them all.

- We don't have to *achieve* a dream in order to find fulfillment—we need only actively *pursue* the dream to attain satisfaction.

- By living our dream, we can contribute not only to ourselves, but to everyone and everything around us.

And yet, with all this good news, most people are not pursuing their dreams.

When we're not pursuing our dreams, we spend our time and abilities pursuing the things we *think* will make us happy, the things we *believe* will bring us fulfillment: the new house, the new car, the new cashmere jump suit.

There's an old saying: "You can't get enough of what you don't really want." When the new car doesn't make us happy, we tend to blame the new car for not being "enough," and set our

> *I stopped believing in Santa Claus*
> *when my mother took me*
> *to see him in a department store,*
> *and he asked for my autograph.*
>
> SHIRLEY TEMPLE

sights on a "better" new car. Surely *that* will make us happy.

Many people are so far away from living their dream that *they have forgotten what their dream truly is.*

It is sad. It is unnecessary. It is wasteful. And yet, it's so common an ailment that it's become a cliché. We have abandoned our heart's desire—and somewhere, deep down, we know it. Even if we don't remember quite what it is—we miss it.

Why aren't we living our dreams?

Because there is something we are trained to honor more than our dreams: the comfort zone.

The comfort zone is all the things we have done often enough to feel comfortable doing again.

Whenever we do something new, it falls outside the confines of the comfort zone. In even *contemplating* a new action, we feel fear, guilt, unworthiness, hurt feelings, and/or anger—all those emotions we generally think of as "uncomfortable."

When we feel uncomfortable enough long enough, we tend to feel discouraged (a form of exhaustion), and we return to thoughts, feelings, and actions that are more familiar, more practiced, more predictable—more, well, *comfortable.*

The irony is that the feelings we have been taught to label "uncomfortable" are, in fact, among the very tools necessary to fulfill our dreams. As it turns out, the bricks used to build the walls of the comfort zone are made of gold.

Why don't we know this?

The training we received as children—which, for the most part, is appropriate for children—is not appropriate for adults. What is useful for a dependent, limited child can be counterproductive for an independent, productive adult. As adults, we live our life as though it were a bicycle with the training wheels still in place—limiting, entirely *too* safe, and somewhat boring.

We no longer believe in Santa Claus, but we still believe that "being uncomfortable" is reason enough not to do something new. The Easter Bunny hopped out of our lives years ago, yet we still let "what other people might think" affect our behavior. The tooth fairy was yanked from our consciousness long before adolescence, but we still feel we can justify any personal failure by blaming someone or something outside ourselves.

> *There are some people*
> *that if they don't know,*
> *you can't tell 'em.*
>
> Louis Armstrong

Most people are drifting along in a childish sleep. To live our dreams, we must wake up.

In reading that last sentence, did you feel your comfort zone being challenged? If I do my job, that will happen a lot in this book. That tingling we feel when we contemplate waking up and living our dreams we can label either "fear" or "excitement." No matter what we call it, it's the same feeling. If we call it fear, it's an uncomfortable feeling, and we tend to find reasons not to read any further. If we call it excitement, we turn it into energy that makes the process of learning and doing an active, enjoyable one.

It's your choice. It's always your choice. The trouble is, many of us have delegated that choice to habits formed long ago, formed when we knew far less about life than we know now. We let habits from when we were two or four or six or ten or fifteen years old control our lives today.

To change a habit requires work. Make no mistake about it: reading this book will not change your life, just as reading a guidebook to France will not show you France. It may give you a *sense* of France, but France is France and can only be experienced through *action*.

And so it is with your dreams. This book will show you *how* to discover your dreams, *how* to select the dreams you choose to pursue, and *how* to fulfill those dreams—but if you don't *act* upon those *hows*, you will never see Paris from atop the Eiffel Tower.

Although fulfilling our dreams requires *work*, the process can also be *fun*. Which reminds me of a joke. I heard it at, of all places, Disneyland.

An Indian chief greeted a friend by raising his hand in the traditional salute and saying, "Chance!"

"Chance?" his friend asked, "You must mean 'How!'"

"I know how," the chief responded, "I'm looking for chance."

If you like, this book can be your chance—a chance *you* are giving *yourself*. Imagine for a moment that you are powerful enough to have had this book written *just for you*. When you get a sense of that power, you'll know that you have all it takes to fulfill your dream. *Any* dream. *Your* dream.

> *If you're not playing*
> *a big enough game,*
> *you'll screw up*
> *the game you're playing*
> *just to give yourself*
> *something to do.*

F. Scott Fitzgerald met Joan Crawford at a Hollywood party. He told her that he had been hired to write the screenplay for her next film. She looked him straight in the eye and said, "Write hard, Mr. Fitzgerald, write hard."

Imagine that I am looking you straight in the eye and saying, "Dream big, dear reader, dream big."

The truth is, pursuing a Big Dream of your own choosing is the same amount of work as gathering more and more of the things you don't really want. You're going to spend the rest of your life doing *something*—it might as well be something *you* want to do.

"But what about money? But what about time? But what about this? But what about that?" I'll get to all that (and all this, too). There are a lot of *buts* to "get off" before we can even *consider* living our dreams.

Let's bring this Introduction to a close by answering the question I posed at the beginning: "How do you do?"

That's easy. You do by learning.

"Great. And how do you learn?"

You learn by doing.

A chicken-and-egg conundrum, to be sure; yet one that can easily be penetrated by this deceptively simple thought: "The willingness to do creates the ability to do."

For now, simply be *willing* to do. Be willing to do what it takes to read this book. That takes the willingness to finish this page and turn to the next. That takes the willingness to finish this paragraph. That takes the willingness to finish this sentence (which you have just done).

Where does the willingness come from?

From you.

As Joni Mitchell pointed out, "It all comes down to you."

I certainly agree, and would only add, "It all comes down to *do.*"

"Let's go."
"Yes, let's go."
STAGE DIRECTION:
They do not move.

Last Lines of *Waiting for Godot*
Samuel Beckett

PART ONE

WHY WE'RE NOT
LIVING OUR DREAMS

You may find this first part of the book depressing. I'm going to explain why most people aren't living their dreams—and I'm not going to pull any punches.

It's not a pretty picture.

The reason we aren't living our dreams is *inside ourselves*. We *pretend* it's people, things, and situations *outside ourselves* that are to blame.

On the other hand, you may find this an uplifting section. You may say, "So *that's* why that happens!"

Further, when we know that the *cause* of something is in ourselves, and that we (ourselves) are one of the few things in this universe that we have the right and the ability to change, we begin to get a sense of the choices we really do have, an inkling of the power we have, a feeling of being in charge—of our lives, of our future, of our dreams.

Pithy quote to come.

This Was Going to Be a Truly Great Opening Chapter, But . . .

This was going to be the best opening chapter you could possibly imagine, but so many things got in the way.

I was going to spend lots of time writing it, but, well, you know how time goes!

I was going to get lots of touching and poignant and humorous examples of people not getting things done, but I never got around to interviewing the people.

I was going to gather lots of wonderful quotes to illustrate my points, but I left the quote book at home, and this chapter is being written at a lecture hall outside Carmel, California. (Besides, I think the dog ate it.)

I was going to make sure that this chapter was so informative, so readable, and so wonderful that if you were reading it in a bookstore, you'd buy the book, or, if you were reading it in a library, you'd check it out, or, if you were reading it at home, you'd decide, "Boy, I'm certainly going to enjoy reading *this* book!" but I decided to watch this movie on TV last night, and I was going to work on the chapter afterward, but then I went out for ice cream, and I was tired, and decided to start fresh in the morning, but then I slept late, and then I went out for breakfast and took a drive past an aquarium and decided to stop in, then I went for lunch, and then thought I'd take a nap and start fresh in the

note:
find
quote

evening, but then I started watching a documentary on TV, then, of course, it was time for dinner, then I was invited to the movies, and I don't want to be rude to my friends, and besides I sort-of wanted to see the movie anyway, then I was going to go right back and work on this chapter, but then I remembered how good the ice cream was the night before . . .

If this
page goes to press
without a quote,
it will be
<u>*most*</u> *embarrassing.*

Do or do not.
There is no try.

Y<small>ODA</small>

But

But—that three-letter, four-letter word. It permeates our language. It's a nasty little word. It allows us to lie to ourselves and to severely limit ourselves without even knowing it. Let's look at a typical sentence containing "but."

"I want to visit my sick grandmother, but it's too cold outside."

"But" usually means: "Ignore all that good-sounding stuff that went before—here comes the truth." You might even consider BUT as an acronym for Behold the Underlying Truth. (And Buts can be shortened to BS.)

The truth is that grandma is not getting a visit. The lie is that I *care* so much about my sick grandmother that I *really want to* pay her a visit. (Note my *sensitivity* to her need for visitation, and my *compassion* for wanting to visit her.)

At this point, entering stage right, are two of *but's* dearest friends—*if only* and *try*.

"*If only* it were a fine spring day, I'd be into the woods and on my way to Grandmother's house. *If only* it weren't so darn *cold*, I'd be at Granny's side right now. I'm going to *try* to get there tomorrow!"

Unless, of course, we are too busy, too poor, too tired, too _____ (please fill in the blank with one of your favorites), or perhaps not feeling all that good ourselves.

But even if we and everything else were fine and dandy, let's not forget the about the *wolves* . . .

*Success is simply
a matter of luck.
Ask any failure.*

EARL WILSON

Yes-But

The naked "but" is what we use when ignoring our own good advice. When ignoring the unbearably good advice of others, we use the hyphenated version: "yes-but."

"You really should pay your car insurance."

"Yes-but, I don't get paid until next week."

"You could get an advance on your credit card."

"Yes-but, I owe so much already."

"You have no insurance!"

"Yes-but, I'll drive *real careful.*"

And on and on.

When we argue for our limitations, we get to keep them. *Yes-but* means, "Here come the arguments for my limitations." Or, if you favor acronyms, YES-BUT = "Your Evaluation is Superb—Behold the Underlying Truth."

The only activity more foolish than a person pouring forth a stream of "yes-buts" is the person who continues to give good advice in the face of obvious indifference.

"Yes-but, I thought if I tried *just once more,* it might be the bit of wisdom that would *make the difference.*

Uh huh. As Jesus of Nazareth said, "Give not that which is holy unto the dogs, neither cast ye your pearls before swine, lest they trample them under their feet, and turn again and rend you" (Matthew 7:6).

"Ouch."

Results!
Why, man,
I have gotten a lot of results.
I know several thousand
things that won't work.

THOMAS A. EDISON

Reasons or Results

In life, we have either reasons or results—excuses or experiences, stories or successes.

We either have what we want, or we have iron-clad, airtight, impenetrable reasons why it was not even *marginally possible* to get it.

We use one of the most powerful tools *at* our disposal—the mind—*for* our disposal. Rather than dispose of the barriers to our dreams, the mind disposes of the *dreams.*

In the amount of time it takes for the mind to invent a good excuse, the mind could have created an alternate way of achieving the result—rendering excuse-making unnecessary.

But, alas, as John Kenneth Galbraith pointed out, "In the choice between changing one's mind and proving there's no need to do so, most people get busy on the proof."

While I'm on the subject of the mind, allow me to give the mind something to ponder—a premise I'll be considering throughout the book . . .

It is hard to fight an enemy
who has outposts in your head.

Sally Kempton

We Live the Life We Choose

Here's the premise: We are all, right now, living the life we choose.

This choice, of course, is not a single, monumental choice. No one decides, for example, "I'm going to move to L.A., and in five years I will be a waiter in a so-so restaurant, planning to get my 8-by-10's done real soon so that I can find an agent and become a star," or "I'm going to marry a dreadful person and we'll live together in a loveless marriage, staying together only for the kids, who I don't much like, either."

No. The choices I'm talking about here are made daily, hourly, moment by moment.

Do we try something new, or stick to the tried-and-true? Do we take a risk, or eat what's already on our dish? Do we ponder a thrilling adventure, or contemplate what's on TV? Do we walk over and meet that interesting stranger, or do we play it safe? Do we indulge our heart, or cater to our fear?

The bottom-line question: Do we pursue what we want, or do we do what's comfortable?

For the most part, most people most often choose comfort—the familiar, the time-honored, the well-worn but well-known. After a lifetime of choosing between comfort and risk, we are left with the life we currently have.

And it was all of our own choosing.

*The only thing I can't stand
is discomfort.*

GLORIA STEINEM

The Comfort Zone

The comfort zone is our arena of thoughts and actions within which we feel comfortable—all the things we've done (or thought) often enough to feel comfortable doing (or thinking) again. Anything we haven't done (or thought) often enough to feel comfortable doing lies outside the parameters of the comfort zone. When we do (or think) these things (basically, anything new) we feel uncomfortable.*

For example, most people reading this book find little difficulty reading English—it's within their comfort zone. But how comfortable are you at reading code? Here's a sentence in code:

Dpohsbuvmbujpot! Zpv'wf kvtu dsbdlfe uif dpef!

Can you crack the code? Each of the letters stands for another letter in the alphabet. They are arranged in a logical way so that when you know the code, you'll be able to decipher the sentence. What does the sentence say?

How do you feel? Uncomfortable? Overwhelmed? Have you given up? Did you give up before even starting? What if I told you there was $100,000 riding on solving the puzzle? In addition to *money*, what if you had to solve it *on television?* And,

---

*For the purpose of simplicity, while talking about the comfort zone, when I mention "actions," assume I've included "thoughts," too. It will save cluttering up the next few chapters with several hundred "(or thoughts)."

> *We act as though comfort*
> *and luxury were*
> *the chief requirements of life,*
> *when all that we need*
> *to make us happy*
> *is something*
> *to be enthusiastic about.*
>
> CHARLES KINGSLEY

in addition to that, what if there were a *time limit* imposed? Say, three minutes. What if something *really bad* were to happen to someone you love if you couldn't crack the code in three minutes? What if he or she were *really counting on you?*

How do you feel? If you played along with my questions, you probably felt some tinges of fear, guilt, unworthiness, hurt feelings, and/or anger— the feelings I lump into the general category of *uncomfortable*.

After feeling uncomfortable enough long enough, we tend to feel discouraged; we give up. Some people gave up before they even began. They were permanently discouraged about word puzzles. They told themselves, "I'm no good at this sort of thing," and skipped to the next paragraph. Unfortunately, there I was in the next paragraph—waiting for them—reminding them of the puzzle—making them feel uncomfortable.

Other people, who love puzzles, jumped right in. They weren't uncomfortable; they were *challenged*. They hung in there, and some of them solved it (and are now wondering how they can collect the $100,000 prize). Perhaps the "doers" felt the same emotion the uncomfortable felt—that tingling we feel when rising to a challenge—and labeled it "excitement" instead of "fear." Maybe they *used* that energy to help solve the puzzle.

Okay. Try again. This time I'll give you a clue: The first letter is a C.

Dpohsbuvmbujpot! Zpv'wf kvtu dsbdlfe uif dpef!

Compare the relationship between C and the first letter of the puzzle (D) and see if you can see a pattern. If you see one, try it on the next several letters and see if something approaching a word emerges. If not, look for another pattern.

Some people are now actively involved in the process of figuring it out. Others are still saying, "I can't do these things." As Henry Ford said, "If you think you can do a thing or think you can't do a thing, you're right." If we say we can't do something, we don't spend any time on it; therefore we can't. A self-fulfilling prophecy.

So, if you're still in the "can't" category, switch it around. Tell yourself, out loud, "I *can* solve this!" Become involved. Invest a little *time* in the process. "The willingness to do creates the ability to do."

> *You have to leave*
> *the city of your comfort*
> *and go into the wilderness*
> *of your intuition.*
> *What you'll discover*
> *will be wonderful.*
> *What you'll discover*
> *will be yourself.*
>
> ALAN ALDA

Give yourself the willingness. (A pencil might help, too.)

What is the relationship between C and D? Where have you seen them together before? Where are they *always* together, one right after the other?

Dpohsbuvmbujpot! Zpv'wf kvtu dsbdlfe uif dpef!

Another clue? ("I'd like to buy a vowel, please.") The second letter is O. What's the relationship between O and P? It's the same relationship as between C and D. ("Living together, no children.")

Most people have, of course, figured it out by now. (There. Does *that* make you feel uncomfortable? Those who haven't figured it out don't like to think they're *behind* most people, and those who have figured it out don't like to be thought of as "most people.")

My final clue: the alphabet. The alphabet looks like this:

ABCDEFGHIJKLMNOPQRSTUVWXYZ

Now, can you see the relationship between C and D and between O and P? Apply that to the other letters of the puzzle and see what you get. Congratulations! You've just cracked the code!

You'll note that when you move *past* your comfort zone you find adventure, excitement, satisfaction, and the answer to some questions you may never have known to ask before.

How often have you heard someone say, "I don't want to do that; I feel uncomfortable"? It is a *given*—for most people an *accepted fact*—*that being uncomfortable is sufficient reason for not doing.*

The primary sensations we encounter when approaching the "walls" of the comfort zone are fear, guilt, unworthiness, hurt feelings, and anger. When feeling any one—or, especially, a combination of them—we say we're uncomfortable. After tilting the windmills of our comfort zone for a time, we tend to feel discouraged—and discouragement is the primary barrier to living our dreams.

Let's take a closer look at fear, guilt, unworthiness, hurt feelings, anger, and discouragement. (Just what you wanted, huh?)

HOW TO BEHAVE IN AN ELEVATOR

1. *Face forward.*
2. *Fold hands in front.*
3. *Do not make eye contact.*
4. *Watch the numbers.*
5. *Don't talk to anyone you don't know.*
6. *Stop talking with anyone
   you do know when anyone
   you don't know enters the elevator.*
7. *Avoid brushing bodies.*

LAYNE LONGFELLOW

Fear

We all know fear. It is probably the most common limiting emotion—and, for many people, the most common emotion, *period*. As Shakespeare pointed out, we are often "distilled almost to jelly with the act of fear."

Not only do we fear new things; we also feel fear *in addition to* other negative emotions. We feel guilt, *and we're afraid to feel the guilt*. We feel pain, *and we're afraid to feel the pain*. Even when we feel fear, we're often afraid to feel the fear. (That's known as "worrying about your worries," "an anxiety attack," or "the screaming meemies.") Shakespeare, again: "Of all base passions, fear is the most accursed."

Because it's so common, fear has many other names: apprehension, misgiving, trepidation, dread, horror, phobia, terror, alarm, consternation, foreboding, qualm, suspicion, fret, uneasiness, distress, panic, worry.

Physically, we tend to feel fear in the area we generally call the stomach. Although it's lower than the biological stomach (more in the area of the lower abdomen), for the sake of locating fear—and going along with the popular use of the word—I'll define "the stomach" as a large, circular area with the navel at its center.

In its more intense forms, the feeling of fear is accompanied by a quickening of the pulse, a widening of the eyes, and a sharpening of the senses.

Someone once described FEAR in an acronym: False Expectations Appearing Real. For the most

> *The thing I fear most is fear.*
> MICHEL EYQUEM DE MONTAIGNE
> 1580

> *Nothing is terrible except fear itself.*
> FRANCIS BACON
> 1623

> *The only thing I am afraid of is fear.*
> DUKE OF WELLINGTON
> ("THE IRON DUKE")
> 1831

> *Nothing is so much to be feared as fear.*
> HENRY DAVID THOREAU
> 1841

part, what we fear is not real—it is merely our mind *imagining* something awful that has not yet happened. ("Fear is pain arising from the anticipation of evil," Aristotle said.)

Seldom do we do the thing we fear, so we seldom discover whether or not our projection of disaster was accurate. In fact, when we *don't* do the thing we are afraid of, we breathe a sigh of relief *as though it actually would have taken place.* "That was a *close* one!" we say, even though we never actually got *close* to anything but a string of our own negative thoughts.

Fear breeds lack of experience; lack of experience breeds ignorance *(ignore*-ance); ignorance breeds more fear. It is a vicious circle.

As Lucretius described it more than two centuries ago, "For as children tremble and fear everything in the blind darkness, so we in the light sometimes fear what is no more to be feared than the things children in the dark hold in terror and imagine will come true."

Put another way: fear is interest paid on a debt you may not owe.

When we feel fear, we look around for something *to* fear. Considering all there is to look at (the media, the environment, our body, our memory, our imagination), we have little trouble finding *something*. The fear grows, our perception of the world darkens, and it becomes an increasingly terrible place.

Sophocles (fifth century B.C.) knew this when he wrote, "To him who is in fear, everything rustles."

Eventually, we begin to avoid all things and thoughts that even *might* produce fear, or that *might* produce the fear of fear, or that *might* produce the fear of fear of fear. It becomes a many-layered fortress—fear defending fear defending fear defending fear—and inside: nothing.

It is one of the great jokes of existence. When people have the courage to journey into the center of their fear, they find—*nothing*. The terror was only layers of fear, being afraid of itself.

This realization is either tragic or comic—often both. People are often seen laughing and crying si-

> *Fear is the main source*
> *of superstition,*
> *and one of the main sources*
> *of cruelty.*
> *To conquer fear is*
> *the beginning of wisdom.*
>
> Bertrand Russell

multaneously. The unenlightened nearby may fear that the newly enlightened have gone mad.

When unreal fears become extreme, it's known as *paranoia*. As Tennessee Williams warned an interviewer, "I'm a paranoiac, baby, so I hope you don't make the mistake of laboring under the false impression that you are talking to a sane person."

Anytime we let unreal fears (and that includes untested fears) keep us from moving toward our dreams, it is a form of madness.

If the madness makes us furious, that might not be so bad: "To be furious is to be frightened out of fear." (Shakespeare, yet again.) But for most, the insanity of fear only produces discomfort and inaction.

And more fear.

Fear is that little darkroom
where negatives are developed.

MICHAEL PRITCHARD

Hail to you gods,
On that day of the great reckoning.
Behold me, I have come to you,
Without sin, without guilt, without evil,
Without a witness against me,
Without one whom I have wronged.
I am one pure of mouth, pure of hands.

THE BOOK OF THE DEAD
THE ADDRESS TO THE GODS
1700–1000 B.C. (NOT USED IN SEVERAL
CENTURIES—OBVIOUSLY)

We find the defendants incredibly guilty.

THE FOREMAN RETURNING THE VERDICT
ON ZERO MOSTEL AND GENE WILDER
IN MEL BROOKS'S THE PRODUCERS

Guilt

Guilt is the anger we feel toward ourselves when we think we do something "wrong." The trouble is, most of us haven't explored what *we* think is truly "right" and "wrong" in years—maybe ever.

Even if we *have* explored our own sense of right and wrong, often we *still* feel guilty for things we don't personally think are wrong. It's a habit. So, even if we know that kind of guilt is a waste of time, we feel it anyway. Then we feel guilty about *that*.

Guilt is something we get so *clever* about. We always seem to be able to find subtler and subtler levels of self-judgment. "The only reason I still feel guilty about masturbation," David Steinberg said, "is that I do it so badly."

The process of limitation and immobility is *fear before* we do something new, and *guilt after*. (Maybe that's why they're both felt in the stomach area.) Guilt is the remorse—the shame, the regret—we feel at having done something "different." We feel so bad we promise ourselves, "I'll never do that again!" even if it's the very thing we need to do, over and over again.

When we've had enough blaming ourselves, we often find someone or something else to blame— "The devil made me do it" in all its various forms. In addition to purging the offending *action* from our lives, we also promise to avoid the person (situation, thing, etc.) that "caused" our "downfall."

> *Last night at twelve*
> *I felt immense,*
> *But now I feel like thirty cents.*
>
> GEORGE ADE
>
> 1902

And so our circle of activity becomes smaller and smaller. The comfort zone closes in.

Guilt is tricky. It's not always a deep, painful feeling—a desperate need for atonement. It has other methods. It can, for example, rewrite the *memory* of an experience. We may do something new, enjoy doing it (or the result of doing it), and guilt will actually convince us that we *didn't like it* (or got nothing from it).

We can say to someone, "I'm not going to do that again; I didn't really like it," and *believe it*—although, in fact, the experience itself (not the fear before the experience or the guilt after, but the *actual experience*) was enjoyable (or profitable).

Keep in mind I'm not talking about hurting yourself or others. I'm talking about the guilt we feel when we do something new (submitting a manuscript to a publisher, say, or taking a high school equivalency test) and fail. Although we learned something from the failure, guilt steps in and convinces us, "The lesson wasn't worth the cost."

I'm also talking about feeling uneasy about trying something new and *succeeding*. Remember that guilt is not rational. Many of us have irrational beliefs that we should not be *too* successful.

"Who do you think you are?" guilt asks, "Someone special? What's wrong with the way things are? You have no *appreciation*. Why can't you fit in? Why do you always have to do it *your way*? Can't you learn to *cooperate*?" And on and on.

It's guilt's job to make us feel bad when we violate even a *limiting* belief about ourselves. A limiting belief such as unworthiness, for example.

(More about guilt on page 383, "Guilt (again).")

You have no idea
what a poor opinion
I have of myself—
and how little I deserve it.

W. S. GILBERT

Unworthiness

Unworthiness is the deep-seated belief that tells us we're undeserving, not good enough, inadequate, fundamentally deficient.

It's the primal doubt we feel in the pit of our stomach when we consider living a dream. "Don't try it," unworthiness warns. "Don't even *think* about it."

And so, we don't even think about it. Our mind goes off on one distraction after another—*anything* rather than having to face even the *possibility* of our own elemental inadequacy.

Of all the components of the comfort zone, unworthiness is the most hideous, and therefore, the most hidden—especially from ourselves. We can stand feeling *bad,* but to feel that we are lacking even the most meager spark of goodness—that we are condemned to never have what we truly want, *and that we deserve that condemnation*—is beyond pain and terror; it's unthinkable.

We don't want to know that there's even a *possibility* that what unworthiness says is true. We camouflage and cover and avoid any thought about our unworthiness. We act *as if* we *might* be unworthy, which, eventually, convinces us that it *must* be true—otherwise, why would we spend so much time *pretending* we're good and *pretending* we're happy and *pretending* we're worthy? It seems we'll quickly abandon the thought of fulfilling a dream as long as we can momentarily calm the center, comfort the Doubt of Doubts.

I grew up to have my father's looks,
my father's speech patterns,
my father's posture,
my father's opinions,
and my mother's contempt for my father.

JULES FEIFFER

My vigor, vitality and cheek repel me.
I am the kind of woman I would run from.

NANCY, LADY ASTOR

Physically, unworthiness resides in the area of the solar plexus—an area just below the breast bone where the rib cage forms an inverted "V." In some Eastern traditions, they call this the center of *Chi,* a fundamental point for focusing energy and moving ahead in life. Unworthiness inhibits that energy.

As Abraham Lincoln pointed out, "It is difficult to make a man miserable while he feels he is worthy of himself and claims kindred to the great God who made him."

Paraphrasing Lincoln in the negative (which is what unworthiness always does): "It is easy to make a man miserable while he feels he is unworthy of himself and not good enough to claim kindred to the great God who made him."

When reading "Be free, all worthy spirits, and stretch yourselves, for greatness and for height," (George Chapman, 1608), unworthiness says, in what seems our own voice, "That obviously doesn't apply to me."

When offered something we really want, unworthiness says, "No, I couldn't."

One of the most popular of unworthiness's comments, however, is, upon hearing of our own good fortune, "I don't believe it! That's too good to be true!" It's often spoken with such enthusiasm—and such self-limitation—that the good that's "unbelievable" soon disappears.

Unworthiness can destroy relationships. When we don't feel worthy, we can't love ourselves—how can we love ourselves knowing our Dark Secret? And all the games we play to cover the unworthiness—how insincere, how phony, how deceptive we are. No, we are not worthy of our love.

If someone loves us, we sometimes resent that person—how can we respect anyone who falls for the facade we slapped together so haphazardly and manipulate so desperately? Anyone loving us must be easily deceived, and not worthy of our attention. Conversely, the people who dislike us we might (sometimes secretly) admire—they must be very wise to see to the truth of our very being.

Unworthiness is the foundation of the comfort zone.

I buy women shoes,
and they use them
to walk away from me.

MICKEY ROONEY

Hurt Feelings and Anger

How much closer to living our dreams we'd be if everyone who ever promised us something delivered. How much fuller our lives would be if, any time we asked people for something, they would give it to us. When we don't get what we want from others, when they fail to keep their promises, when they let us down, we often have hurt feelings.

Even deeper (and more frequent) are the times we have let *ourselves* down. How much greater are our imagination and desires than our physical abilities to fulfill them.

The result of all this letdown is often hurt feelings—sadness, loss, grief.

In our bodies, hurt feelings are usually felt in the center of the chest, in the area most people refer to as the heart. (As with the stomach, it's not located directly over the physical heart, but close.)

A common "cover-up" for hurt is anger. We blame whatever or whoever let us down, and we get *steamed*. ("How *dare* you!" "Why *didn't* you?") Some people have anger as the *automatic response* to disappointment. In almost all cases, however, hurt is just underneath.

After enough hurt and anger, people tend to decide, "I'm not going to do anything that causes me any more pain." That would, of course, include any dream-fulfillment behavior that includes asking people (including ourselves) for things—some of which we'll get, and some of which (let's be honest: *most* of which) we won't.

*Do not be too timid
and squeamish
about your actions.
All life is an experiment.*

RALPH WALDO EMERSON

Discouragement

Over time, the result of all this fear, guilt, unworthiness, hurt feelings, and anger is discouragement.

There is a story told of Beelzebub, who had a meeting with a few of his sub-Beelzebubs (subbubs). Beelzebub asked for ideas on the best way to keep people constantly frustrated by not being able to follow their dreams. All sorts of physical barriers were suggested by the subbubs, but Beelzebub rejected them all, citing examples of human beings overcoming one physical obstacle after another.

Finally, one of the subbubs suggested something that would keep human beings from even *attempting* to overcome the barriers between themselves and their dreams—*discouragement*. It was such a profound and innovative idea that Beelzebub put this subbub in charge of Strategic Planning to Make Humans Even More Miserable. Since that time, this subbub has invented, among other things, elevator music, tamper-resistant packaging, and commercials in movie theaters.

It's hard to imagine anything more pernicious—and effective—than discouragement. Discouragement promotes inaction, and inaction guarantees failure—a life of not living our dreams.

Baby elephants are heavily chained to stakes driven deep in the ground. Pull as they might, they remain firmly tethered. Soon, the baby elephant becomes discouraged and stops pulling. It learns to stay put. Over time, the trainer uses lighter and lighter restraints. Eventually, a small rope attached

Don't ask the barber
whether you need
a haircut.

DANIEL S. GREENBERG

to a stick barely anchored in the earth is sufficient to stop a fully grown elephant from moving.

In a sense, discouragement makes us all like elephants. Although we, as adults, have the power we didn't have as children to pursue our dreams, discouragement keeps us from using it.

If you cannot catch
a bird of paradise,
better take
a wet hen.

NIKITA KHRUSCHEV

Why should we
take up farming
when there are
so many mongongo nuts
in the world?

AFRICAN BUSHMAN

Intermission

This section on the comfort zone is becoming *uncomfortable*. All these elements of the comfort zone *do* have a positive side. I'll discuss that in Part Two. In this part I'm talking about how people use these tools to limit themselves. It's not easy to write about, and it might not be easy to read about, but imagine how uneasy it is to continue *living* it.

So, I thought I would pause here and take a breather before going on.

Let's see . . . with what shall we take a breather? What fun things do I have lying around here? Ah, quotes!

> Quotations are comfortable.—*The author*

> Life is like a dogsled team. If you ain't the lead dog, the scenery never changes.— *Lewis Grizzard*

> I've always thought that the stereotype of the dirty old man is really the creation of a dirty young man who wants the field to himself.—*Hugh Downs*

> Father, each of your sermons is better than the next.—*Anonymous churchgoer*

> Destiny is not a matter of chance; it is a matter of choice. It is not a thing to be waited for; it is a thing to be achieved. — *William Jennings Bryan*

> The denunciation of the young is a necessary part of the hygiene of older people, and greatly assists the circulation of the blood.—*Logan Pearsall Smith*

> *I don't want any*
> *yes-men around me.*
> *I want everybody*
> *to tell me the truth*
> *even if it costs them their jobs.*
>
> SAMUEL GOLDWYN

Eighty percent of success is showing up.—*Woody Allen*

Almost every man wastes part of his life in attempts to display qualities which he does not possess.—*Samuel Johnson*

Once you accept your own death all of a sudden you're free to live. You no longer care about your reputation. You no longer care except so far as your life can be used tactically—to promote a cause you believe in.—*Saul Alinsky*

It matters not whether you win or lose; what matters is whether *I* win or lose.—*Darin Weinberg*

My idea of an agreeable person is a person who agrees with me.—*Benjamin Disraeli*

Good behavior is the last refuge of mediocrity.—*Henry S. Haskins*

God is really only another artist. He invented the giraffe, the elephant, the ant. He has no real style. He just goes on trying other things.—*Pablo Picasso*

Not as bad as you might have imagined.— *Motto suggested for New Jersey by Calvin Trillin*

Having your book turned into a movie is like seeing your oxen turned into bouillon cubes.— *John LeCarre*

I've been promoted to middle management. I never thought I'd sink so low.—*Tim Gould*

Condoms aren't completely safe. A friend of mine was wearing one and got hit by a bus.— *Bob Rubin*

A "Bay Area Bisexual" told me I didn't quite coincide with either of her desires.—*Woody Allen*

Your request for no MSG was ignored.— *Fortune cookie*

Advice to expectant mothers: you must remember that when you are pregnant, you are eating for two. But you must remember that the other one of you is about the size of a golf ball, so let's not go overboard with it. I mean, a lot of pregnant women eat as though the other person they're eating for is Orson Welles.— *Dave Barry*

Life is to be lived. If you have to support yourself, you had bloody well better find some way that is going to be interesting. And you don't do that by sitting around wondering about yourself.—*Katherine Hepburn*

> *Cats are intended to teach us*
> *that not everything in nature*
> *has a function.*
>
> GARRISON KEILLOR

When I can no longer bear to think of the victims of broken homes, I begin to think of the victims of intact ones.—*Peter De Vries*

When I played pro football, I never set out to hurt anybody deliberately—unless it was, you know, important, like a league game or something.—*Dick Butkus*

I'm not a vegetarian because I love animals; I'm a vegetarian because I hate plants.—*A. Whitney Brown*

If at first you don't succeed, find out if the loser gets anything.—*Bill Lyon*

My wife and I were happy for twenty years. Then we met.—*Rodney Dangerfield*

Please give me
some good advice
in your next letter.
I promise not to follow it.

EDNA ST. VINCENT MILLAY

I learned the way
a monkey learns—
by watching its parents.

QUEEN ELIZABETH II

Childhood: The Psychological Basis of the Comfort Zone

No, this is not going to be one of those chapters in which our parents are blamed for *everything* we are and are not. Parents seldom look in the eyes of a newborn baby and say, "How can we screw this kid up?"

Our parents (or whoever raised us) *loved* us—in the most fundamental sense of that word. Maybe they didn't hug us all we wanted, but we are alive today because they (at least minimally) *fed* us.

The primary reasons parents don't raise their children free from trauma are

1. *Parents don't know any better.* Most parents have as much training for being parents as children have for being children.

2. *Children learn by example.* If parents knew how to live their own lives better, naturally they would—and that learning would be passed on to the child.

3. *Parents have other things to do besides raising children:* making a living, keeping house, maintaining a relationship with their spouse, dealing with *their* parents. Life can be overwhelming even without children.

4. *Who on earth knows what a child needs when?* Some complain their parents ruined them by not enough attention—they needed more loving; others claim their parents gave them too much attention—they needed more freedom. Many complain about both. To have

> *I owe my success*
> *to having listened respectfully*
> *to the very best advice,*
> *and then going away*
> *and doing the exact opposite.*
>
> G. K. CHESTERTON

given us precisely what we wanted, precisely when we wanted it, our parents would have had to be psychic—which some children would have considered painfully intrusive.

5. *Children require different rules than adults.* Children are not as capable as adults. The less capable we are, the more rules we need. This, of course, can *seem* terribly unfair.

Given this preamble, let's look at childhood—the place where we learned to use the elements of the comfort zone to limit ourselves.

Fear. Young children don't know the difference between playing in the street and playing on a playground, between drinking poison and drinking milk, between petting the nice neighbor's poodle and petting the nasty neighbor's pit bull. In order to let their children out of their sight, parents must teach them not to do things that *might* cause themselves physical harm. The parents' tool is fear.

In turning children loose on the world (and vice-versa), parents give the basic message, "Don't do anything I haven't personally shown you how to do." In other words, *"Don't do anything new."* While most of the "new" a child could do is perfectly safe, a small percentage of it is deadly, and that small percentage is what the parents want to protect their child from.

Guilt. Naturally, children sometimes ignore the warnings of parents—curiosity is more powerful than rules. So, the parents "lay down the law." (Actually, the law already *has* been laid down; now they're laying down the *punishment.*)

Punishment can include yelling (which includes the perceived removal of love), deprivation (of freedom, food, toys), or physical pain. From a *parent's* point of view, this may not be much, but from a *child's* point of view, this can be devastating.

To children, parents are (a) big (imagine someone thirty feet tall, weighing a thousand pounds); (b) the source of love, caring, comfort, dry diapers, etc.; and (c) the ones who protect them from all those *other* thirty-foot, thousand-pound monsters. In addition to all that, parents control the *food*.

Little wonder, then, that when parents exact punishment—even though they're doing it for "your own good"—the child reacts strongly. Sometimes the child hates the parents, and sometimes he or she feels self-hatred for doing whatever provoked

> *If you want a place in the sun,*
> *you must leave the shade*
> *of the family tree.*
>
> OSAGE SAYING

the parent's wrath. When the latter happens, it's called guilt. First, we learn to use fear as a reason not to do anything new; then if we do it anyway, we learn to feel guilty afterwards.

Unworthiness is programmed in at the same time. If the child plays for two hours within the parents' comfort zone (toys in the living room, for example), all is well. There is little interaction with the parents; they're reading or watching TV or whatever parents do when children are being "good." When the child goes beyond the parents' comfort zone and starts playing with, say, a can of shoe polish, the interaction with the parents becomes suddenly intensified—and almost entirely negative. Bad, wrong, nasty, naughty, no good.

What does the child remember from an evening at home with "the folks"? The hours of harmonious play, worthy of a Rockwell painting? Or the moments of intense, negative interaction? The intensity, probably. After enough negative memories, a child can build a self-image of being bad, wrong, nasty, naughty, and no good—in a word, *unworthy.*

Hurt feelings. From a very early age, we are taught that what happens *outside* us should affect what happens *inside* us. Someone jangles keys, and that's supposed to make us fascinated. Someone makes faces and silly noises, and that's supposed to make us happy. Someone gives us a Teddy bear, and that's supposed to make us feel loved. Eventually, our inner feelings are linked to external events. When those external events don't go the way we want them to go, we feel hurt.

We also learn by watching. Father arrives late; mother's feelings are hurt. Mother doesn't cook father's favorite food; father's feelings are hurt. Mother's choice in food has some *direct connection* to father's emotional condition.

Anger. If we respond to hurt feelings with anger, we could have learned it by watching how our parents responded to hurt. And what *kind* of anger? Lashing out, or withdrawal? Noisy blame or quiet revenge? Do you see any of your patterns in your parents?

We are a spectacular,
splendid manifestation of life.
We have language . . .
We have affection.
We have genes for usefulness,
and usefulness is about as close
to a "common goal" of nature
as I can guess at.

LEWIS THOMAS

Hi, Genes

All that said about childhood programming, the way we were *raised* actually has less influence on us than what we *are*. I'm not being philosophical—much less metaphysical—when I discuss "who we are" in this chapter. I mean who we are physically, biologically, genetically.

The old debate over which is more powerful, heredity or environment, is pretty much ended. The winner: heredity. Yes, extremes in environment can cause significant shaping—for good or ill—but most of "us" was created when the genetic code of our mother and the genetic code of our father combined at conception to form the unique genetic code that determines our height, eye color, personality, and thousands of other characteristics.

A study of identical twins separated at birth (only identical twins have precisely the same genetic code) revealed that—even if the environments in which they were raised were radically different—they were, essentially, the same person. Even if they spoke a different native language or had vastly different levels of learning (that is, *what* they knew), their personalities were basically the same. They didn't necessarily use what they had in the same way—a tendency toward creativity, for example, might express itself in painting for one and writing for the other—but the fundamental personality structure was almost identical.

Our comfort zones and our willingness to overcome them, then, are largely genetic. Which of the comfort zone's limitations—fear, guilt, unworthi-

> *Don't try to take on*
> *a new personality;*
> *it doesn't work.*
>
> RICHARD NIXON

ness, hurt feelings, or anger—you seem to specialize in was determined before you were born. Also, the tendency toward courage or complacency—to *do* something about life rather than have life do it unto you—is also genetic.

What does this mean practically?

First, acceptance seems the only rational course. To fully accept who and what you are—limitations *and* gifts—is essential to success. This acceptance does not mean complacency toward your Big Goal, but it does tell you what you have to work with—and against.

Second, genetics underlines the fact that if you are going to actually *change* yourself, then you must *choose wisely* what you plan to change. For the most part, you are who you are and that's that. The microscopic fraction of what you want to change had better be what you *really* want to change—more than anything else, because changing it will require an enormous effort.

In this context, allow me to restate two points: (a) a deep desire—especially one as deep as the genetic code—also comes with an inborn ability to achieve that desire, and (b) people don't read books with titles such as *DO IT! Let's Get Off Our Buts* unless they have a genetic predisposition to do more, become more, and achieve more than the average skinny dipper in the gene pool.

More on the ramifications of "I am what I am and that's all what I am" as the book progresses. For now, know that you are who you are, there's no one to blame for it, and who you already are is enough to get what you want.

Help!
I'm being held prisoner
by my heredity
and environment!

DENNIS ALLEN

The Fight or Flight Response:
The Physiological Basis
of the Comfort Zone

Human beings, as a species, have an in-built, automatic, biological response to perceived danger: to fight or to flee. It's called, not surprisingly, the fight or flight response.

The cave dwellers who could outfight the neighbors and outrun the tigers prevailed. Those who could not became trophies and tigerfood.

In a survival-of-the-fittest sense, we are the offspring of the fittest. For the most part, the fittest were the ones who could fight the fiercest or run the fastest—or both (often at the same time). We inherited that. It's genetic.

The emotion of fight is anger; the emotion of flight is fear. Anger and fear—two mainstays of the comfort zone.

The key word in the definition of the fight or flight response is *perceived*. We don't have to actually *be* in danger to trigger the fight or flight response; we merely have to *perceive* danger. Given the power of our imagination, that's not hard to do.

Once the fight or flight response is triggered, it becomes self-perpetuating. Fear feeds anger and anger feeds fear, and both fire the imagination to "perceive" new dangers which stoke the fear-and-anger fires. Some people haven't been *out* of the fight or flight response for *years*.

> *Human beings yield*
> *in many situations,*
> *even important and spiritual*
> *and central ones,*
> *as long as it prolongs one's well-being.*

ALEXANDER SOLZHENITSYN

It's little wonder, then, that we look for any degree of comfort we can find—even at the cost of our dreams.

*Our greatest pretenses are built up
not to hide the evil and the ugly in us,
but our emptiness.
The hardest thing to hide
is something that is not there.*

ERIC HOFFER

*I don't want
to achieve immortality
through my work.
I want to achieve it
through not dying.*

WOODY ALLEN

*Either this man is dead
or my watch has stopped.*

GROUCHO MARX

Death: The Ultimate Discomfort

Beneath the psychological programming is the physiological fight or flight response, and beneath all *that* is The Big One: *death*.

Death is so final, so ultimate—so *mysterious*. ("The grand perhaps," Robert Browning called it.) Death doesn't just *feed* the various aspects of the comfort zone; it positively *inspires* them. It gives them *life*.

Fear. One small misstep, and boom—we're history. Job called it "The king of terrors" (18:14). As Professor Sydney Hook said, "Fear of death has been the greatest ally of tyranny past and present." To quote the proverb, "It is better to be a coward for a minute than to be dead the rest of your life."

Anger. The unfairness of death can make us furious. As Mel Brooks explained, "Why do we have to die? As a kid you get nice little white shoes with white laces and a velvet suit with short pants and a nice collar and you go to college, you meet a nice girl and get married, work a few years and then you have to *die!* What is this shit? They never wrote that in the contract!"

Guilt. Somehow, no matter when we die, we know we'll have *something* to do with it. We'll drive too fast or eat the wrong thing or ignore our intuition. We will probably cause our death by doing something our mother told us not to do. Even if we repent, it's hopeless. As Johnny Carson said, "I know a man who gave up smoking, drinking, sex,

> *Do not fear death so much,*
> *but rather the inadequate life.*
>
> BERTOLT BRECHT

and rich food. He was healthy right up to the time he killed himself."

Unworthiness. If being alive is the ultimate proof of worthiness, then death must be the ultimate proof of unworthiness. No matter how much good we do, no matter how many lives we save or starving mouths we feed, someday we wind up dead.

Hurt Feelings. To lose someone or something you love hurts. Imagine how much losing *everyone* and *everything* all at the *same time* would hurt. No, don't imagine it. It's too uncomfortable.

Discouragement. No matter how much we build up, no matter what we acquire, no matter...what's the point of finishing this sentence—

we're just going to *die* someday anyway. And everybody who reads it is going to die someday, too. So what's the point in finishing this paragraph? In fact, what's the point in finishing this chapter?

He not busy being born
is busy dying.

Bob Dylan

The Bad News about the Comfort Zone

The comfort zone is never static. It is dynamic—always expanding or contracting. If you're not consciously expanding your comfort zone, it contracts.

In the heating
and air conditioning trade,
the point on the thermostat
in which neither heating nor cooling
must operate
—around 72 degrees—
is called
"The Comfort Zone."
It's also known as
"The Dead Zone."

The Worst News about the Comfort Zone

The comfort zone is not just a collection of "uncomfortable" emotions—it has its own personality, character, and individuality. It is a complex psychological-physiological entity unto itself.

If this sounds like some sort of science fiction horror story, consider the horror the comfort zone wreaks on people's lives.

Many don't see the comfort zone as a limitation at all. They call it "intuition," "morality," or "conscience." Some connect it with religion—they think the limiting rantings of the comfort zone are the voice of God.

(I won't even discuss what happens when these people put their self-limitations on others—by force, if necessary. Well, take a look at history; take a look *around!*)

The comfort zone knows us intimately and hits us at our weakest point. It wouldn't dream of using an excuse we could see through. It uses the reasons we find reasonable, the rationales we find rational (the rational lies), the realizations we find most real (real lies). It takes our greatest aspirations and turns them into excuses for not bothering to aspire.

Only two things are infinite,
the universe
and human stupidity,
and I'm not sure
about the former.

ALBERT EINSTEIN

The Even Worse News about the Comfort Zone

To the degree we're not living our dreams, our comfort zone has more control over us than we have over ourselves.

*Love your enemies
just in case
your friends turn out to be
a bunch of bastards.*

R. A. DICKSON

The Very Worst News about the Comfort Zone

In order to truly master the comfort zone, we must learn to love it.

I once complained to my father
that I didn't seem to be able
to do things the same way
other people did.
Dad's advice?
"Margo, don't be a sheep.
People hate sheep.
They eat sheep."

MARGO KAUFMAN

PART TWO

BUILT FOR SUCCESS
(programmed for failure, perhaps, but)
BUILT FOR SUCCESS

Life moves on, whether we act as cowards or heros. ¶ *Life has no other discipline to impose, if we would but realize it, than to accept life unquestioningly.* ¶ *Everything we shut our eyes to, everything we run away from, everything we deny, denigrate or despise, serves to defeat us in the end.* ¶ *What seems nasty, painful, evil, can become a source of beauty, joy and strength, if faced with an open mind.* ¶ *Every moment is a golden one for him who has the vision to recognize it as such.*

HENRY MILLER

The Good News about the Comfort Zone

The good news about the comfort zone is that all the energy that makes up the comfort zone is *yours*.

People often want to "get rid of" a "negative" emotion before attempting something new. That's the same thing as saying, "I want to get rid of some of my energy."

Fear, guilt, unworthiness, hurt feelings, and anger are, in fact, *tools*. Tools are neutral—they can be used either for us or against us. A knife can be used to heal or to hurt. A hammer can be used to build or to destroy. It is not the tool itself, but *the way the tool is used* that determines its benefit or detriment.

The difficulty lies in a fundamental *misperception* of "limiting" emotions. The limitation is not in the emotions themselves, but in the way we've been taught to *perceive* these emotions. We've been programmed with certain attitudes about certain feelings, and in the *attitudes* lie the limitations, not in the feelings.

In a sense, we play isometrics with our feelings and our attitudes. A certain feeling arises. An attitude says we shouldn't have that feeling, and pushes it down. It's like arm wrestling with ourselves—we can expend a lot of energy and work diligently, but not much is accomplished.

When we see how little gets done, we wonder (a) why so little was accomplished ("I tried *so*

> *They shall beat their swords*
> *into plowshares,*
> *and their spears into pruninghooks:*
> *nation shall not lift up sword*
> *against nation, neither shall*
> *they learn war any more..*
>
> ISAIAH
>
> 2:4

hard"), (b) why we're so tired, or (c) both.

The energy pushing up and the energy pushing down is all *our* energy. Imagine moving toward a goal and not just *removing* the inner resistance to achieving that goal, but *adding* all the energy that was part of the resistance to the forward motion of achievement. Whew!

Imagine if all the energy of fear, guilt, unworthiness, hurt feelings, and anger were available to help us achieve anything we wanted.

Well, it is.

Using fear, guilt, unworthiness, hurt feelings, and anger as allies in the journey toward our dreams is not difficult. It is a matter of *under-*

standing their true use and function—and *remembering* that we now know it. (The habit of treating them as "the enemies" to be "gotten rid of" can be strong.)

It's as though someone hung a large rock around our neck. "Oh, how heavy," we'd complain. Later we were told the rock was really a diamond in the rough. "Oh! How heavy!" we'd exclaim.

Fear, guilt, unworthiness, hurt feelings, and anger are diamonds in the rough. They're valuable now, and with a little cutting and polishing, they become priceless.

The next few chapters reveal these gems for what they are. The rest of this book suggests cutting and polishing techniques.

And neither shall we learn to war with ourselves any more.

It's all right to have
butterflies in your stomach.
Just get them to fly
in formation.

DR. ROB GILBERT

Fear Is the Energy to Do Your Best in a New Situation

Think about entering a new situation. To meet the new situation, imagine you received an extra burst of energy, your senses sharpened, there was a tingling—an excitement—in your body, and you became more sensitive and aware.

Doesn't that sound great? It seems to be the very thing we need in order to do our best in a new situation. Well, it's precisely what *does* happen each time we enter a new situation. Most of the time, however, we call it "fear" and we don't like it.

Contrary to popular belief, our parents didn't teach us to feel fear. Our parents *did* teach us to use fear as a reason *not* to do something. As I explained earlier, they did this from love. Children cannot logically determine whether their physical well-being is or is not endangered when attempting a new activity.

Alas, at eighteen-or-so, when we *do* know the difference between the truly dangerous and the merely new and untried, no one draws us aside and says, "That fear you've been using as a reason *not* to do things—it's *really* part of the energy to get things done."

The first thing we need when entering a new situation (whether physically or in our imagination) is more energy. A new situation, by definition, will be *different*, and extra energy will help us meet the challenges of whatever "different" may hold.

> *You gain strength, courage*
> *and confidence by every*
> *experience in which you really*
> *stop to look fear in the face.*
> *You are able to say to yourself,*
> *"I've lived through this horror.*
> *I can take the next thing*
> *that comes along."*
> *You must do the thing*
> *you think you cannot do.*
>
> ELEANOR ROOSEVELT

When we feel fear, adrenaline, glucose, and other energy-producing chemicals are released into the bloodstream. This physiological energy is available to support our thoughts and actions.

In a new situation, naturally we want to get all the information we can. This is where the sharpened senses, sensitivity, and heightened awareness associated with fear are useful—they help us absorb and more quickly process the new information.

Fear also forces us to *let go of irrelevancies*. We automatically focus on what's most important, "and let the rest of the world go by." When in a new situation, we want to focus on what's central, what's significant. Fear drives thoughts about whether or not grapefruit will be on sale right out of our awareness.

Part of doing our best in a new situation involves learning. There is so much to learn from a new experience—so much to learn about the experience and, more importantly, so much to learn about ourselves. Fear provides a good environment for learning—not an *ideal* environment (fear is not known for its abundance of patience)—but a *good* environment nonetheless. Energy, clarity of mind, and ability to focus are excellent tools for learning.

With enough work (doing), we will eventually—without even thinking about it—use fear as the energy to do our best. In the interim—as we break the habit of thinking this energy is a reason not to do anything new—the suggestion is: feel the fear and do it anyway.

Once you know something is not physically dangerous, go ahead and *do* the thing. It may feel uncomfortable (count on it), but keep moving one step after another in the direction of doing it. As you move—as you *use it*—the energy will transform from barrier to blessing. You'll have *energy*, not limitation.

Feeling the fear and doing it anyway reprograms our attitude from, "Fear means, 'Don't'" to "Fear means, 'All systems go!'"

My parents have been visiting me
for a few days.
I just dropped them off
at the airport.
They leave tomorrow.

MARGARET SMITH

Guilt Is the Energy for Personal Change

Guilt is anger directed toward ourselves, and anger is the energy for *change*.

Alas, few of us were trained to use anger for change (except, perhaps, in athletics). Mostly, we use anger for *blame* and *feeling bad*. As we will explore in a later chapter, the gift of anger is the physical, mental, and emotional strength to make change.

When we feel guilty and want to use the anger for change (for a change), we have two options: we can either change our *actions,* or change our *beliefs* about those actions.

If we feel guilty about something that hasn't yet happened (that twinge of guilt we feel when premeditating a "wicked" action), we can use the anger in the guilt to *not* do it (or, if it's an act of omission, to do it).

If we feel guilty about something that's already taken place, we can use the anger to make amends, to clean things up. (Atonement leads to at-one-ment.)

If there's nothing we can do, then we can use the energy of guilt to change the *belief* about how bad, wicked, terrible, immoral, despicable, disgusting, and downright slug-like our action was.

Most people use guilt (a) to make half-hearted (but often heated) promises to "never do it again," which they don't really believe any more than any

> *When such as I cast out remorse*
> *So great a sweetness flows*
> *into the breast*
> *We must laugh and*
> *we must sing,*
> *We are blest by everything,*
> *Everything we look upon*
> *is blest.*
>
> W. B. YEATS

of their close acquaintances do, and/or (b) to feel bad.

Feeling bad is an important part in the *mis*use of guilt. Part of the "contract" for violating our beliefs is that we must feel bad. We tell ourselves, "Good people are _____ (fill in the perfect human behavior violated by the guilt-producing action), *and when they're not, they feel guilty.*"

In this limiting system, feeling guilty *proves* our goodness. Good people feel bad when they do something bad. (After all, bad people feel *good* when they do something bad.) So, guilt allows us to maintain a mistaken (but admirable-sounding) *belief* about ourselves while *acting* in a way that violates the belief.

A more productive use of guilt's energy is to *change the belief*. Once the belief is changed, the self-judgments stop—the energy is no longer directed toward feeling bad when doing (or failing to do) certain activities.

I'm not saying change your belief about yourself from "I am a good person . . ." to "I am a bad person . . . ." I'm suggesting, add a qualifier to the too-rigid ("perfect") beliefs you have about yourself. "Good people are kind to others . . . and sometimes they're not." "Good people stick to their diet . . . and sometimes they don't." "Good people don't yell in public . . . and sometimes they do."

Making these changes is not easy. The habit of using the energy of guilt in a limiting rather than expansive way is deep seated. As B. F. Skinner pointed out, "Society attacks early, when the individual is helpless." It takes enormous energy and perseverance to change our response to guilt.

Fortunately, there's a lot of energy available in the anger of guilt. It's a matter of remembering to redirect it from *blame* to *change—over and over*.

You may be wondering, "When do I use the energy to change the *action*, and when do I use it to change the *belief* about the action?"

It's an important question. Here are some thoughts.

1. If you change the *belief* first, changing the *action* is easier. Taking the pressure off by changing the belief allows for the freedom of movement necessary to change the action.

> *The wages of sin are death,*
> *but by the time*
> *taxes are taken out,*
> *it's just sort of a tired feeling.*
>
> PAULA POUNDSTONE

2. Realize you're not going to change all the actions about which you currently feel guilty. We're not perfect, we're human. Nonetheless, in our childhood we are given a seemingly infinite number of perfect images to live up to. We add to these the perfect images we have as adults. I'll discuss this perfection syndrome later, but for now realize that you can change *anything* you want, but you can't change *everything* you want.

3. Change first the actions that *physically harm* others. I'm not talking about hurting someone's *feelings;* I'm talking about activities such as hitting people, stealing, child abuse, drunk

driving, in which another is or is very likely to be *physically* harmed by your actions.

4. Change next the actions that *physically harm* you—smoking, extreme overeating, high-risk sexual activities, drug or alcohol abuse, and so on. Again, these are not the things that might *emotionally* harm you (that's quite often the comfort zone), but things that do significant physical harm.

5. Later in the book, you'll have the opportunity to make a list of your wants, desires, and dreams, then to prioritize them in such a way that you'll know which you have time to pursue, and which you (for now) do not. Work next on changing the actions that go against your primary goals.

6. If you've handled *all those* and are *still* looking for more, well, you're a far better person than I am, Gunga Din!

≈

When used to produce guilt, the statement, "I could have done better!" is false. If we *knew* better, we'd *do* better. I don't just mean *intellectually* knowing better. I'm talking about *knowing* in the full sense of the word—the way you *know* to walk, speak, and breathe.

A more accurate statement when we *intellectually* know better (and do it anyway) is to say, "This will remind me to do better next time—I'm still learning."

Because, of course, we are.

*There are three reasons
why lawyers are replacing rats
as laboratory research animals.
One is that they're plentiful,
another is that lab assistants
don't get attached to them,
and the third is that there are
some things rats just won't do.*

LAWYER JOKE NUMBER 3,479,153(C)

Unworthiness
Keeps Us On Track

Just as "We can have *anything* we want; we just can't have *everything* we want," so, too, we are worthy of *anything* we want, but not worthy of *everything* we want.

Why? Unless our list of wants is truly meager, or, unless we plan to live forever, we simply don't have the *time* to fulfill them all. (More on this in the chapter, "You Can Have *Anything* You Want, but You Can't Have *Everything* You Want.")

Say I want to be a lawyer (God knoweth why, but let's suppose for the sake of an example I do). I commit to being a lawyer and sign up for law school. If one day I think, "I'd like to be a doctor," I might feel unworthy. While I'm studying law, the part of me that feels unworthy to be a doctor is *accurate.*

I *chose* something else, something that takes a lot of time, money, and perseverance. My sense of unworthiness about being a doctor keeps me on the lawyer track.

Even if I *did* declare a double-major—the nightmare of the insurance industry—and were (very) busy becoming an M.D., Esq., then feelings of unworthiness about being, say, a nuclear physicist would be accurate. Even if I declared a *triple* major . . . well, you get the idea.

Somewhere along the line, my plate will be full. At that time, everything *not* on my plate I am un-

> *The important thing in acting*
> *is to be able to laugh and cry.*
> *If I have to cry,*
> *I think of my sex life.*
> *If I have to laugh,*
> *I think of my sex life.*
>
> GLENDA JACKSON

worthy of. There's plenty to eat (do) right in front of me.

When you discover your dream—your Big Dream—know that you are worthy of that dream. Tell yourself you are worthy of that dream. Program that worthiness in. (Lots of techniques for that later.) Act upon that worthiness. Be content knowing that your dream is yours. Accept that everything that's not part of your dream is not yours.

Worthiness and unworthiness keep us on our path. It is our path. We selected it—it leads to our dream. Unworthiness is a friend that says, "Your path is this way, not that way." If we listen and move back onto our path, we feel worthy again.

If we continue to stray, we will continue feeling unworthy until we (a) get back on our path, or (b) choose another dream and another path.

Seen in this way, the feeling of unworthiness is better described as *humility*. We know what we want, we know the direction we're going, we know that we are entitled to our dream, and we let the rest of the goals go by.

Humility comes with maturity. Children want this and this and this and this and that—practically everything pleasurable they see, smell, touch, or hear. Many adults do the same: "I want a career *and* a marriage *and* children *and* a house *and* a car *and* save the whales *and* stop pollution *and* write a book *and* find God. Then, next week, I want . . . ."

I'll talk soon about how to choose which dream you pursue and which to consider "good ideas I might get to someday." (In other words, which goals you choose to become worthy of and which you do not.)

Remember—the choice of which to be worthy of is *yours*.

*Don't go around saying
the world owes you a living;
the world owes you nothing;
it was here first.*

MARK TWAIN

Hurt Feelings Are a Reminder of How Much We Care; Anger Is the Energy for Change

We only feel hurt about what we care about. Yes, when anger covers the hurt we say, "I don't care about them (it); I *hate* them (it)." That's part of the caring, too.

If we want A, and B stops us from having it, it's not that we subconsciously care about B. We still love A. It's easy, however, to get lost in the hurting and hating of B and forget about the caring we have for A.

Hurt feelings are a reminder to find A, refocus on A, feel the caring we have for A, and find alternate ways to get A, even if B, C, D, E, and F get in the way.

Most people use hurt as a reason to stop doing. If we let this happen, we truly *are* hurt—we hurt ourselves by letting hurt keep us from attaining our heart's desire.

Another word for caring, of course, is love. Love is powerful. Keep it directed toward your goal.

Feel the *passion* of the caring. Put that passion behind your goal. If you feel *anger*, remember this is the energy for change. *Use* it; *do* something with it. What you do may or may not work. If it does work, great. If not, you've learned something. If nothing else, you've learned one more thing that

> *Vex not they spirit*
> *at the course of things;*
> *they heed not they vexation.*
> *How ludicrous and outlandish*
> *is astonishment*
> *at anything that may happen*
> *in life.*
>
> MARCUS AURELIUS

won't work. Even if you can't do anything physically, use the passion to *imagine* success.

Another excellent use for hurt and anger is to change the *beliefs* we have about the way the world *should* treat us.

As with guilt, add ". . . and sometimes they don't (won't, can't, etc.)" to each belief about things and people that includes the notion of "should," "must," "have-to," "ought-to," or "supposed-to." Adding these qualifiers not only makes life easier; it makes changing easier, too.

Hurt feelings and anger—like fear, guilt, and unworthiness—are there as energy to be used *toward* your goal, not as reasons to stop.

Our *feelings* don't say stop—our *programming* says stop. It's time to rewrite that programming to say, "Here's the information and the energy I need to make necessary corrections and continue moving toward my dreams."

The great French Marshall Lyautey
once asked his gardener
to plant a tree.
The gardener objected that
the tree was slow growing and
would not reach maturity
for 100 years.
The Marshall replied,
"In that case, there is no time to lose;
plant it this afternoon!"

JOHN F. KENNEDY

Death—
The Ultimate Deadline

Deadlines help us get things done. Deadlines get us going, moving, and motivate us to do things sooner rather than later. There's no greater—or more certain—deadline than death.

Parkinson's Law states that work either expands or contracts to fill the time available. Death lets us know that there's only a certain amount of time available—the span of a lifetime—in which to get done whatever we want to do.

Of course, none of us knows how long that time will be, but most of us know it's not going to be longer than, say, another 100 years. So, whatever we want to achieve during our lifetime, we had better start today.

There are some who consider death *bad*. Death is neither good nor bad—it merely *is*. It is a fact of life, like gravity. ("Gravity isn't easy, but it's the law.") We can use death *for* ourselves or *against* ourselves. The choice is ours.

The first step in seeing death as an ally is removing the childhood fears we have concerning death. Children learn about death in a limited (and limiting) way. They see someone (or, in the case of a pet, something) go from warm, active, moving, and alive to cold, inactive, and motionless. Dead. This death stuff does not look very appealing.

Children then see the reaction adults have to death. Although grown-ups may *say* things such as,

> *In the last analysis*
> *it is our conception of death*
> *which decides our answers*
> *to all the questions*
> *that life puts to us.*
>
> DAG HAMMARSKJÖLD

"He is with God," or "She is at peace at last," the emotional *attitudes* of adults (weeping, moaning, wailing) indicate that death is not a welcome guest in anyone's home.

The last straw for children concerns what happens to dead bodies. If a body is buried, the child thinks death must be eternal blackness, darkness, aloneness. If a body is cremated, the child thinks death is fire, flames, and pain.

For children, asking adults about death is about as useful as asking adults about sex—adults become uncomfortable and give conflicting answers to simple questions—answers they don't seem to believe themselves.

It's little wonder, then, that many children decide, "Death is not a good thing, and so I won't think about it any more." And most people don't. Death is such a taboo in our culture that we don't even talk about the fact that it's a taboo. We pretend death doesn't exist.

This is too bad, because there are only three beliefs about death in our culture—none of them bad.

1. *Life is purely biological, and when we die, we're dead.* There's nothing bad in this view of death—we simply are not, so there's nothing to worry about. As Einstein explained, "The fear of death is the most unjustified of all fears, for there's no risk of accident for someone who's dead."

2. *After life, there is heaven or hell through eternity.* If this is one's belief, then there's nothing to worry about, either. Heaven is for good people and hell is for bad people. Who but a good person would believe in heaven and hell? So, if you believe, then a place in heaven awaits you.

3. *We keep coming back, life after life, until we learn all we need to know.* This, too, is not a view of death to fear. Here, death is no more significant than moving from one grade to another in the same school, or from one house to another within the same town. We may not know all that will happen there, but that's part of the fun. "Life is a great surprise," Vladimir Nabokov said, "I do not see why death should not be an even greater one."

> *Even very young children need*
> *to be informed about dying.*
> *Explain the concept of death*
> *very carefully to your child.*
> *This will make*
> *threatening him with it*
> *much more effective.*
>
> P. J. O'ROURKE

When questioned about life and death, almost all adults will describe one of these beliefs, or a close variation thereof. As none of these views of death is *bad* nor inherently *scary*, it's clear that the views of death formed as a child still control the emotional reactions many adults have toward death.

Many believe that young people have no sense of death; that they live their lives as though they will live forever. This may be true in some cases, but only because they have not been taught the inevitability of death, and the value of the interval between now and the inevitable. One's own mortality need not come as a shock later in life; it can be a fact of life, considered in all of life's choices.

When seen as a deadline, death can be used as a tool for doing. Some of the positive uses for this tool include

- When we know "our days are numbered," we see that we can only accomplish a certain amount in this lifetime. This knowledge once again stresses the importance of *choice* in the planning and living of life.

- Death encourages action. We only have so much time left, so let's get going.

- Death encourages risk. The downest of the downside in any risk is death. Since we're going to die anyway, why not take the risks that make life more exciting, enjoyable and, well, alive? Near San Francisco, a group of people with AIDS gather regularly for sky diving, rock climbing, and all those things they wanted to do but at one time considered "too dangerous." The name of their organization? The What-The-Hell-Do-We-Have-To-Lose-Anyway? Club. Life is a sexually transmitted terminal disease.

- Death reminds us how much we owe the past and the future. Those who went before us knew they wouldn't be here forever, and yet they left us a rich legacy. We, too, have many gifts to leave the generations yet unborn. Death says we only have a certain number of

> *Death is nature's way of saying,*
> *"Your table is ready."*
>
> ROBIN WILLIAMS

years in which to appreciate the past and to leave our gift for the future. When Isaac Asimov, who has written hundreds of books, was asked what he would do if he had only six months to live, he responded, "Type faster."

Death, for the doer, is the ultimate reason to do—and to enjoy the doing—*now.*

When you cease
to make a contribution
you begin to die.

ELEANOR ROOSEVELT

*Courage is doing
what you're afraid to do.
They can be no courage
unless you're scared.*

EDDIE RICKENBACKER

Discouragement Reveals Our Courage

The power of discouragement is available for obtaining our goals (or illuminating a small Southern town) by simply dismissing the *dis*.

Courage, contrary to popular belief, is not the *absence* of fear. Courage is the wisdom to act *in spite of* fear. In time, courage becomes the ability to use all the elements of the comfort zone as energy to move toward our goal. When we add *en* to courage, we have *encourage*. *En* is a prefix meaning "to be at one with."

We can think of encouragement as a cheerleader. Whereas discouragement says, "Give up! Give up! Give up!" encouragement says, "Keep going! Keep going! Keep going!" or "DO IT! DO IT! DO IT!"

Along the way, *expect* to be discouraged—to hear and to follow the voices of discouragement. The goal is *not* to never be discouraged again. The goal is to (a) catch the discouragement sooner, (b) call it for what it is, and (c) get out of it faster. How do we get out of it? You simply call on encouragement.

Oh, encouragement!

In fact, here's a scene from the play *Oh, Encouragement!*

SCENE: YOU are about to do something new—a necessary step along the path to your dream. DISCOURAGEMENT has convinced you not to take the

> *Very few people possess*
> *true artistic ability.*
> *It is therefore both unseemly*
> *and unproductive to irritate*
> *the situation by making an effort.*
> *If you have a burning,*
> *restless urge to write or paint,*
> *simply eat something sweet*
> *and the feeling will pass.*
>
> FRAN LEBOWITZ

step. You call . . .

YOU: Oh, encouragement!

ENCOURAGEMENT: Yes.

YOU: Over here.

ENCOURAGEMENT: I thought you'd never ask.

DISCOURAGEMENT: *(Imitating your voice)* I didn't ask. Stay over there where you belong.

YOU: No, encouragement. Come here! That was discouragement talking.

ENCOURAGEMENT: I know. Here I am.

DISCOURAGEMENT: *(Imitating your voice)* Thank you, now go away.

DO IT!

YOU: Don't listen; that was discouragement again.

ENCOURAGEMENT: I'm not going—and don't you listen to discouragement, either. You can do the thing you want to do. You know you can.

YOU: But I'm afraid.

DISCOURAGEMENT: You know fear means: "Don't do it!" *Everybody* knows that.

ENCOURAGEMENT: Fear is the energy to do your best in a new situation. You're in a new situation, so, naturally, you're afraid. *Use* the energy.

YOU: Oh, right.

DISCOURAGEMENT: Oh, wrong. Besides, if you do it you'll feel guilty.

ENCOURAGEMENT: Quiet.

YOU: But discouragement is right. *I will* feel guilty.

DISCOURAGEMENT: You'll feel guilty and miserable and you'll *deserve* to feel guilty and miserable.

ENCOURAGEMENT: Guilt is being angry with yourself, and anger is the energy to make change. Is this new experience something that physically harms yourself or another?

DISCOURAGEMENT: Yes.

YOU: No. It's just new and different.

DISCOURAGEMENT: It'll hurt.

YOU: How?

DISCOURAGEMENT: It'll hurt you *emotionally.* You shouldn't feel uncomfortable. It's dangerous. It can kill you. You can have a heart attack. You can have a stroke.

ENCOURAGEMENT: Give us a break.

> *Every human being on this earth*
> *is born with a tragedy,*
> *and it isn't original sin.*
> *He's born with the tragedy*
> *that he has to grow up.*
> *A lot of people don't have*
> *the courage to do it.*
>
> HELEN HAYES

DISCOURAGEMENT: Never! Speaking of breaks, you might break your leg, you might break your neck . . .

ENCOURAGEMENT: (TO YOU) Is this step you're afraid to take moving you in the direction of your dreams?

YOU: Yes.

ENCOURAGEMENT: Then DO IT!

DISCOURAGEMENT: There you go, advertising that lousy book again. (TO YOU) You're not worthy to do this! Who do you think you are? Do you always have to be so *special*?

ENCOURAGEMENT: Quiet.

DISCOURAGEMENT: No. I'm going to stay right here and ruin everything. It's my job, and I love it. Even if it *wasn't* my job, I'd *still* do it.

ENCOURAGEMENT: (To YOU) Is this a step toward your heart's desire?

DISCOURAGEMENT: No.

YOU: Yes.

ENCOURAGEMENT: Then you're worthy of it.

DISCOURAGEMENT: You'll fail.

YOU: Yeah, I might fail.

ENCOURAGEMENT: If you do, then you'll learn from the failure, but I don't think you'll fail.

DISCOURAGEMENT: You'll be let down. Your feelings will be hurt. You'll feel bad, terrible, miserable, deserted.

ENCOURAGEMENT: You'll be fine. You don't have to respond to *anything* that happens to you with hurt, and, if you do, you can remember that beneath the hurt is loving. Refocus on the loving. Redirect that toward your goal.

DISCOURAGEMENT: You'll be pissed off, furious, seething—you might have a heart attack.

YOU: Heart attack!

ENCOURAGEMENT: Use the energy of anger to make a positive change. Or change the belief you have that people should treat you in a certain way. Beneath the anger is the loving. Let that loving attack your heart. You'll be fine.

DISCOURAGEMENT: Will not! Will not! Will not!

ENCOURAGEMENT: Give it a rest, huh?

DISCOURAGEMENT: No, I won't.

> *Our doubts are traiters,*
> *and make us lose the good*
> *we oft might win*
> *by fearing to attempt.*
>
> WILLIAM SHAKESPEARE

ENCOURAGEMENT: (To YOU) Shall we pull out the big guns?

YOU: Sure.

DISCOURAGEMENT: No! No!

ENCOURAGEMENT: Ready?

YOU: Yes.

ENCOURAGEMENT: Set?

YOU: Uh-huh.

DISCOURAGEMENT: Wait! No!

ENCOURAGEMENT: Go!

YOU: I love you!

DISCOURAGEMENT: Arrrgghh!

YOU: I love you! I love you!

DISCOURAGEMENT: Stop! Stop! You'll have a heart attack!

YOU: I love you! I love you! I love you!

DISCOURAGEMENT: You're crazy! I'm getting out of here. I'll come back when you've settled down. *(Exits)*

YOU: I love you!

ENCOURAGEMENT: Okay, so let's DO IT!

YOU: There you go, advertising that book again.

The longer I live
the more I see that
I am never wrong about anything,
and that all the pains
I have so humbly taken
to verify my notions
have only wasted my time.

GEORGE BERNARD SHAW

The Imagination Is for Rehearsing Our Dreams and Reliving Our Joys

The imagination is a fascinating, powerful place. For example, remember any incident from elementary school—perhaps the face of a teacher, the smell of crayons, the feel of finger-paint, or writing with a fat pencil. (Remember those fat pencils?) Now, think of someplace you plan to go in the next month and imagine yourself there. Good. Now, imagine yourself on the moon, looking back at the earth—a big blue marble in the blackness of space. Excellent.

This is the power of the imagination: we can return to the past, rehearse the future, and zoom off on flights of fancy—all within seconds.

The images you had may not have been well-detailed, or held in the imagination for very long, but you probably had some *sense* of each. Some people primarily *see* in their imaginations, others primarily *hear*, others primarily *feel*. Whichever you do is fine.

When the comfort zone has control of our imagination, it is vigorously and creatively used *against* us. We relive the horrors of the past—fears that were justified, guilts that were especially foul, unworthinesses at their worst, hurt feelings at their most painful, anger at its most destructive. Considering the false history created by the comfort zone's careful selection and occa-

> *The ancestor of every action*
> *is a thought.*
>
> EMERSON

sional rewriting, it's easy to feel discouraged about ourselves and anything we might even *consider* doing.

The comfort zone also uses the imagination to create a future of not just failure, but *monumental* failure, *embarrassing* failure, *public* and *unconditional* failure. Considering the power of our imagination, it's amazing that we ever get out of bed.

The comfort zone also uses news stories and other fictional accounts of disaster to show us *why* we had better not do anything new.

It's time to recapture the imagination from the comfort zone.

The comfort zone *claims* to have complete ownership, or maybe a 99-year lease, but, in fact, it doesn't even have squatter's rights.*

Evict it! Out! Your imagination is yours. You can remember the past you choose, rehearse the future you want, relate to the real and fictional events you select, identify with the heroes you hold dear.

When we remember the good things from our past (and all our pasts are filled with both good and bad), we build an image of ourselves as doers and achievers—charmed, kind, and terrific. This self-esteem forms a solid base for future action.

When we project our dreams into a positive future, we see that we *can* have what we want. A positive image of the future not only shows us how to get there; it *draws* us to it, attracting us toward our dreams like a magnet.

When we hear some good news, read an inspirational story, or see an uplifting movie, we can use our imagination to put ourselves in the center of the action. This allows us to *identify* with all the good, happy, and wonderful aspects of our culture—and know that we're one of them.

The positive use of the imagination is often called *visualization*. The word *visual* in *visualization* does not necessarily mean "to see." *Visual* is used in the general sense, as in, "See what I mean?" As mentioned before, some people *see*, while others primarily *hear* and others primarily

---

*Although it's been squatting there for some time, doing what often is done in a squatting position.

> *I am certain of nothing*
> *but the holiness*
> *of the heart's affections,*
> *and the truth of imagination.*
>
> KEATS

feel. Any one, or any combination, is fine.

An excellent way to reclaim property is to *build* on it. I suggest building a *sanctuary* in your imagination. If you don't already have a sanctuary, you might want to take some time and do it now. We'll be using the sanctuary later in this book. If you do have a sanctuary, you might want to do a little revisiting—or even remodeling—as you read the next few pages.

Imagine immensely enjoying the process of building a sanctuary.

*It is the spirit of the age
to believe that any fact,
however suspect,
is superior
to any imaginative exercise,
no matter how true.*

GORE VIDAL

When love and skill
work together,
expect a masterpiece.

JOHN RUSKIN

The Sanctuary

A sanctuary is an inner retreat you build with visualization in your imagination. Here you can discover the truth about yourself, and work to affirm it. ("Make it firm.")

I call it a sanctuary. Some call it a workshop, or an inner classroom. You can call it whatever word gives you the sense of asylum, harbor, haven, oasis, shelter—a place you can go to learn your lessons in peace and harmony, or just take a rest and get away from it all.

There are absolutely no limits to your sanctuary, although it's a good idea to put *some* limits on it. In this way, the sanctuary is a transitional point between the limitations of our physical existence and the unlimited.

The sanctuary can be any size, shape, or dimension you choose—large and elaborate or small and cozy. It can be located anywhere—floating in space, on a mountain top, by an ocean, in a valley, anywhere. (You are welcome to combine all these, if you like.) The nice thing about the sanctuary: you can change it or move it anytime—instantly.

The sanctuary can contain anything. I'll suggest some things here, but consider this just the beginning of your shopping list. Before giving my design tips (you can consider me your *interior* designer), I'll talk about ways in which you might want to "build" your sanctuary.

Some people will build theirs by simply reading the suggestions: as they read each, it's there. Others

> *I can believe anything,*
> *provided it is incredible.*
>
> OSCAR WILDE

might read them over now for information, and then put on some soft music, close their eyes, and let the construction begin. Still others may want to make this an *active* process. With their eyes closed (and being careful not to bump into too much furniture), they might physically move as each area of the sanctuary is built. Any—or any combination—of these is, of course, fine.

While reading through my suggestions, you will probably get ideas for additions or alterations. By all means make notes of these, or simply incorporate them as you go. Have I gotten across the idea that this is *your* sanctuary? Okay, let's go.

Entryway. This is a door or some device that

responds only to you and lets only you enter. (I'll suggest a way to bring others into your sanctuary in a moment.)

Light. Each time you enter your sanctuary, a pure, white light cascades over you, surrounding, filling, protecting, blessing, and healing you—for your highest good, and the highest good of all concerned.

Main Room. Like the living room of a house or the lobby of a hotel, this is the central area. From here, there are many directions you can go and many things to explore.

People Mover. This is a device to move people in and out of your sanctuary. No one ever enters without your express permission and invitation. You can use an elevator, conveyor belt, *Star Trek* beam-me-up device, or anything else that moves people. Let there be a white light at the entry of the mover as well, so that as people enter and leave your sanctuary, they are automatically surrounded, filled, protected, and healed by that white light, and only that which is for their highest good and the highest good of all concerned takes place.

Information Retrieval System. This is a method of getting any kind of information—providing, of course, it's for your highest good (and the highest good of all concerned) that you have it. The information retrieval system can be a computer screen, a staff of librarians, a telephone, or any other device that will answer your questions.

Video Screen. This is a video (or movie) screen on which you can view various parts of your life—

> *I am looking for a lot of men*
> *who have an infinite capacity*
> *to not know what can't be done.*
>
> HENRY FORD

past, present, or future. The screen has a white light around it. When you see images you don't like or don't want to encourage, the light is off. When the screen displays images you want to affirm, the light glows. (Those who are old enough to remember Sylvania's Halo of Light television know just what I mean.)

Ability Suits. This is a closet of costumes that, when worn, give you the instant ability to be anything you want—great actor, successful writer, perfect lover, eager learner, Master of your Universe; any and all are available to you. When you're done with an ability suit, just throw it on the floor in front of the closet—ability suits have the ability to hang themselves up.

Ability Suit Practice Area. This is a place you can try new skills—or improve on old ones—while wearing your ability suits. Leave lots of room, because there's an ability suit for flying and another for space travel. In your sanctuary, not even the sky's a limit.

Health Center. Here the healing arts of all the ages—past, present, future; traditional and alternative—are gathered in one place. All are devoted to your greater health. The health center is staffed with the most competent health practitioners visualization can buy. Who is the most healing being you can imagine? That's who runs your center.

Playroom. Here, all the toys you ever wanted—as a child or as an adult—are gathered. There's lots of room—and time—to play with each. As with ability suits, you never have to worry about "putting your toys away." They put themselves away.

Sacred Room. This is a special sanctuary within your sanctuary. You can go there for meditation, contemplation, or special inner work.

Master Teacher. This is your ideal teacher, the being with whom you are the perfect student. The Master Teacher knows everything about you (has always been with you, in fact).

The Master Teacher also knows all you need to learn, the perfect timing for your learning it, and the ideal way of teaching it to you.

You don't *create* a Master Teacher—that's already been done. You *discover* your Master Teacher.

To meet your Master Teacher, simply walk over to your people mover, ask for your Master Teacher

> *Advice is what we ask for*
> *when we already know*
> *the answer*
> *but wish we didn't.*
>
> ERICA JONG

to come in, and from the pure, white light of your people mover comes your Master Teacher.

(I'll leave you two alone for a while. More uses for the sanctuary later. See you both in Part Three!)

It is the supreme art
of the teacher to awaken joy
in creative expression
and knowledge.

ALBERT EINSTEIN

Use your weaknesses;
aspire to the strength.

SIR LAURENCE OLIVIER

New-Found Friends

Fear, guilt, unworthiness, hurt feelings, and anger are really our *friends*. Hmmm. That may take some getting used to. We have, in the past, treated them as enemies. In running from these enemies, people have abandoned their dreams and ransomed their futures.

Yet friends they are, and friends they'll stay. Our *perception* of their friendship might not always be up to par, but they'll continue doing their friendly activities whether we realize those activities are friendly or not.

Here are some suggestions on ways to work with your new-found friends:

1. When you're using fear, guilt, unworthiness, hurt feelings, anger, or discouragement to limit yourself, pause for a moment and remember:

   - Fear is the energy to do our best in a new situation.
   - Guilt is the energy for personal change.
   - Unworthiness keeps us on track.
   - Hurt feelings remind us how much we care.
   - Anger is the energy for change.
   - Discouragement reveals our courage.

   Review the chapter for each of these if, in the midst of a comfort-zone binge, you ask, "What on *earth* does he mean by *that*?"

2. Observe your personal process of discourage-

> *Since nothing we intend*
> *is ever faultless,*
> *and nothing we attempt*
> *ever without error,*
> *and nothing we achieve*
> *without some measure*
> *of finitude and fallibility*
> *we call humanness,*
> *we are saved by forgiveness.*
>
> DAVID AUGSBURGER

ment. What makes *you* give up before you even start (or shortly thereafter)?

- Where in your body do you feel fear? Guilt? Unworthiness? Hurt feelings? Anger?
- What are your thoughts ("I'm too tired," "I'm no good at this sort of thing") when you use these emotions in a limiting way?
- Which of these limiting friends is your "favorite"? Do they gang up? Which ones always appear with which others?

3. Forgive yourself for treating your friends as enemies. Forgive yourself for all the things you could have done *if only* you had learned this years ago. Forgive yourself in general.

(Lack of forgiveness is the mortar that holds the wall of the comfort zone in place.) Forgiveness is an easy process. Simply say, "I forgive myself for _____" and fill in the blank with the transgression. Then say, "I forgive myself for judging myself for _____" and fill in the blank with the same transgression. Forgiving is also forgetting. Let it go.

4. Love it all—the fear, the excitement, the guilt, the power for change, the unworthiness, the worthiness, the hurt feelings, the euphoric feelings, the anger, the movement, the discouragement, the encouragement—it's called life. ("Life!" as Cynthia Nelma exclaimed, "Can't live with it, can't live without it.") And when you're not loving it all, love that, too.

≈

The key is *awareness*. At this point, simply be *aware* of the comfort zone and its effect on you.

Soon, we'll get to *expanding* the comfort zone enough to include your dreams—and maybe even a dance floor. For now—what *is* your dream, anyway?

*Everything I did in my life
that was worthwhile
I caught hell for.*

EARL WARREN

PART THREE

DISCOVERING AND CHOOSING OUR DREAMS

Often, what we *really* want is hidden beneath what we've settled for. When the comfort zone doesn't allow the expanded behavior necessary to fulfill our dream, we tend to forget the dream.

It's too painful otherwise.

When we know we *can* have what we want—that the comfort zone is under our control—we can remember what we truly want.

This section will explore the idea that we can have *anything* we want (though not *everything* we want) and offer suggestions for discovering our heart's desire.

*The only true happiness
comes from squandering
ourselves for a purpose.*

WILLIAM COWPER

1731–1800

On Purpose

People often confuse "goal" and "purpose."

A goal is something tangible; a purpose is a direction. A goal can be achieved; a purpose is fulfilled in each moment. We can set and achieve many goals; a purpose remains constant for life.

If the purpose were "west," for example, the goals while heading west (from New York, say) might include Philadelphia, Chicago, Los Angeles, Hawaii, the Philippines, Japan, Korea, China, Turkey, Spain, Portugal, Boston, and New York. Many goals, same purpose.

From there, although we had already traveled 25,000 miles, we would still have as much "west" to go (as much of our purpose to fulfill) as when we first began.

A second journey toward the west, again from New York, might include these goals: Detroit, St. Louis, Denver, Salt Lake City, San Francisco, Midway Islands, Mongolia, Greece, Italy, France, Ireland, Newfoundland, Nova Scotia, and New York. Even after another 25,000 miles, there is still as much west to go as there was in the beginning.

At any point in the journey, in fact, there was (and is) always an infinite amount of movement—and goals—available while living "on purpose."

You'll note that, even though the goals are numerous, there can be many goals within a goal, and lots of freedom within each. While in France, for example, one could travel north, south, east, and west. As long as Ireland were the next major goal, even traveling

> *Strong lives are motivated*
> *by dynamic purposes.*
>
> KENNETH HILDEBRAND

east could be a fulfillment of the purpose "west."

Looking at the life of someone whose purpose is, say, "I am a grateful giver," the goals along that purpose might include nursing home attendant, school teacher, physical therapist, writer, and foundation president. These would, of course, only be *career* and *professional* goals. Marriage/family, social/political, and religious/spiritual goals might interweave that life, all aligned with the purpose, "I am a grateful giver."

While goals are *chosen*, a purpose is *discovered*. Our purpose is something we have been doing all along, and will continue to do, regardless of circumstances, until the day we die.

When I refer to a "dream" in this book, I mean a goal—a significant goal that would, in a profound and vital way, fulfill one's purpose. As that dream is realized, another dream is chosen, and as that is satisfied, another. When I refer to "living your dreams," I mean a life of movement from dream to dream, always on purpose.

People can misdefine a purpose (as something to get to) or misdefine a goal (as something one is always doing no matter where one is), and feel frustrated with both. When people confuse "purpose" with "goal," they often have trouble reaching a goal, which, in turn, can interfere with living on purpose.

Someone may think, for example, that his goal is to be "an actor." This is fine, except whenever he is acting—no matter what, where, how, or with whom—his goal is fulfilled. The automatic goal-fulfillment mechanism within him says, "That's done. What's next?"

"What's next?" the actor puzzles. "I want to be an actor."

"You just acted," the inner goal-filler says, "in that class you took. And very well, too."

"No. I want to be *paid* for acting." So the goal-fulfillment mechanism rallies its considerable resources and finds the actor a job as an avocado in a supermarket Vegetable-of-the-Week promotion. Pay: $250 for the week. The goal of being a paid actor having been met, the goal-fulfillment mechanism shuts down for a while.

"Hey," the actor complains, "Why aren't I getting work?"

> *The great thing in this world*
> *is not so much where we are,*
> *but in what direction*
> *we are moving.*
>
> OLIVER WENDELL HOLMES

"You got work," says the goal-fulfillment mechanism. "You acted. You got paid. Two goals, two goals fulfilled."

"I want *more* work."

"Want to try for carrot? Radishes are next week. You can go out for radish."

"No. Enough with the vegetables. Actors have agents. I want an agent."

So, the goal-fulfillment mechanism finds an agent, and the agent finds nothing.

"I want an agent who will get me work. Regular work. Performing."

An agent is found who also manages a restaurant, and the actor gets regular work performing as a singing waiter.

"No! I want to be an actor! A *big* actor!"

So, the actor puts on 100 pounds.

The actor's problem is that he is confusing purpose with goal. If he discovered that his purpose was, say, "I am a joyful entertainer," then the week as an avocado could have been a fun-filled, fulfilling one.

It would also free him to set clearly defined goals within his purpose: "I want a major role in a feature film," "I want to star on a network sitcom," "I want to make $100,000 this year acting in commercials," and so on. These are the kinds of goals to which the goal-fulfillment mechanism within says, "Yes! Let's go!"

There'll be a lot more on goal setting later. For now, let's focus on the purpose. *Your* purpose.

*Nothing contributes so much
to tranquilizing the mind
as a steady purpose—
a point on which the soul
may fix its intellectual eye.*

MARY WOLLSTONECRAFT SHELLEY

1797–1851

What Is Your Purpose?

This is the first of several exercises in this book that involves *doing*—in this case, writing. Please decide now if you're reading this book just for information, or if you're reading this book to make a significant improvement in your life. Although I'd like to flatter myself that I could write a book that would make indispensable advancements in the lives of everyone who even brushed past it, I know that change comes through involvement, and involvement means doing. My recommendation, then, is to *do* the exercises, starting with this one. If you read the book and later decide to do the exercises, please start with this one. It is the foundation of all the others.

To discover your purpose, get a piece of paper and start listing all your positive qualities. You might want to write each positive quality on a 3x5 card. This will make shuffling them easier later. If no 3x5 cards are handy, listing the qualities on paper will do.

(Do pick up 500-or-so 3x5 cards the next time you're out. We'll be using them later. If you're someone who tends to put off physical tasks until "later," and then never gets to them, you might want to put down this book and go get some 3x5 cards *now*. While you're out, consider your positive qualities. And have fun!)

Don't be shy listing your positive qualities. This is no time for false modesty. Are you kind? Considerate? Compassionate? Joyful? Loving? Loyal?

> *One doesn't discover new lands*
> *without consenting*
> *to lose sight of the shore*
> *for a very long time.*
>
> ANDRÉ GIDE

Happy? Tender? Caring? Write them down.

A purpose usually begins with *"I am,"* followed by an attitude ("joyful" "happy" "caring") and an action ("giver" "explorer" "nurturer").

On another page (or another set of cards), start listing *actions* you find fulfilling—the positive things you like doing most. Giving? Sharing? Exploring? Teaching? Learning?

Take some time with this process. Reflect on your life. Explore its motivation.

If you get stuck, call a few friends and ask for suggestions. Tell them you're filling out an application for the Peace Corps. You need help with the questions, "What are your best qualities?" and

"What activities give you the most satisfaction?"

You might also go to your sanctuary and ask your Master Teacher for some ideas. Or, go to the video screen and review some scenes of satisfaction, joy, or fulfillment from your life. What were the qualities you embodied in those situations?

Consider the people you admire most. What is it you admire about them? What qualities do they embody? Those same qualities are most likely true about you, too, so write them down.

Eventually, a pattern will emerge on the "Qualities" and the "Actions" lists. Begin grouping qualities and actions under general headings. For you, "Compassionate" might include "caring," "loving," and "kind" while, for another, "Kind" might encompass "compassionate," "loving," and "caring." The idea is not to discover which is "right" from Mr. Webster's or Mr. Roget's point of view, but which resonates most clearly within *you*.

Start to play around with the qualities and actions in a sentence that starts, "I am . . . ." A purpose is short, pithy, and to the point. There's usually room for only one or two qualities and an action. "I am a cheerful giver," "I am a joyful explorer," "I am a compassionate friend."

Please consider my grammatical structure as a starting point. "I am a minstrel of God," "I sing the song of life," or "I serve the planet" are outstanding purposes that don't fit the "I am a [quality] [action]" format. Go to the *spirit* of what a purpose is—the *purpose* of a purpose, if you will—and find your purpose there.

> *Here is the test*
> *to find whether your mission*
> *on earth is finished:*
> *If you're alive, it isn't.*
>
> RICHARD BACH

After a while of rearranging qualities and actions, something will click. A voice inside will say, "Yes, this is what I've always done, and this is what I'll always be doing." (This discovery can come with equal parts joy and resignation—joy at seeing that our life has had a direction all along; resignation in noticing it may not be as *glamorous* as we had secretly hoped.)

And that's your purpose.

You might want to place your purpose in a prominent place in your sanctuary—emblazoned on the wall in letters of fiery gold, or, perhaps, on a hand-sewn sampler.

I suggest you not tell your purpose to anyone.

DO IT!

That's why I suggested—as a joke, of course—the Peace Corps ruse. (You didn't *really* tell your friends you were joining the Peace Corps, did you? Oh, dear. All right. Well, call them back, and tell them it wasn't the Peace Corps. It was really the Nobel Selection Committee. Yeah, that's it. The Nobel Selection Committee has been asking a lot of questions about you, and you wanted to have a few comments prepared, should you unexpectedly be invited to Stockholm.)

Keeping your purpose to yourself is not so much *secret* as it is *sacred*. Consider it a beautiful plant. Keep the roots (the essence of the purpose) deep within yourself, and let the world share in its fruits.

Please save your lists (stacks) of qualities and actions. We'll be using them later.

*Perfections of means
and confusion of goals seem
—in my opinion—
to characterize our age.*

ALBERT EINSTEIN

Intention vs. Method

An intention is what we want. Methods are the ways of getting it. An intention is our heart's desire. Methods are the actions, information, things, and behaviors we use to get it.

The intention may be "Go to Chicago." The method might be car, train, walking, flying, roller skating, pogo sticking, etc. For each intention, there are many methods.

Unlike our purpose, which is discovered, an intention is *chosen*. If our purpose is west, our intention (goal) can be any destination west of wherever we happen to be. The choice of that destination is ours.

When you ask some people why they're not living their dream, they usually respond with a listing of unavailable methods: not enough money, looks, information, contacts, breaks, and so on. All these are just methods. Excuses of not having them may sound rational, but are, in reality, rational lies.

Most people let their methods decide their intentions. This is a fundamental mistake. Those who look at what they already *have* before selecting what they *want* are involved in *making do*, not *doing*.

The reason many people feel bored and unfulfilled is that they spend their lives shuffling and reshuffling the methods they already have. This can be like rearranging deck chairs on the *Titanic*—no matter how well it's done, the result is the same. As someone said, "If you do what you've always done, you'll get what you've always gotten."

> *The way you activate the seeds of your creation is by making choices about the results you want to create.* ¶ *When you make a choice, you mobilize vast human energies and resources which otherwise go untapped.* ¶ *All too often people fail to focus their choices upon results and therefore their choices are ineffec- tive.* ¶ *If you limit your choices only to what seems possible or reasonable, you disconnect yourself from what you truly want and all that is left is a compromise.*
>
> ROBERT FRITZ

When choosing a dream, look to your heart, not to your "reality." That's why it's called a dream. Make that dream your intention. Commit to it. Act upon that commitment. The methods to fulfill that dream will appear.

An intention might be a method to achieve a greater intention, and that greater intention might be a method for obtaining a greater intention still.

For example, a taxi might be the method to get to the airport, the airport being the intention. The airport might be the method of getting to Chicago, a larger intention. Chicago might be a method of traveling west, which is a larger intention still, all of which fits within the purpose, "I am joyfully traveling west."

We can add new methods to our lives regardless of age, circumstances, situation, or anything else. All it requires is a *willingness* to learn. And learning methods that can radically improve our lives doesn't necessarily take a lot of time.

Imagine the difference between a newborn infant and a two-year-old. An infant cannot walk, talk, coordinate its body, control its bowels, eat solid food, understand language, or see very well. By two, the child is well on the way to mastering all these. That's how much learning a human can do in two years.

That same transformational amount of learning can take place in any similar period of time. In fact, adults can learn even *faster.* All it takes is commitment and willingness.

I'll discuss the techniques of commitment and willingness later. For now, feel free to choose a goal that seems "impossible." *Possible* and *impossible* are simply terms to describe how many methods one has available that already fit the goal. In fact, why not choose for yourself the intention to create a perfect intention?

Meanwhile, here is some Good Advice:

> Never eat anything whose listed ingredients cover more than one-third the package.— *Joseph Leonard*

> Have a place for everything and keep the thing somewhere else; this is not a piece of advice, it is merely a custom.—*Mark Twain*

> *When I was born*
> *I was so surprised*
> *I didn't talk*
> *for a year and a half.*
>
> GRACIE ALLEN

Write injuries in dust, benefits in marble.—*Benjamin Franklin*

People will accept your ideas much more readily if you tell them Benjamin Franklin said it first.—*David H. Comins*

Let your intentions create your methods and not the other way around.—*The author—although Benjamin Franklin said it first*

Follow your bliss.—*Joseph Campbell*

After ecstasy, the laundry.—*Zen statement*

(For more advice, please read Jon Winokur's book *Good Advice*. Lots of fun.)

Poor is the man
whose pleasures depend
on the permission of another.

MADONNA

*Love is but the discovery
of ourselves in others,
and the delight
in the recognition.*

ALEXANDER SMITH

Needs vs. Wants

Let's be clear about this—any time I refer to "wants" in this book, I mean *wants*, not *needs*.

Our needs are already fulfilled, and have been fulfilled—consistently—from the time we were born, until this very moment.

I can make this seemingly bold statement, and include you in it, because, if it *weren't* true, you wouldn't be reading this book. In fact, you wouldn't be here at all. When human needs are not fulfilled, death occurs. Period.

Needs are food, shelter, clothing, air, water, and protection. (Even this may be a long list: "shelter," "clothing," and "protection" cover pretty much the same ground—keeping the elements and the elephants at bay.) Everything else we *think* we need is a want.

The rule of thumb: if you can live without it for even a short period of time, it's a want. I didn't say *happily* live without it, or *comfortably* live without it—just *live* without it, as in *exist*.

"Not love?" some might protest. Whoever or whatever is providing you with food, clothing, shelter, air, water, and protection loves you beyond measure. Romantic love ("I love you. Sigh." "I love you, too. Sigh.") is all very nice—but it's a want, not a need.

We get into trouble when we call a want a need—it begins to corrupt our integrity. When we say we *need* something, the body goes into red alert. Need? That's like food, water, air! The body—the

> *This above all:*
> *to thine own self be true,*
> *And it must follow,*
> *as the night the day,*
> *Thou canst not then be false*
> *to any man.*
>
> SHAKESPEARE

whole being, in fact—uses all its resources to meet the need *right away*. After too many false alarms, it becomes the story of the little boy who cried "Wolf!" once too often. Eventually, the body ignores our urgent pleas of "I need!"

Meanwhile, a part of us is patiently waiting to help us fulfill our *wants*. The simple statement, "I want . . . ," committed to and acted upon, can move mountains. When we call our wants "needs," however, a part of us says, "Okay, let's just see how much you *really* need this."

As a poet once put it, "My needs destroy the paths by which those needs could be fulfilled."

Yes, we do need, but those needs are entirely

physical. Emotionally, we are whole and complete just as we are (although we may not yet *realize* that fully).

Saying we need something outside ourselves in order to have a positive feeling within (joy, happiness, love) implies that we are somehow *lacking*. This is simply not the case. In this sense, saying "I need . . ." is an affirmation of personal deficiency— even if it is followed by very nice words.

Take, for example, "I need to give my love to others." The giving of one's love to others is all very nice, but the inherent lack in the "I need . . ." part of the sentence pollutes the whole thing. "I want to give my love to others" is less desperate and somehow *nicer.*

It's fine to want something *a whole lot.* That's part of manifesting your dream. Passion. The next section of this book, in fact, is about becoming more passionate about our dream. When we start calling a want a need, however, we step over the line from being passionate to being impoverished.

What we *need* is always supplied to us, and always will be, until the day we die. Let us be grateful for that. And let's pursue our wants and desires from this platform of fulfillment and gratitude.

*We forfeit three-fourths
of ourselves to be
like other people.*

ARTHUR SCHOPENHAUER
1788–1860

Selfish vs. Selfing

Yes, I'm going to coin a word here. (What would a self-help book be without a coined word or two?) The word I'm going to coin is *selfing.*

Selfing means doing for one's Self, in the larger sense of Self, as in True Self, or "To thine own self be true." It means fulfilling our inherent dreams, goals, and aspirations. It means living our life "on purpose."

Selfish, on the other hand, describes the petty, endlessly greedy gathering of stuff (houses, cars, boats, clothes), stuff (husbands, wives, children, lovers), and more stuff (power, fame, money, sex). It's the relentless pursuit of glamour at all costs. It's worshiping the god of other people's opinion.

Selfing is knowing what you want—what *you* want, not what you *should* want because others *say* you should want it—and moving toward it. Others may call you selfish, but you know that you are selfing—"being yourself."

As Ralph Waldo Trine explained,

> There are many who are living far below their possibilities because they are continually handing over their individualities to others. Do you want to be a power in the world? Then be yourself. Be true to the highest within your soul and then allow yourself to be governed by no customs or conventionalities or arbitrary man-made rules that are not founded on principle.

Those who do fulfill their dreams *naturally*

> *The only man*
> *who is really free*
> *is the one who can turn down*
> *an invitation to dinner*
> *without giving an excuse.*
>
> JULES RENARD

share that fulfillment with all those around them. Inviting others to enjoy the advantages of one's goal is inherent in the process of realizing a dream; it's an organic part of the process.

Someone studying to be a doctor may spend all her time, energy, and resources on learning. For several years, she may appear to others as "selfish." She will, however, spend the remainder of her life applying what she has learned during this "selfish" period to benefit others. Was it truly selfish after all?

George Bernard Shaw explained the difference between selfing and selfish when he wrote,

This is the true joy in life, the being used for a

purpose recognized by yourself as a mighty one; the being thoroughly worn out before you are thrown on the scrap heap; the being a force of nature instead of a feverish selfish little clod of ailments and grievances complaining that the world will not devote itself to making you happy.

Shaw's first use of "self" ("a purpose recognized by yourself as a mighty one") would be the large Self; his second use ("a feverish selfish little clod") would be the petty self.

In moving toward your goal, it may be necessary to use all your available resources toward the fulfillment of that goal. That's to be expected, and that's selfing. Others (especially people who are now receiving less of your resources) may call you selfish. The question is, "What's more important—your goal, or others' opinions of your goal and you?"

It's amazing how many people—through their actions—answer "others' opinions."

When the eagles are silent
the parrots begin to jabber.

S<small>IR</small> W<small>INSTON</small> C<small>HURCHILL</small>

You Can Have *Anything* You Want, but You Can't Have *Everything* You Want

Here it is, the chapter that was foretold to you many times. The phrase "you can have anything you want, but you can't have everything you want" sums up this whole section of the book.

You can have anything you want: No dream is too big to achieve. If *one other* person has achieved it, you can be the second. If *no other* person has achieved it, you can be the first. Dream big, dear reader, dream big.

But you can't have everything you want: We live in a finite world for a finite period of time, but with an infinite imagination. Our imagination can create more wants than a computer can generate random numbers. We're not going to have time for all the wants we want.

There are those who say, "I want it all!" I wonder, if they ever got it all, where they would put it. When would they find the time to use it all, or even the time to *learn* how to use it all? One begins to get images from *Citizen Kane*—warehouse after warehouse stuffed with treasures, purchased but never uncrated.

In fact, we *can't* "have it all"—there's simply not enough time. To make "having it all" a goal is not realistic. Long before we get "it all" we run out of

> *People are always blaming*
> *their circumstances*
> *for what they are.*
> *I don't believe in circumstances.*
> *The people who get on*
> *in this world are the people*
> *who get up and look for*
> *the circumstances they want,*
> *and, if they can't find them,*
> *make them.*
>
> GEORGE BERNARD SHAW
>
> 1893

time, energy, and resources. Maybe that's why people who "want it all" often look so *tired*.

More often, however, I encounter people who don't want enough. Oh, they may want *enough* in the sense of a little here and a little there and all the littles add up to "enough." Unfortunately, many of those littles aren't what the people *really want*—they only think they *should* want them because somebody once said they should. If these people had their heart's desire—the Big Want—they would gladly "sacrifice" most of the little littles.

We have only so much time and so much energy and so many resources, and we're going to spend them on *something*. The tragedy in most people's lives is that they spend their time, energy, and resources *doing something other than their heart's desire.*

We are, of course, never given more time. We all have twenty-four hours each day. We're going to spend that time doing *something.* Why not spend it pursuing our dreams?

When we have *too many* goals ("I want to visit Los Angeles, New York, Chicago, and Denver, all in one day"), or goals that *conflict* (try starting from Kansas and going to New York *and* Los Angeles simultaneously), we run up against "you can't have *everything* you want."

Yes, we are worthy of visiting *any* of those cities, but not *all* of them at once. Most people, however, rather than *choosing* one, just give up and stay in Kansas. "I can't have anything I want," they sigh.

They *can* have anything they want, but they *can't* have everything they want. There is more to life than Kansas. The key is choosing what we want most (our heart's desire), letting go of everything else we want (for now), and moving (mentally, emotionally, and physically) toward our goal.

The choosing, letting go, and moving is what we're going to look at next. It is, in fact, the essence of how to DO IT!

If someone says "can't,"
that shows you what to do.

JOHN CAGE

The Biggest Lie in Choosing

The biggest lie in choosing is, "I can't."

It is simply not true.

We *can* do anything we want. If we *don't* do something, it is because we have committed our time, energy, and resources elsewhere.

The next time you hear yourself saying, to another—and especially to yourself—"I can't," take a deep breath and say instead, "My resources are otherwise engaged."

Because that's the truth.

*Lots of folks confuse
bad management
with destiny.*

KIN HUBBARD

Life's Four Basic Areas of Activity

When choosing a dream to pursue, it's good first to consider the four basic areas in which people live. They are

- Marriage/Family

- Career/Professional

- Social/Political

- Religious/Spiritual

Naturally, in the course of a lifetime, people spend some time in each. Looking back, however, most people can say, "Yes, I gave the majority of my time and attention to _____" and mention one of the categories. Sometimes, it's the area they *wanted* to spend most of their time in. Other times, they spent their life in an area other than the one closest to their heart.

In choosing *now* which area you feel most drawn to, you can either (a) spend more time in that area, or (b) realize that the draw you feel ("I really want to do this, but I think I *should* do that") is from programming other than your own. Now is a good time to start reprogramming yourself so that the goals you follow are your own.

Here's where the "I want it all" syndrome comes in. We somehow think we're *entitled* to fulfill a *significant* goal from *each* of the four categories. All at once. Sorry. I haven't seen it. You can have *any*

> *The heights by great men*
> *reached and kept*
> *Were not attained*
> *by sudden flight,*
> *But they,*
> *while their companions slept,*
> *Were toiling upward*
> *in the night.*

HENRY WADSWORTH LONGFELLOW

category you want, but you can't have *every* category you want.

Life is easier if one faces this hard reality sooner, rather than later. (Some people are reading this book because the hard reality came knocking on their door . . . or repossessed the house, or filed divorce proceedings, or got them fired, or, or, or.)

You *can* spend equal amounts of time in each category, but, if you do, don't expect to go very far in any of them. You will live "a balanced life." People will remark, "My, what a balanced life you live."

If, while you're imagining this, a part of you says, "I don't want a balanced life! I want to be a rock star!" (Career/Professional) or "All I care about is my family!" (Marriage/Family) or "What difference does a balanced life make if we can't breathe the air?" (Social/Political) or "This world is but the shadowlands; the greater world is beyond!" (Religious/ Spiritual), then perhaps you're not looking for the balanced life after all.

The narrower your goal—and the more fully you supply that goal with your time, energy, and resources—the farther you'll go and the faster you'll get there. Think of a rocket. All its energy is pinpointed in one direction, and it can zoom off to distant planets.

The downside of rocket travel? You can't bring your house *and* your family *and* report for work on time *and* save the whales *and* take all your religious and spiritual books *and* . . . . Very little fits in the capsule of a rocket. If, however, seeing the moon close-up and in-person is your heart's desire, letting go of all but that "very little" is the price you must pay.

"All right. I'll settle for *pictures* of the moon."

Much less investment is required for that. You can even have a *video* of the moon. In color. Let go, however, of the dream of seeing the moon in-person and up close. Letting that dream go will free up energy you can put toward the dream you *do* choose to achieve.

In the next four chapters we'll take a look at each of the four basic areas of activity. Along the way, I'll do what I can to dispel a few of the myths that have grown around each.

Before discussing the four areas, let me mention

> *The only service*
> *a friend can really render*
> *is to keep up your courage*
> *by holding up to you a mirror*
> *in which you can see*
> *a noble image of yourself.*
>
> GEORGE BERNARD SHAW

a concept called the mirror.

This concept says that all life is a mirror, and by looking into the mirror, we can learn a great deal about ourselves. The mirror concept asks, "What if everything you like in people and things around you is really reflecting back to you something you like about yourself?" If you admire people who are kind, for example, they are reflecting back to you the kindness within yourself.

On the other hand, the mirror also reflects back what we don't like about ourselves. When we dislike someone for being selfish, perhaps there's a selfishness within ourselves that we don't like.

The mirror works just as well with things as

with people. In fact, it's sometimes easier to see that we're projecting our feelings about ourselves onto something else when the object is inanimate. If we're moved by the grandeur of the sky, it's obvious that the grandeur is our projection. The sky is the sky. No grandeur there other than the grandeur we put there.

Using the mirror concept, we can use everything in life to teach us more about ourselves. Each area of life acts as a magnifying mirror to one aspect or another of ourselves. The area of ourselves we find most intriguing—the one we would most like to explore—often leads us to become involved in the corresponding area of life.

*If you want to sacrifice
the admiration of many men
for the criticism of one,
go ahead, get married.*

KATHERINE HEPBURN

Marriage and Family

The myths about marriage and family are omnipresent in our culture. The myths are perpetrated in almost every movie, TV show, song, magazine, book, billboard, and advertisement.

The mythical scenario goes something like this: You are trudging along in life—lonely, but coping. Some Enchanted Evening (across a crowded room) you meet The Perfect Stranger (as opposed to a total stranger). Fade in music. Fade out loneliness. You are lifted to the pinnacle of bliss, where you and Prince Charming or Cinderella live happily ever after. The end.

This is the most popular version of the larger, underlying myth that says things and people outside ourselves make us happy. ("You made me love you, I didn't want to do it . . .")

In fact, *we* make us happy. ("If you are lonely when you are alone," cautioned Jean-Paul Sartre, "you are in bad company.") The joy we see in others is a reflection of the joy in ourselves. We feel uncomfortable, however, giving ourselves credit for our own joy. It's easier to say, "You're wonderful, and I'm so happy you're with me," than to say, "I'm wonderful, and I'm so happy to be me." The first version may be easier to *say*, but it's not (a) honest, and (b) easy to live with.

It's not easy to live with because, if we feel happiness only when the other person is around, then we have to keep that other person around in order to be happy. If that person happens to be lost in the

> *Seldom or never does*
> *a marriage develop into*
> *an individual relationship*
> *smoothly and without crisis.*
> *There is no*
> *birth of consciousness*
> *without pain.*
>
> C. G. JUNG

same illusion, that's called "being in love," and everything is hunky dory—for a while. (As Cher observed, "The trouble with some women is that they get all excited about nothing—and then marry him.")

Eventually, no matter how hard we try to keep up the facade, one partner or the other will peek behind it and see the Dark Side, which is not at all lovable. "He loved me absolutely," wrote Frieda (Mrs. D. H.) Lawrence, "that's why he hates me absolutely."

The Dark Side is, of course, only something we see in another that we don't like about ourselves, and, again, are not honest enough to admit. If A sees B's Dark Side, but B fails to see A's Dark Side, it's Dump City. B sings a medley of torch songs and A cries, "Free Again!" If both see it at once, the perfect lovers become perfect enemies.

Am I being harsh on love and marriage? Look at the statistics. In the United States, more than half the marriages end in divorce within five years. *Half!* ("In Hollywood all the marriages are happy," Shelley Winters observed. "It's trying to live together afterwards that causes all the problems.")

Remember, these are the couples who stood before God, friends, and in-laws, *swearing* to love one another 'til death did them part. Imagine how many others—who at one time or another thought they were in love forever—never made it to the altar. ("My boyfriend and I broke up," Rita Rudner explained. "He wanted to get married and I didn't want him to.")

Which brings me to children. Children are a twenty-four-hour-a-day commitment, for a minimum of eighteen years—probably longer. With children, you can learn something very important: how to give for the sheer joy of giving. If you give to children with any hope of return, you're inviting misery all around. ("Before I was married I had three theories about raising children," John Wilmot, the Earl of Rochester, wrote. "Now I have three children and no theories.")

In fact, that's one of the primary lessons one learns—not just from children but from intimate relationships of all kinds—how to give.

The myth is that marriage is for *receiving*. It's

> *I have known more men*
> *destroyed by the desire*
> *to have wife and child*
> *and to keep them in comfort*
> *than I have seen*
> *destroyed by drink and harlots.*
>
> W. B. YEATS

not. It's for giving. ("Marriage is not merely sharing the fettucini," Calvin Trillin explained, "but sharing the burden of finding the fettucini restaurant in the first place.")

But don't take my word for it. Ask anyone who's been in a successful relationship for, oh, at least two years. They'll almost certainly describe themselves as *giving,* with no thought of return. If they go on and on about how much fun it was to *receive,* you're probably talking to Zsa Zsa Gabor.

(When Zsa Zsa was on a call-in radio show, a caller asked, "I want to break up with a man, but he's been so nice to me. He gave me a car, a diamond necklace, a mink stole, beautiful gowns, a stove, expensive perfumes—what should I do?" Without having to think, Zsa Zsa said, "Give him back the stove.")

Another cultural myth is that we are somehow *incomplete* if we do not reproduce. This notion may have had some validity when being fruitful and multiplying was necessary for a species or tribe to continue. Today, however, one of the great problems in the world is overpopulation. Let those who really *want* to reproduce reproduce (and that includes providing the eighteen-year environment in which the reproductions can grow into functioning, creative, healthy humans). Those who want to leave their legacy in another way can feel free to do so.

Another value of relationships is learning about *ourselves*—the good, the bad, the beautiful, and the ugly. Marriage is like a dinner with dessert first. The falling in love portion shows us the beauty within us. Everything else shows us everything else. It's a package deal. When the Dark Side presents itself and says, "I'm in you, too," many people panic.

"Wait a minute. This isn't part of the contract."

"Yes, it is. For better or for worse. This is worse."

"This is *the worst*. Where's the lovey-dovey stuff?"

"Maybe that bird will return when you learn to love this one."

"I have to learn to love it?"

"You only *have to* learn to *accept* it. Loving it, however, feels better."

> *As to marriage or celibacy,*
> *let a man take which course he will—*
> *he will be sure to repent it.*
>
> SOCRATES

People seldom want to face the Dark Side of themselves. Instead, they (choose one or more)

1. Deny it's a mirror and pretend it's the other person. (One must be careful not to strike out too severely at a mirror, for, as we all know, if you break a mirror, it's seven years bad luck— perhaps in jail.)

2. Pretend *really hard* that everything is all right, and "play house." ("Welcome to *At Home with the Ostrich Family.* Here's mother, Heroic Pretender; and father, General Denial. Here are their children, Make Believe, Gloss Over, and Feign Affection. Don't they all look *happy?* The Ostrich Family!")

3. Realize that the reflected Dark Side they see in the mirror is true about themselves and hate themselves even more.

4. Run!

For those looking for an intensive workshop in self-discovery, self-acceptance, and the perfect place to learn the joy of giving—like it or not—Marriage/Family is an area of life to consider.

(If you thought I was perhaps too hard on marital bliss, let me close with a romantic thought from Britt Ekland: "I know a lot of people didn't expect our relationship to last—but we just celebrated our two months anniversary.")

I don't have anything against work.
I just figure, why deprive somebody
who really enjoys it?

DOBIE GILLIS

NAPOLEON SOLO: Are you free?
ILLYA KURAKIN: No man is free
who has to work for a living.
But I am available.

THE MAN FROM UNCLE

Career and Professional

Did you ever hear parents placing a curse on their child? "Someday, something's going to straighten you out!" That's what a career is—The Great Straightener.

Next to gravity, there's very little as constant as the business world—it will drag you down if you slip too often, or hurl you to the moon if you understand how to use it. (Most of the energy used in traveling to the moon and back was the gravitational pull of the moon and Earth.) Wernher von Braun found the business side of putting a man on the moon more difficult than the functional side. "We can lick gravity," he said, "but sometimes the paperwork is overwhelming."

A job is what you have when you want to take the money to some other area of life in order to buy the necessities. Someone whose primary focus is marriage, for example, leaves the marriage only long enough to make the money to support the marriage—baby needs a new pair of shoes, and all that. That's a job.*

---

*Not that staying home and working isn't a job. To illuminate, here's Roseanne: "As a housewife, I feel that if the kids are still alive when my husband gets home from work, then hey, I've done my job. When Sears comes out with a riding vacuum cleaner, then I'll clean the house." One could follow Quentin Crisp's advice, "There is no need to do any housework at all. After the first four years the dirt doesn't get any worse. It's simply a question of not losing your nerve."

> *Drive thy business,*
> *or it will drive thee.*
>
> BENJAMIN FRANKLIN

You have a *career* or *profession* when what you love doing most is what you also get paid for doing. As Noel Coward said, "Work is much more fun than fun." Or, as Richard Bach remarked, "The more I want to get something done, the less I call it work."

"But I am an artist," some may say. "I only want to create." If you plan to get paid for creating, then you're in business. "But someone will discover me and take care of all that." Right, and if you have nothing to wear to the ball, your fairy godmother will supervise the mice and the birds in making you a gown.

The days of being "discovered" in the arts went

out with Diaghelev. Artists—and that includes actors, singers, writers, dancers, musicians, painters,
and so on—must become their own supporters,
must champion their own cause. To succeed, they
must become patron *and* protégé all in one. In
other words, if you're a creative person, you must
create your own creative outlet. And that means
being in business.*

The secret of success in a career? Same as success in any other area. As John Moores explained,
"Work seven days a week and nothing can stop
you." Not only is success hard work, it's hard, *challenging* work. "If you have a job without aggrava-
tions," Malcolm Forbes pointed out, "you don't
have a job."

One must, however, not just work *hard*. One
must work *smart*. As the saying goes, the efficient
person gets the job done *right;* the effective person
gets the *right job done*. "The really idle man gets
nowhere," Sir Heneage Ogilvie observed. "The per-
petually busy man does not get much further."

Of course, a career is not for everyone. Lily
Tomlin said, "The trouble with the rat race is that
even if you win, you're still a rat."

And, yes, in addition to long hours and hard

*In 1988, twenty publishers turned down *You Can't Afford the
Luxury of a Negative Thought,* so I published it myself. I then
published *LIFE 101* myself, and this one, too, because I realized
there's a lot more to getting a book into a reader's hands than
merely writing it.

> *It is your work in life that is*
> *the ultimate seduction.*
>
> PABLO PICASSO

work, each career has its Dark Side. "The price one pays for pursuing any profession or calling," James Baldwin explained, "is an intimate knowledge of its ugly side."

When one peeks through the glamour, one sees reality, and one may not like it. As Fred Allen said, "When you get through all the phony tinsel of Hollywood, you find the genuine tinsel underneath." David Sarnoff remarked, "Competition brings out the best in products, and the worst in people."

One *especially* may not like a career's Dark Side when one remembers the mirror—the things we don't like about our career are also what we don't like about ourselves. Is your career insincere? Dishonest? Heartless? Gulp. Behold, the mirror.

If one is willing to see a career as a great, big mirror (career and mirror—they even rhyme, if you pronounce them with a vague Southern accent), there's a lot to learn—facts most people don't want to learn about themselves.

Rather than looking in either the relationship or career mirror, some spend time looking in one until it becomes uncomfortable, then run off to look in the other. Back and forth, endlessly.

The career vs. marriage struggle has been going on since the caveperson who invented the first wheel decided to open *Wheels R Us*.

One side of the struggle is expressed by George Jean Nathan: "Marriage is based on the theory that when a man discovers a brand of beer exactly to his taste he should at once throw up his job and go to work in a brewery."

Representing the other side of the debate, Bertrand Russell: "One of the symptoms of an approaching nervous breakdown is the belief that one's work is terribly important."

"Can't I have both a career and a marriage?" Well, some can. And some can juggle seven balls while eating a tuna fish sandwich.

What happens at the end of a long, successful career? You'll be glad you chose career over everything else, brimming with pride over all you've accomplished, right?

Well . . .

T. S. Eliot, poet, Nobel Laureate—but better known as the lyricist for *Cats*, heaven help his

> *The easiest kind*
> *of relationship for me*
> *is with ten thousand people.*
> *The hardest is with one.*
>
> JOAN BAEZ

memory—wrote,

> As things are, and as fundamentally they
> must always be, poetry is not a career, but a
> mug's game. No honest poet can ever feel
> quite sure of the permanent value of what he
> has written: he may have wasted his time and
> messed up his life for nothing.

And Sir Thomas More, after fifteen years of
practicing law, wrote of an ideal future, *Utopia*,
"They have no lawyers among them, for they consider them as a sort of people whose profession it is
to disguise matters." Or, as Robert Frost put it, "By
working faithfully eight hours a day, you may eventually get to be a boss and work twelve hours a day."

To laugh often and much;
to win the respect of intelligent people
and the affection of children;
to earn the appreciation of honest critics
and endure the betrayal of false friends;
to appreciate beauty;
to find the best in others;
to leave the world a bit better,
whether by a healthy child,
a garden patch
or a redeemed social condition;
to know even one life has breathed easier
because you have lived.
This is to have succeeded.

HARRY EMERSON FOSDICK

A cardinal rule of politics—
never get caught in bed
with a live man
or a dead woman.

J. R. Ewing

Social and Political

If the sentence, "I love humanity, it's people I can't stand," fits you, perhaps you should consider a life of social change and political action.

"The only thing necessary for the triumph of evil," Edmund Burke wrote two hundred years ago, "is for good men to do nothing." The world has any number of good people right now, with the dream to make changes for the better deep in their hearts. The problem is not that they're doing *nothing*; the problem is that they're doing *something else*.

People who are naturally drawn toward social action or politics are often repelled by its name. "Ninety percent of the politicians give the other ten percent a bad reputation," Henry Kissinger said. Here is an area of activity where the *reputation* is worse than the *reality*—a sort of reverse glamour.

"I used to say that politics was the second oldest profession," said Ronald Reagan in 1979, "and I have come to know that it bears a gross similarity to the first." The following year he won the presidency.

"Nobody could sleep with Dick," Pat Nixon revealed. "He wakes up during the night, switches on the lights, speaks into his tape recorder, or takes notes—it's impossible."

John Updike had this explanation for the inconsistency of our leaders: "A leader is one who, out of madness or goodness, volunteers to take upon himself the woe of the people. There are few men so foolish, hence the erratic quality of leadership in

> *I know God will not give me*
> *anything I can't handle.*
> *I just wish that He didn't*
> *trust me so much.*
>
> MOTHER TERESA

the world."

And yet, with all the bad things written about it, some do have a few good words for and about the art of politics.

"True leadership must be for the benefit of the followers," wrote Robert Townsend in *Up the Organization,* "not the enrichment of the leaders." Townsend was speaking of the business world, but it applies to the political world as well.

You may not always be popular, even among those you are helping. Harry Truman asked, "How far would Moses have gone if he had taken a poll in Egypt?"

"Public life is regarded as the crown of a career,

and to young men it is the worthiest ambition," said John Buchan. "Politics is still the greatest and the most honorable adventure."

"Politics," Gore Vidal wrote, with his own enticing twist on Buchan, "is the grim jockeying for position, the ceaseless trading, the deliberate use of words not for communication but to screen intention. In short, a splendidly exciting game for those who play it."

"If you're going to play the game properly," cautioned Barbara Jordan, "you'd better know every rule."

The great social causes that capture the hearts of men and women do not necessarily involve politics. They do, however, involve courage, sacrifice, commitment, and selfless giving—the worst of marriage and career combined.

There are, however, inner benefits. "The great use of life is to spend it for something that will outlast it," William James wrote.

And make no mistake about it: we make social changes because, over time, it makes *us* feel better. We may not appreciate the day-to-day tilting at windmills, but we prefer that to day-by-day observing a condition we know we could somehow make better, get worse.

People often think a social problem is too great and they are too small. I suggest: If drawn to do it, do it. "What one has to do," Eleanor Roosevelt pointed out, "usually can be done."

The reward is the joy of giving, the satisfaction of following your heart's desire, and, perhaps,

> *A pessimist is one who builds
> dungeons in the air.*
>
> WALTER WINCHELL

someone will say of you what Clare Boothe Luce said of Eleanor Roosevelt, "No woman has ever so comforted the distressed—or distressed the comfortable."

The little entourage
of friends and relatives
whom she completely dominated
was fond of saying,
"Becky would give you
the shirt off her back."
And it was true.
The only trouble was that she neglected
to take it off first,
and what you found on your back
was not only Becky's shirt
but Becky too.

MARGARET HALSEY

I am ready to meet my Maker.
Whether my Maker is prepared
for the ordeal of meeting me
is another matter.

SIR WINSTON CHURCHILL

Religious and Spiritual

Here I tread softly. In *LIFE 101*, I put all the religious and spiritual beliefs—from Anglicanism to agnosticism to atheism to Catholicism—in an area I called The Gap.

The contents of anyone's Gap is between the individual and the contents of his or her Gap. I don't get involved with the Gap in these books because the tools I discuss work regardless of what's in anyone's Gap, just as a cookbook or car repair manual works for Baptist and Buddhist alike.

In discussing the areas of life's activity, however, I must touch on an area some people are strongly drawn to—religion and spirit.

There is an interesting ambivalence to religion and spirituality in our culture. On one hand, if people have no beliefs, they are thought odd. On the other hand, if they devote all their time to the understanding and worship of God, they, too, are thought odd.

As with politics, people may hesitate pursuing spirit full time because religion has been so, well, shall I say (tap, tap, tap) has made God to look, uh, um (tap, tap, tap—that's me tap dancing while arriving at a diplomatic, nonjudgmental way of saying this), perhaps some people's behavior has not cast the Deity in the best possible light.

For example, the chief executive of Coca-Cola said, "It's a religion as well as a business." (By the way, do you know that the taste of cola is a combination of three familiar flavors? Which three? If you

> *We live very close together.*
> *So, our prime purpose in this life*
> *is to help others.*
> *And if you can't help them,*
> *at least don't hurt them.*
>
> THE DALI LAMA

want to guess, I'll wait for a bit before telling you.)

Others seem to use God as some great bellhop in the sky—"give me this, send me that, take this away." Dorothy Parker parodied these people when she wrote, "Oh God, in the name of Thine only beloved Son, Jesus Christ, Our Lord, let him phone me *now.*"

All of this—and I haven't even *mentioned* tele-vangelists and their traumas—may have made traditional religion seem a little strange, even to those who feel a calling. My advice, as always: follow your heart.

Of course, there are those who think they *should* spend all their time worshiping God because, after all, God is God and isn't that what I'm *supposed* to do? And, even though these people are off pursuing a goal in another area of life, they feel *guilty* for not *praying* more—as though God were an overanxious mother who hasn't had a phone call in a month. (Although, if that is your image of God, far be it from me to de-Deify you.) Might I suggest to these people that they let their good works in whatever field they choose glorify God? (Cola, by the way, is made up of these three flavors: citrus [lemon or lime], vanilla, and cinnamon.)

And for those who are feeling the Ultimate Unworthiness—not worthy to serve God—I offer you this from Phyllis McGinley:

> The wonderful thing about saints is that they were human. They lost their tempers, scolded God, were egotistical or testy or impatient in their turns, made mistakes and regretted them. Still they went on doggedly blundering toward heaven.

*I can think of nothing
less pleasurable
than a life devoted to pleasure.*

JOHN D. ROCKEFELLER, JR.

Let's Not Forget Fun and Recreation

I'm not sure whether all work and no play made Jack a dull boy, or whether Jack was a dull boy to begin with, so, dullard that he was, he worked too much. Either way, fun and recreation are a necessary part of an undull life.

When I say *recreation*, I mean it in the lighter sense of recreation (tennis, boating, going to the movies), as well as in the deeper sense—*re-creation*. What do you do to "recreate" yourself? This might include meditation, retreats *(re-treats)*, prayer, spiritual work, rest, pilgrimages, massage, silent time—whatever activities recharge your batteries in a deep and powerful way.

I didn't include Fun/Recreation in the other areas of life because I assume this is an area people will want to enjoy no matter what other area they choose. To use the battery analogy, Fun/Recreation charges the batteries; Marriage/Family, Career/Professional, Social/Political, and Religious/Spiritual are the ways in which the batteries are used.

It's important to realize, however, that the endless pursuit of fun and recreation *in and of themselves* is not very fulfilling. In fact, it's something of a curse. When one pursues pleasure *all the time*, the pursuit of pleasure becomes work—it's a job. If pleasure is one's job, then where does one go to recharge the batteries for more work? The pleasure *is* the work. Hence, perhaps, the old saying about

> *A Code of Honor—*
> *Never approach a friend's*
> *girlfriend or wife*
> *with mischief as your goal.*
> *There are just too many*
> *women in the world*
> *to justify that sort of*
> *dishonorable behavior.*
> *Unless she's <u>really</u> attractive.*
>
> BRUCE JAY FRIEDMAN

not mixing business with pleasure.

Fun and recreation form a stable base for fulfilling one's dreams—they're just not a very good dream all by themselves.

*Do not do unto others
as you would that they
should do unto you.
Their tastes may not
be the same.*

GEORGE BERNARD SHAW

Basically my wife
was immature.
I'd be at home in the bath
and she'd come in
and sink my boats.

WOODY ALLEN

Relationships

Please don't think from the tone of the last few chapters that the only way to pursue a dream other than marriage and family is to become a hermit. Far from it.

Relationships are essential to the pursuit of almost any goal. In successfully pursuing a goal, however, it is important to understand the different *types* of relationships that are available. When you do, you can see which types of relationships can best help you pursue your dream.

Before exploring the types of relationships humans tend to have, here are two essential points about relationships in general. First, all relationships are with yourself—and sometimes they involve other people. Second, the most important relationship in your life—the one you'll have, like it or not, until the day you die—is with yourself.

That said, let's look at the various types of relationships.

Recreational Relationships: These are the people we enjoy being with simply because we enjoy being with them. *What* we do together is not as important as *that we are* together.

These are the people we generally call "friends." We love them in a nonpossessive way. "Love without attachment is light," wrote Norman O. Brown. We see people in recreational relationships for what they are. "We don't love qualities," Jacques Maritain explained; "we love a person; sometimes by reason of their defects as well as their qualities."

> *Since I was twenty-four*
> *there never was any vagueness*
> *in my plans or ideas*
> *as to what God's work was for me.*
>
> FLORENCE NIGHTINGALE

Again, the word *recreational* should not be misread as "always superficial." These can be some of the most re-creative and nurturing relationships in our lives.

Among the many things that *can* (although usually doesn't) take place in a recreational relationship is sex. This won't destroy the relationship, as long as neither person sees the other as "the one and only."

Romantic Relationships: Here, sex—or sexual desire—combines with a feeling of, "you are the only one for me," and "if you don't love me, I'm miserable and worthless." We don't have to like— or even *know*—the "love object." Some say ignorance is a *prerequisite* for romantic love. "Of course it is possible to love a human being," wrote Charles Bukowski, "if you don't know them too well."

Romantic love is the most popularized of all relationships. Just about every movie, TV show, novel, and popular song features romantic interaction. It's called the "love interest." It seemingly must be worked into every plot, no matter how silly or tortured.

Why? Because romantic love is a fundamental cultural myth. As George Lucas explained to Steven Spielberg (these are the two who *somehow* squeezed a "love interest" into all of those Indiana Jones movies), "If the boy and girl walk off in the sunset hand-in-hand in the last scene, it adds ten million to the box office."

I call romantic love ("If only I could find the right person to love, I would live happily ever after") a myth because no other human endeavor has failed so miserably, so often—yet continues to have such "good press."

Not everyone, of course, believes "the press." "I can understand companionship," said Gore Vidal, "I can understand purchased sex in the afternoon. I cannot understand the love affair." Margaret Anderson explained, "In real love you want the other person's good. In romantic love you want the other person."

Some people "fall in love" rather than deal with the guilt often associated with sex. "If we love each other, sex is okay," the logic goes. "Love is the drug," wrote Germaine Greer, "which makes sexuality palatable in popular mythology."

> *The consuming desire of most*
> *human beings is deliberately*
> *to plant their whole life*
> *in the hands of some other person.*
> *I would describe this method*
> *of searching for happiness*
> *as immature.*
> *Development of character*
> *consists solely in moving*
> *toward self-sufficiency.*
>
> QUENTIN CRISP

Romantic love is a primary distraction to the pursuit of *any* goal, *including* Marriage / Family. I should say *especially* Marriage / Family. The illusion of "falling in love" can blind one to the suitability of a partner for a venture as delicate, intricate, and important as getting married and raising children. (Or even getting married and raising *orchids.*)

"Many a man has fallen in love with a girl," Maurice Chevalier observed, "in light so dim he would not have chosen a suit by it." And, many a person has chosen a mate in a light of reason dimmer than that.

In addition, the *lack* of romantic love is hardly sufficient reason to eliminate another otherwise-qualified candidate from a list of potential spouses—and yet it's done all the time. People say, "He/she'd be a wonderful husband/wife, but I don't really *love* him/her." You might as well use romantic love as a criterion for going into business, or any other significant partnership.

It is this blindness, as much as anything else, that accounts for the many failures in the pursuit of a successful marriage. If you think running a house and raising children *isn't* a business, you've never run a house and raised children.

"Love is an ideal thing;" said Goethe, "marriage is a real thing. A confusion of the real with the ideal never goes unpunished."

Contractual Relationships: In a contractual relationship, something is exchanged for something else. The "something" could be anything—a product, a service, an experience. Usually the culturally agreed upon *symbol* for energy—money—is involved in the transaction.

When we pay someone for something, or to do something for us, that is a contractual relationship. It could be as basic as buying a box of cough drops at the store (even such a simple transaction involves entering into a contract), or as elaborate as a fifty-year partnership—including marriage.

In a contractual relationship, we are "in relationship" primarily because of the exchange. We can enjoy each other's company or not. If so, that's an extra plus. If not, too bad—we're in it for something else.

"Almost all of our relationships begin," ob-

> *Saddle your dreams*
> *afore you ride 'em.*
>
> MARY WEBB
> 1881–1927

served W. H. Auden, "and most of them continue as forms of mutual exploitation, a mental or physical barter, to be terminated when one or both parties run out of goods."

Common-Goal Relationships: Here people share a common goal, and that goal is the primary reason they relate. This is often the source of work-based relationships. The common goal may be a company goal, a personal goal fulfilled by the company, or, simply, as Sir Noel Coward put it, "your pay packet at the end of the week."

It might be a service goal—relating to fellow Red Cross volunteers, for example. It might be a religious or spiritual goal—the people you know in church, or who pursue the same spiritual dreams as you.

The marriages that continue "for the sake of the children" are also examples of common-goal relationships—the raising of the children being the common goal. "The value of marriage," said Peter De Vries, "is not that adults produce children, but that children produce adults."

Power-Point Relationships: This is a specific form of common-goal relationship. Here one person becomes the "power point." A group feeds its energy (power) to the power-point person, and through this power point, the entire group can fulfill its common goal.

An example is the Olympic athlete training for an event. Power from many people is invested in this one person. The "power" may be in the form of information, encouragement, money, time—anything the athlete needs to meet the goal. A trainer, coach, corporate sponsor, masseur, doctor, nutritionist—and many others—channel their power (in the form of individual specialties) to the athlete. They all have the same goal—winning the event—and send power to a single point so that the goal can be fulfilled.

Think of the point-person as the point of the arrow. The point is the portion of the arrow that "does the work," but the shaft, feathers, bow, and archer are equally important to hitting the target.

The point person never needs to *return* any energy to those giving it. The point person need only do his or her best in the event—the common

> *If the point is sharp,*
> *and the arrow is swift,*
> *it can pierce through the dust*
> *no matter how thick.*
>
> BOB DYLAN

goal. In so doing—win or lose—the investment of power is "paid back."

In addition to sports, power-point relationships are often seen in politics, the arts, spiritual groups, and, less frequently, in business and marriage. In a marriage, a power-point relationship can work as long as it is understood that partner A's success is the goal of both partner A and partner B—and that partner A's success *in and of itself* is sufficient for partner B. If partner B wants something more from partner A or partner A's success, then it's a contract or common-goal relationship.

≈

In relationships—as in all human activity—there is a lot of room for negotiation. As the saying goes, "You don't get what you deserve, you get what you negotiate."

Let's say someone with whom you have a recreational relationship calls you up and asks you out. Although it would be fun to go out, you have committed four hours to stuffing envelopes, the result of which could further your goal. Rather than automatically saying, "No, I can't make it," present the situation to your friend and see if he or she (let's say he) has any creative solutions.

Maybe he'll offer to come over and chat with you as you stuff. This will still take four hours, but it might be more fun. Maybe he will come over and help you get the work done in two hours, which leaves two newly freed hours for other pursuits. Maybe he will *hire* someone to stuff *all* the envelopes, and you are free for the whole evening. The solutions are endless, and creating them is part of relating.

There are few "pure" relationships—most cross lines, combining one type of relationship with another. Relationships also change over time, evolving—or deteriorating—from one type to another.

It's obvious that—far from being a "loner" as you pursue your goal—you will be relating with lots of people for lots of reasons. In fact, you may well be interacting with far more people than you currently are.

Father told me that
if I ever met a lady
in a dress like yours,
I must look her
straight in the eyes.

CHARLES, PRINCE OF WALES

(ON SUSAN HAMPSHIRE'S DECOLLETAGÉ)

What Have You Accomplished?

Thus far in this book, I have written thousands and thousands of words. Now it's your turn.

In the next two chapters, I'll ask you to do some writing, as well as some remembering and observing. If you're reading this book for information now and plan to do the "work" later, when you return to do the work, please begin with the chapter "What Is Your Purpose?" and then return to this one.

In doing this exercise, you might want to use 3x5 cards, as that eliminates the need for rewriting. It's not necessary for this exercise, and you'll need a lot of them—200 to 300, probably. If you're low on 3x5 cards (fewer than 300), please save them for the exercises in the chapter "What Do You Want?"

So, what have you accomplished? As things come to mind, set this book aside and write them down (one per card). I'll make some comments to jog your memory, but when it's jogged, write for a while, and then return for some more jogging.

What have you accomplished? What have you achieved? What things did you want and go out and get? They may be a part of your life now, or they may be long gone. Either way, write them down.

Cars? Jobs? Apartments? Stereos? Furniture? You don't need to list every piece of clothing or can of beans you ever bought, but if some special purchases or exceptional dinners come to mind, write them down.

> *Dust is a protective coating
> for fine furniture.*
>
> MARIO BUATTA

What about schooling? Did you get a high school diploma? What degrees did you obtain? Perhaps you're prouder of the degrees you *didn't* receive. What about night classes, workshops, seminars, or other less traditional forms of education? Have you learned a language? How to change your own oil? Cook? Play ball (any ball)? Dance? Sing? What are your hobbies? Where have you traveled? What about the books you've read? Plays you've seen? Miniseries you've lived through? Tapes you've listened to?

What about people? Of whom did you say, "I want this person for a friend/lover/boss/employee/ teacher/student/roommate/wife/husband/etc.," and got them? Even if you didn't initiate the relationship, for every relationship you've ever had, you had to do *something,* even if it was not saying no.

The fact that a relationship, job—or anything else—may have *ended* poorly doesn't mean it shouldn't be on your list. If it was something you wanted and you got, that counts. Much of our growth comes from getting what we want and finding out we don't want it after all. Even if *they* are the ones who decided the relationships were not what they wanted, include those relationships on your list, too. You had them for a time, and the only difference between a happy ending and an unhappy ending is where they put the closing credits. Go to the happy time, consider it an achievement, and write it down.

What about social or political goals? Did your candidate win? Did the proposal you favored pass? Even if you did nothing more than *vote* for it, that's better than half the people in the United States do during any given election. What giving—directly, or through organizations—have you done?

Yes, this is a lot of remembering and a lot of writing. That's the point. We tend to forget what we've accomplished; we tend to forget how much we have created; we tend to forget how powerful we are.

How about family? Did you create any children? What have you done for members of your family? Perhaps *leaving* a family situation that wasn't doing *anyone* any good was a major achievement.

What about health? What illnesses have you successfully recovered from? What changes in your

> *One can never consent to creep*
> *when one feels*
> *an impulse to soar.*
>
> HELEN KELLER

body image have you made? Do you exercise? *Have* you exercised? Take vitamins? Had body work of any kind done? What bad habits have you overcome (even temporarily)? Have you been in therapy? Whatever the outcome, the fact that you sought help is a major accomplishment.

What about God? Do you go to church? Temple? Meditate? Pray? Whatever connection you have with the Almighty, *you* had something to do with it. (If not, *everyone* would feel connected, and that's not the case.) Perhaps your accomplishments include abandoning one religious or spiritual path to find one closer to your heart.

Keep writing. The pump has been primed. This is a good point to set this book aside and spend some time writing and remembering. It will never be a complete list—the list of your achievements is nearly endless—but at some point, you'll approach the limit of your immediate memory. Pick up the book again and continue reading when the memories run out.

≈

Now, read through your list. Note how much you *have* done, how much you *have* created—and how much more is available to you in the future.

Without regretting anything, imagine what you could have achieved if all these accomplishments had been pointed in a *single* direction—if all this creative energy had been directed toward fulfilling your heart's desire.

Again: no regrets. Don't look at the past and say, "What a waste." As Katherine Mansfield said, "Make it a rule of life never to regret and never to look back. Regret is an appalling waste of energy; you can't build on it; it's only good for wallowing in."

Use the energy to be *excited* about the future. If you're, say, thirty, don't think, "Thirty wasted years!" Most people don't begin making their own decisions until eighteen or twenty.

Let's arbitrarily say, "Life begins when you move out of your parents' house." (Although, for you it might be, "Life began when I got my first full-time job," or, if you're, say, Prince Charles and *never* plan

> *The world is moving so fast*
> *these days that the man*
> *who says it can't be done*
> *is generally interrupted*
> *by someone doing it.*

HARRY EMERSON FOSDICK

to move out of your parents' house or get a job, "Life began when I got married" or "Life began when I got my divorce.")

For the first twenty-or-so years of life, we are in the hands of other people. If, then, you are thirty, and moved out when you were twenty, you really only have ten years of *your* life to consider.

Look at what you've done in those years. Imagine how much you'll accomplish in the next similar period of time. This is something worth getting excited about.

*The man who
tried his best and failed
is superior to the man
who never tried.*

BUD WILKINSON

Happiness?
A good cigar, a good meal,
and a good woman
—or a bad woman.
It depends on how much
happiness you can handle.

GEORGE BURNS

What Do You Have?

This list is a subset of the list you just made. It is a list of everything you're glad to have in your life *now*.

This is an exercise in recognizing what we often tend to take for granted. It is also an exercise in *gratitude*.

As you write this Inventory of Now, begin each item on the list with a phrase such as "I am grateful for . . ." or "I am thankful for . . ." or simply, "Thank you for . . . ."

The list, then, will read,

I am grateful for my health.

I am grateful for my house.

I am grateful for my relationship with . . .

and so on.

If you used 3x5 cards for the last exercise, you can go through those and pull out the ones that apply. Write at the top of each "I am grateful for" or, if the top is already taken, you can add to the bottom, "for which I am grateful."

If you didn't use 3x5 cards, go back over your list and copy those things onto a new list. As you copy to the new list, preface each with "I am grateful for" or "I am thankful for"

Please do write "I am grateful for" before each thing on your list. Writing it once at the top of a page is not as effective—the physical writing of it, over and over, is important. And, if you're doing

> *If I had known my son*
> *was going to be*
> *president of Bolivia,*
> *I would have taught him*
> *to read and write.*
>
> ENRIQUE PENARANDA'S MOTHER

this process on a computer, for heaven sakes don't program it to add the phrase automatically!

(When I say "things," I mean anything—from people to cars to body parts to inner qualities to God. I don't mean to diminish any of them by calling them "things.")

After transferring all the things you have now from the list of your accomplishments, take a look at your current life. What did you leave out? What was so taken for granted you didn't include it on your list of achievements? What would you miss if it were taken from you? List those things, too.

What about your body? Even if some part of it doesn't look the way you'd like or function the way you want, what about the rest of it? Be grateful for those parts, and add them to your list.

How about your abilities? What do you know how to do that you're glad to know? Don't forget the skills you currently use to make money, the skills you *plan* to make money with, and the qualities that keep your friends coming back for more. (Review the list of qualities you made while working on your purpose.)

Speaking of friends, what about people? Who are the friends, lovers, acquaintances, spouses, children, relatives, coworkers, fellow-seekers you're glad to have in your life?

What about physical possessions? Look around. Your insurance agent may have recommended you make a list of this sort for years. Now's a good time to do it.

What about hobbies? Sports? The view from your window? The country, state, city, and neighborhood you live in? What freedoms do you have you'd hate to lose?

This is another of those lists that takes some time. It is, however, finite, and, with some time spent on it, can become fairly complete.

It is time well spent.

The truth is that all of us
attain the greatest success
and happiness possible in this life
whenever we use our
native capacities
to their greatest extent.

DR. SMILEY BLANTON

Choice and Consequences

Life is like *Truth or Consequences*. When we tell ourselves the *truth*, we are better prepared for the *consequences*.

People often fail to tell themselves the truth in the area of choices. Many people *pretend* they have made Choice A, while their actions, behavior, and direction clearly indicate they are moving toward Choice B. When they arrive at B (or see it looming before them), they react with genuine surprise (often coupled with disappointment and/or outrage), "What's this B stuff? I chose A!"

It's bad enough to tell others we're heading toward A when we know we're heading toward B. It's ten times worse to tell ourselves we're heading toward A, when all the while we're making a beeline for B. That's called *confusion, frustration,* and *what's-a-nice-person-like-me-doing-in-a-life-like-this?*

What gets us to our goal is *action*—action in the broadest sense of the word. Mental action, emotional action, and physical action—all focused in one direction. People tell themselves they want one thing—then they think, feel, and move toward another.

Why?

Fear of the Consequences.

Humans are smart—as compared with, say, amoebas. Humans can logically, and fairly accurately, project ahead in time. If we go to the store, we know we will find popsicles there. If we pay a certain amount of money, we can have a popsicle

> *Far better it is*
> *to dare mighty things,*
> *to win glorious triumphs*
> *even though checkered by failure,*
> *than to rank with those poor*
> *spirits who neither enjoy*
> *nor suffer much because*
> *they live in the gray twilight*
> *that knows neither*
> *victory nor defeat.*
>
> THEODORE ROOSEVELT

of our own. If we put it in our mouth, it will taste cold and sweet. If we set forth on that course, in all probability, a popsicle is what will happen.

We can also predict the down side of the future—the potentially negative consequences of the action: it will cost money, it will take time, it will contain so many extra calories, it might spoil our appetite, and so on.

When we consider actually moving toward our heart's desire, a part of us automatically looks ahead to the possible consequences—especially the negative ones. The comfort zone gloms onto these negative consequences. The comfort zone argues that the *actions* will bring on the negative *conse-*

quences. The comfort zone's emotionally backed demand: No Action.

The comfort zone stays fairly quiet as long as we don't seriously contemplate action. We can *want* our dream all we want; we can *think about someday getting it* as much as we like; we can *tell everyone we know how we're one day going to have it* at every opportunity. We can even *make commitments we don't really plan to keep.* The only thing we can't do is DO IT!

If we begin to do it, the comfort zone goes into overdrive—hyperdrive, actually—and gets us back on track. "On track" to the comfort zone is what we've always done before, which means heading (again) toward B, even though our dream is A.

Why are the consequences of action so uncomfortable? Let's take a look:

1. *When we choose, we must let other options go.* If we have enough money for one popsicle, and we choose cherry, we must abandon grape, orange, tangerine, banana supreme, pina colada, watermelon, tutti-fruti, and passion fruit. Naturally, we don't *want* to abandon grape, orange, tangerine, banana supreme, pina colada, watermelon, tutti-fruti, and passion fruit. All that loss! We're miserable. We should have stayed at home. No, the store-keeper won't let us have a bite of each. No, there's no credit. We keep picking up and setting down one flavor after another, feeling rotten, until we get frostbite.

   When we make our Big Choice and go for the Big Dream, it means letting go of all the

> *Procrastination is the fear of success.*
> *People procrastinate because*
> *they are afraid of the success*
> *that they know will result*
> *if they move ahead now.*
> *Because success is heavy,*
> *carries a responsibility with it,*
> *it is much easier*
> *to procrastinate and live on the*
> *"someday I'll" philosophy.*
>
> DENIS WAITLEY

other Big Dreams, even though those dreams may be as appealing as grape, orange, tangerine, banana supreme, pina colada, watermelon, tutti-fruti, and passion fruit. I don't like hearing this news any more than you do, but if I don't tell it to you, life will. (Life probably already has.)

If we make *no choice,* we end up with *nothing.* (Actually, we end up with what randomly comes our way that's "not too bad." Compared with *any* of our Big Dreams, however, it's nothing. *And* we have to pay for it, just as though it were a Big One.)

2. *When we choose, we risk losing.* If we boldly walk into the store and say, "I want a cherry popsicle," we run the risk of the storekeeper saying, "We're all out," or, even worse, "We sold the last one five minutes ago. You *just missed it.*" (Why do people *say* things like that? Why do they add torture to torment?)

   If we commit to the Big One, the Big Dream, we might not get it. We might lose. And not only will *we* know, but *everyone else* will know, too. It's the "agony of defeat." When we never really choose—never really commit—if we don't get it, we can always say, "Oh, I didn't really want it anyway."

3. *When we choose, we risk winning.* We stride in! We put down our money! We get the cherry popsicle! We claim it! It is in our hand! It is ours! The storekeeper says, "Congratulations!" Now what?

   Many people find the Big Now-What? more intimidating than "the agony of defeat." Defeat is part of most people's comfort zone. But *winning?* "What would I do? What would happen to me? How would I cope?" It's called the fear of success.

   Not only do we have to make changes to become successful, but success itself brings even more changes. The greater the success, the greater the changes. Imagine being very, *very* successful at your dream. Would you live where you're living now? Would you do the same things, go the same places, wear the

> *Quit now,*
> *you'll never make it.*
> *If you disregard this advice,*
> *you'll be halfway there.*
>
> DAVID ZUCKER

same clothes, have all the same friends? Would *any* part of your life be the same?

Even more startling than the external changes, however, are the inner changes brought on by success. What do we do with the concept that we're not *worthy* of success? How about the cultural programming most of us have that we're just an "ordinary person"? How can an ordinary person be capable of *extra*ordinary success? What's wrong with this picture?

An even deeper reason we fear success is that we fear our own power. We are much more powerful than we let ourselves believe. If we knew how powerful we were, "the slings and arrows of outrageous fortune" would be about as troublesome as being attacked by a frustrated two-year-old.

This sense of personal power is not comfortable. It's much easier to believe the cultural conditioning that things "out there" affect us "in here," that what happens to us is inseparably linked with how we feel, that dreams don't come true, and that our lot in life is not to have a lot in life.

≈

So, what do we do about all this?

1. Know it's there. Know what happens when you make choices, and be prepared for the consequences. *Expect* the comfort zone to have a fit. That's its job.

2. Be prepared to let go of grape, orange, tangerine, banana supreme, pina colada, watermelon, tutti-fruti, and passion fruit *for now*. Make your slogan, "Cherry today, tutti-fruti tomorrow!" Success in one area quite often clears the way for success—both inner and outer—in others. If cherry is the one you want most *now*, get that. Later look around and choose again.

3. If we choose, we *may* lose, but if we don't choose, we almost *certainly* lose. Some people tell themselves, "If I don't play, I can't lose. As long as I don't lose," they say, "then everything's okay." The problem with playing not

> *Always listen to experts.*
> *They'll tell you what*
> *can't be done and why.*
> *Then do it.*
>
> ROBERT HEINLEIN

to lose is that you can never *win*. The risk of losing is part of winning, but *never* losing also means never getting what we want.

4. Accept the fact that winning is not all it's cracked up to be—*but what else is there?* Would you rather be in the store, eating your popsicle, saying, "This doesn't taste quite cherry enough to me," or be outside the store, your nose pressed against the window, thinking how wonderful it must be to have a popsicle?

5. Know that you are worthy. (We're all worthy of our dream.) Yes, you *are* special. (We all have a dream, the doing of which will make us special to a great many people.)

6. You are powerful. Sorry. Hate to be the bearer of bad news. You are. You can continue arm wrestling with yourself, or you can use both arms, your whole heart, and all your strength to wrestle with greatness.

The choice is yours.

What's money?
A man is a success if he
gets up in the morning
and goes to bed at night
and in between
does what he wants to do.

Bob Dylan

The Myth of Money, Fame, and Power

Money, fame, and power—for their own sake—all spell one thing: *glamour.*

Glamour is one of the biggest traps in life. It is a sweet, sticky snare, like the petals of a Venus-flytrap. "Come to me," it beckons; "all happiness lies within."

What lies there are lies. The allure of glamour all rests on the myth we discussed earlier—that someone or something outside us can make us happy; that we are somehow incomplete without certain externals; and that if we have enough externals, we will never be unhappy again.

"You don't seem to realize that a poor person who is unhappy is in a better position than a rich person who is unhappy," explained Jean Kerr, "because the poor person has hope. He thinks money would help."

Money, fame, and power, as intentions, are deadly. People pursue them, get them, and are not happy (in fact, are usually more unhappy). Then they decide, "This must not be *enough.* I need more; *then* I'll be happy." So they set their sights higher, get more of what didn't make them happy in the first place, and are unhappier still.

As with any addictive substance, by now they're hooked. Life becomes the relentless pursuit of more! More! *MORE!*

Am I saying money, fame, and power are intrinsically evil? No. They have their place. They are

> *Pleasure is a shadow,*
> *wealth is vanity,*
> *and power is a pageant;*
> *but knowledge*
> *is ecstatic in enjoyment,*
> *perennial in frame,*
> *unlimited in space and*
> *infinite in duration.*
>
> DE WITT CLINTON

tools—*methods* for obtaining goals. As goals themselves, however, they are nothing. Less than nothing. Distractions at best; addictions at worst.

Take money, for example. Let's say I'm hungry and I don't have any money. I think, "If I only had money, I could eat. I want some money. I'm hungry and I want some money." So, someone says he'll give me all the money I could want, and locks me in a warehouse with one billion dollars in cash. Now what? Am I still hungry? Yes. Do I have lots of money? Yes. Perhaps a few lower forms of life that thrive on paper and ink could find nourishment, but within a few weeks I would probably trade the whole pile for a hamburger.

That's what it's like to go after money for money's sake. You get the money, and then what? "I'd see the world." Then make seeing the world your goal. If money is the necessary method for doing that, fine. It will come. There could, however, be other methods. You could, for example, meet someone who wants to hire a traveling companion; then you could *get paid* to see the world.

"I've had an exciting life," Rose Kennedy wrote. "I married for love and got a little money along with it." That's another method. Of course, *do* marry for love. Remember the old saying, "The one who marries for money, earns it."

"Money won't buy happiness," Bill Vaughan said, "but it will pay the salaries of a huge research staff to study the problem."

Some people who want to write a book wonder how to get the money to buy a word processor. When I point out to them that several very fine books were written before the advent of computers, they usually frown and say, "You don't understand."

I *do* understand. I was writing books back when the *cheapest* computer cost a million dollars. Did I wait to get a million dollars before writing? No. I wrote with the "word processor" at hand—a pen. Shakespeare didn't even have that. He used a *quill*.

Many people use money as the *rational lie* for not doing something they want to do. It sounds *so good:* "As soon as I get all the money I need to _____, I'll be living my dream!" Other people listening to these excuses believe them, because they, too, have their collection of rational lies.

I don't know much about
being a millionaire,
but I'll bet I'd be <u>darling</u> at it.

DOROTHY PARKER

It's a conspiracy: I won't challenge your rational lies if you don't challenge mine.

"When you do what you love, the money follows," is probably a phrase you've heard before. It's true, but incomplete.

The complete statement is, "When you do what you love, the *necessary* money will follow." The money that's *needed* to fulfill your goal will appear, in the proper timing, as you prove yourself worthy of that goal (that is, as you do the work necessary to fulfill that goal). What will *not* appear is all the money that would make everything all comfortable and cozy to do what you love at precisely the moment you want to do it.

If you want to write a book, you may, for a start, have enough money to buy a pencil, a notebook, and be given fifteen free minutes each day. If you use the fifteen minutes each day writing, when you fill the notebook, you will have enough money for another notebook and be given thirty minutes a day. And so on. Eventually, you'll have a book. What will the person who's waiting for a computer before even beginning to write have? Waiting. And resentment.

To make the phrase "Do what you love and the necessary money will follow" even more accurate: "Do what you love, and the necessary *resources* will follow."

In some cases, the resource will be money. In other cases, it will be time. It might be information, tools, connections, opportunities. Another word for *resources,* of course, is *methods.*

It's the same with fame: Fame itself is a hollow goal, but if fame is the natural result of doing what you love to do, then so be it. Most famous people consider fame a burden. The "burden of fame" is something of a joke, of course. "A celebrity is a person who works hard all his life to become well known," said Fred Allen, "then wears dark glasses to avoid being recognized."

Imagine not being able to go *anywhere* without being *mobbed.* It may sound nice, and for a time it might be fun, but, after a while, you'd probably agree with Lewis Grizzard: "Being a newspaper columnist is like being married to a nymphomaniac. It's great for the first two weeks."

> *Fame is only good*
> *for one thing—*
> *they will cash your check*
> *in a small town.*

TRUMAN CAPOTE

"If I were famous," some not-famous people say, "I'd get on TV and raise money to feed the homeless." A double-glamour whammy! *Fame* to get *money* to get something done. To someone saying this, I suggest: If feeding the homeless is your calling, go out and feed *one* homeless person *now*. Tomorrow, feed two. Keep it up. Maybe you'll become famous for that. If so, use it as a tool. If not, at least you'll be fulfilling your dream. As Mother Teresa said, "We can do no great things—only small things with great love."

You can easily see how power baits the glamour trap. What's the point of power if you don't use it for something? Nothing. So, what is the something

DO IT!

you would do if you had the power? Then go do that now.

"Do the thing and you will have the Power," Emerson wrote.

No, your action may not be as grand, sweeping, and dramatic as your imagination might conjure, but if you don't get satisfaction from doing it on a small scale, you won't get satisfaction doing it on a global scale. Nothing, multiplied by six billion, is still nothing.

*Men for the sake
of getting a living
forget to live.*

MARGARET FULLER

1810–1850

The Myth of the 40-Hour Work Week

Most people think they "need" to work forty hours per week. For some, that's true. For others, it's sixty hours per week. For still others, eighty. (Ask any spouse whose "job" it is to care for the house, or creative person working on a project, or monk in a monastery, or social activist working for change). For some others, it might be five or ten.

Just as "the work expands to fill the time available," so, too, the "needs" expand to consume the money available. ("Expenditure rises to meet income." —C. Northcote Parkinson) If we are bringing home forty-hours' worth of money, we will spend it. As John Guare pointed out, "The rich live hand-to-mouth, too—just on a higher level." If that forty-hours' worth of work amounts to $150 or $1,500 or $15,000 or $150,000, or $1,500,000—it will be spent.

Many people are trapped in the myth of a 40-hour work week.

If we define "job" as what we do that we don't really want to do to get money to do what we really want to do, then the number of *hours* we work depends upon (a) what it costs us to do what we want to do, and (b) how much per hour we get.

What about our basic needs? Good question. Basic needs are often dictated by what we want to do. For example, someone who wants to pray all day and serve God might be able to combine that

> *Never keep up*
> *with the Joneses.*
> *Drag them down to your level.*
> *It's cheaper.*
>
> QUENTIN CRISP

with life in a monastery and not have to work for even *one* hour per week at the local fast-food emporium.

People wanting to serve humanity could find the same all-expenses-paid fulfillment of a goal in the Peace Corps, or, if they wanted to do it domestically, in VISTA or AmeriCorps. The examples go on and on.

Our basic needs should be based on the fulfillment of our heart's desire, not on the latest style, or how to intensely fill the few "leisure" hours we have when not working at a job we hate.

To significantly raise your standard of living sometimes requires significantly lowering it for a while. Say you want to write a book, and you have a $25,000 car and a $2,000 per month apartment. You don't need those to write a book. A $5,000 car (or even a $500 moped) and a $500 per month apartment are all you need.

"Yes, but . . ."

Do I hear the comfort zone stirring?

People who plan to "make it" had better plan to sacrifice—and that *starts* with creature comforts. It might mean a smaller living space, bringing in a roommate, or turning the current living space into an office. Either way—discomfort, ho! It may mean fewer dinners out, fewer trips, fewer new clothes, not as many CDs, domestic wines, domestic sparkling water (aka club soda), domestic pasta, domestic vinegar—and no domestics.

Remember the New England maxim? "Use it up, wear it out, make it do, or do without." Instead of doing without the comfort, many people do without their dreams.

One of the toughest things to sacrifice is the idea that we *should* be comfortable all the time. I said you would find *satisfaction* pursuing your dreams, not comfort.

When we want all the creature comforts the Joneses have, we trade our *time* for those comforts—the time we spend making money at a job—time we could be spending to live our dreams. Time is precious. It is given each day in equal measure to us all. What we do with that time determines what we achieve in our lives.

TIME = DREAMS

> *Only a fool*
> *would make the bed*
> *every day.*
>
> NANCY SPAIN

Also, let go of the myth that we only have one career, profession, marriage, religious belief, etc. per lifetime. Person after person (you may be one of them) has demonstrated that this is simply not true. Abandon, too, the deadly myth that there is a certain *age* at which it's too late to take new paths.

This is your *life*—not a myth. Let your life be one that *inspires* myth making—don't make your life a slave to the myths of the past.

*While you're saving your face,
you're losing your ass.*

LYNDON B. JOHNSON

In the afternoons, Gertrude Stein and I
used to go antique hunting in the local shops,
and I remember once asking her
if she thought I should become a writer.
In the typically cryptic way
we were all enchanted with, she said, "No."
I took that to mean yes
and sailed for Italy the next day.

WOODY ALLEN

You have to know what you want to get.

GERTRUDE STEIN

What Do You Want?

Here it is, the chapter you've been awaiting with eagerness, anxiety, or both. Here you'll discover what *you* want. You'll get to choose which of those wants you'll pursue, which you'll let pass, and which you'll postpone.

The underlying question of this chapter was best stated by Dr. Robert Schuller: "What would you attempt to do if you knew you could not fail?"

The answer to this question may require some reflection. I use the word *reflection* rather than *thought* because, as William James once said, "A great many people think they are thinking when they are merely rearranging their prejudices."

We all have prejudices. We think we don't know what we want, and that becomes a prejudice. We think we know *for sure* what we want, and that becomes a prejudice. We think we'll discover what we want sometime—but not now—and that becomes a prejudice.

To the degree you can, clear the slate. Start fresh. If a dream is truly your dream, it will survive the questions I am about to ask you. And if it is not your time to know, nothing I can ask will part the veil. You and your dream are safe. How well you learn about your dream in this process is entirely up to you.

If you happen to have some 3x5 cards lying around (ha!), get them. And a pen or pencil. If you're not using 3x5 cards, get three pads or piles of paper and make lists. Without 3x5 cards, you'll have to do a bit more recopying.

> *The only way*
> *to avoid being miserable*
> *is not to have enough leisure*
> *to wonder whether you*
> *are happy or not.*
>
> GEORGE BERNARD SHAW

Let's start by returning to the sanctuary.

Imagine going to the entryway. It opens. You step inside and bathe under the pure, white light just inside the entryway. You know that only that which is for your highest good can take place while you are in your sanctuary and during this process.

It's important to ask this for, as Cicero said, "the highest good." It's usual for various glamour-seeking parts of us to want something, not because *we* want it, but because it would be impressive to have. Obtaining these things only leads to woe. As St. Teresa of Avila said, "More tears are shed over answered prayers than unanswered ones." Or, to quote Oscar Wilde, "When the gods choose to punish us, they merely answer our prayers." Asking for the highest good of all concerned allows your true dreams to surface.

Go to the people mover and invite in your Master Teacher. See your Master Teacher appear through the white light of the people mover. Welcome your Master Teacher. Chat for a while about the process you are about to do.

This is a special process using your sanctuary. You can open your eyes, write things down, do things, and when you close your eyes again, you're immediately back in the sanctuary, precisely where you were when you opened your eyes. In fact, this entire process is done *in* the sanctuary—some of it with your eyes open, some with your eyes closed.

Open your eyes. You're about to make three piles of cards (or three lists). Each card will contain one item. As you write each item on a card, place the card in the appropriate pile.

Write a card to identify each pile. The first is labeled "WANTS," the second "QUALITIES and ABILITIES," and the third "LIMITATIONS."

Now, start filling out the cards. Free associate. A WANT ("Move to New York") might spark some of your QUALITIES and ABILITIES ("Adventurous," "Flexible," "Cultured"), and also some LIMITATIONS ("Not enough money," "Fear," "Leaving friends behind").

An ABILITY ("Talented") might prompt a WANT ("Become an opera singer"), which may inspire a LIMITATION ("Can't sing").

> We must select the illusion
> which appeals
> to our temperament and
> embrace it with passion,
> if we want to be happy.
>
> CYRIL CONNOLLY

Once a card has been filled out on a given subject, it need not be repeated. One card containing the limitation "Fear," for example, is enough. (Might as well fill that one out right now and get it over with.)

Don't bother sorting or prioritizing the cards. If you "want" a hot fudge sundae, write it down. And, despite the rattlings of an earlier chapter, if money, fame, and power pop into your mind, by all means fill a card with them (three cards, in fact).

Tiny Tim, in listing his wants, said, "I'd love to see Christ come back to crush the spirit of hate and make men put down their guns. I'd also like just one more hit single." That's how our wants seem to go—some cosmic and grand; others personal and tiny.

In the process of decision-making and organization, putting it *all* down in writing is known as a "data dump." Dump all the data onto cards, and the only sorting to be concerned about now is whether something is a WANT, a QUALITY and ABILITY, or a LIMITATION.

In writing all this down, remember that you're not committing to any of it. You'll have the opportunity to do that in a later chapter. For the purposes of this chapter, everything is just a "good idea."

And don't forget to have fun. Yes, it's your life you're looking at, and what you'll be doing with it, but that doesn't mean you have to be too *serious*. What we do to fill the time between our first cry and our last sigh is all a game, anyway. Treat this list with the same gravity you'd spend deciding what to do next Saturday afternoon. Shall we play football, baseball, or stage a ballet?

Take some time now and fill out the cards. If you run out of ideas, close your eyes and return to the sanctuary. Ask the Master Teacher for suggestions. Get all your WANTS, QUALITIES and ABILITIES, and LIMITATIONS on cards. Spend at least an hour doing this, although you may choose to take longer.

Do it 'til it's done, and return to this place in the book when your piles (or lists) are complete.

≈

> *You've got to be very careful*
> *if you don't know*
> *where you are going,*
> *because you might not*
> *get there.*
>
> YOGI BERRA

Excellent. Congratulations.

Now go through the cards (or lists) you made during the earlier process *What Is Your Purpose?* Write your purpose on a card and place it where you can easily see it. Does this remind you of other WANTS, QUALITIES and ABILITIES, or LIMITATIONS? When you discovered your purpose, you made a list of qualities about yourself, and also actions you enjoyed. These can be added to the QUALITIES and ABILITIES or WANTS piles.

Now, look at the earlier listing of all the things you already have for which you are grateful. Add those things you want to include in your future to your WANTS list. Yes, you already have them, but *maintaining* them will probably take some time.

Almost *everything*—except perhaps that rock you brought back from Yosemite—requires *some* maintenance. To *maintain* what you currently have must be considered a goal for the future. So, add "Maintain house," "Maintain car," "Maintain relationship with _____," etc. to your pile of WANTS. If any ABILITIES and QUALITIES or LIMITATIONS arise while adding these wants, make cards for them, too.

That done, let's turn to the WANT pile. Sort each want into one of five categories: Marriage/Family, Career/Professional, Social/Political, Religious/Spiritual, and Recreation/Fun.

I am making the assumption that *everyone* will want *some* recreation and/or fun in their lives regardless of which area of life they choose to primarily pursue. It seems to me that even the most serious devotee of a given path will want *some* recreation—in the sense of re-creation. So I'm making this a *parallel* category, one that can complement whatever major life area you choose to pursue.

In choosing the category (Marriage/Family, Career/Professional, Social/Political, Religious/Spiritual, or Recreation/Fun) in which to put each WANT, remember, "to thine own self be true." There may be an *obvious* category, but your personal *motivation* may make a particular WANT part of another category.

If one of your WANTS is, say, "Become a minister," is that because you want to be closer to God (Religious/Spiritual), you feel it would be a good

> *There is no security*
> *on this earth,*
> *there is only opportunity.*
>
> GENERAL DOUGLAS MACARTHUR

platform from which to make social change (Social/Political), you think it would be a rewarding occupation (Career/Professional), or you want to intensify your relationship with someone who has a decided fondness for persons of the cloth (Marriage/Family)?

We must look closely at our motivations. As Madonna explained, "Losing my virginity was a career move."

You could, for example, put "Get married" under Career/Professional because everyone in the career you intend to pursue is properly espoused. Or, perhaps you're doing it for Religious/Spiritual reasons, following the dictate of Paul when he wrote,

"It is better to marry than to burn" (I Corinthians, 7:9). You could be getting married for primarily societal reasons: "Any young man who is unmarried at the age of twenty-one," said Brigham Young, "is a menace to the community." Or, you might want to get married just because you want to get married (Marriage/Family).

There will be some overlapping, of course, but put each WANT card in the category that *most* fits your motivation.

That done, review each of the Marriage/Family, Career/Professional, Social/Political, and Religious/Spiritual categories. (We'll look at Recreation/Fun a little later.)

Now, let's look ahead for the next, say, five years.

Take each category of wants separately, read them over, then close your eyes. Imagine what your life would be like in the next five years if you had a good number of those wants. Explore both the good *and* the bad, the up side and the down. Be neither too romantic nor too cynical. Take a look at it "straight on."

Use all the elements of your sanctuary to explore your life in that category. You can use the **people mover** to invite experts in the field and discuss the pros and cons; the **information retrieval system** to gather any facts or data you might find useful; the **video screen** to see yourself living that life. You can put on **ability suits** for each of the wants, and experience what that ability is like in the **ability suit practice area;** visit your **health center** and

> *JANE HATHAWAY: Chief,*
> *haven't you heard of the saying*
> *"It's not whether you win or lose,*
> *it's how you play the game"?*
>
> *MR. DRYSDALE: Yes,*
> *I've heard it.*
> *And I consider it*
> *one of the most ridiculous*
> *statements ever made.*
>
> THE BEVERLY HILLBILLIES

check on the health risks and advantages of each want; contemplate the category in your **sacred room;** and, of course, take your **Master Teacher** along with you throughout the whole process, discussing your reactions as you go.

And in all cases, ask yourself, "Would this direction in life fulfill my purpose?"

After spending time in your sanctuary with each of the four main areas of life, ask yourself, "During the next five years, within which *category* does my heart's desire lie? During the next five years, which would give me the most satisfaction?"

If no answer is forthcoming, return with your Master Teacher to your sanctuary and explore. Is the choice between two? Examine them both, alternately. Which is most "on purpose"? Which category thrills your heart the most?

When you've chosen the category, go through all the wants within the category and select the one WANT you want the most. Again, use all the tools in the sanctuary to explore the pros and cons of each WANT, and choose the Big Want, the Big Goal, the Big Dream.

Why do I have you choose a category first, then a goal within that category? Usually, going for the Big Goal within a category automatically fulfills many of the smaller goals within that category—not all, of course, but many. If you pick the *area* of life first, you will, by pursuing a Big Dream within that area, have more of what you want in the area of life you choose.

You are, of course, free to choose a Big Dream *outside* the area of life you are most drawn to. I have found, however, that most people tend to be more fulfilled by obtaining several goals within the area they prefer, rather than one big goal in an area they don't prefer as much. This is just an observation. Please make your choice of Big Dream yourself. Your Master Teacher will not steer you wrong.

One method of choosing between two Big Dreams that *seem* equally appealing is to make a list of all the pros and cons for each choice. As you read over these lists and compare them, one dream usually takes the lead.

Is this it? Is this your dream? The Big Dream? If yes, read on. If no, keep choosing.

> *I always wanted*
> *to be somebody,*
> *but I should have*
> *been more specific.*
>
> LILY TOMLIN

Congratulations! But our work is not yet over.

When you have chosen, then *quantify* your dream. That is, make it a goal with *specific results* so that you'll know when you've achieved it.

This can be tough. People like to keep their dreams vague. "I want a family," is easier to say than, "I want a spouse, two children and a rottweiler." But one is obtainable, one is not.

"I want a family" is not obtainable because the goal does not define what a family is. You could have a family of mice in your kitchen and your goal is fulfilled. "That's not what I mean." You could have eighteen children and *still* not reach the goal, because some families have nineteen children. "That's not what I mean, either."

Then what *do* you mean?

Put something countable, something quantifiable in your goal so that you'll *know* when you've obtained it. You are not saddled with this goal forever and ever. When you reach it, you can choose a bigger one. For now, however, it's important to know what your goal is and be able to tell when you've reached it. (Remember: you haven't committed to anything yet.)

Here is where money often comes in. Although money is not a great goal *by itself,* as an indicator of whether or not you've obtained a goal, it can be excellent. As the people who understand money say, "Money is just a way of keeping score."

Rather than, "I am a singer," say "I am a singer making $50,000 (or $100,000, or $1,000,000) per year singing." Make the goal big enough to be a dream (if you're already making $40,000 at something, $42,000 is hardly a Big Dream), but small enough to be at least *partially* believable (if you're making nothing at something, jumping to $100,000,000 per year might be a bit too much for *any* of you to believe).

Some goals are quantifiable by time: "I am spending six months per year traveling." Others by amount: "I weigh 150 pounds." Others by degrees or recognition: "I have my medical license."

In setting a goal, it's fun to remember the movie *Bedazzled.* In a reworking of Faust, Peter Cook plays the devil and Dudley Moore—a short-order cook—sells his soul to be with a waitress who is indifferent

> *Ours is a world*
> *where people don't know*
> *what they want*
> *and are willing to go through hell*
> *to get it.*
>
> DON MARQUIS

to him. The devil catches the cook in one loophole after another. Moore wants to be married to his beloved, live in the country, and be rich. He gets his wish. *However,* she is in love with someone else. Moore asks for another chance. This time he wants to live in the country and have his beloved in love with him, too. The devil finds a loophole and makes them both nuns in a convent. And on it goes.

Be careful of the loopholes. If in doubt, add, ". . . for the highest good," to the end of your goal.

Write down your goal, your Big Dream.

Phrase your goal as though you already had it: "I am . . ." "I have . . . ." If your goal begins, "I want . . ." then your goal is *wanting,* not *being* or *having.*

Now, for a slight aside. Do you know how many minutes there are in a week? 10,080. That's 168 hours. That's your wealth in time. What you spend it on is your choice. No matter what you spend it on, however, you never get more than 10,080 minutes (168 hours) per week.

On a clean sheet of paper, or a new set of cards, write "168 Hours" at the top. Now, let's plan the next year.

Let's start with the basics. How many hours do you sleep each night? Multiply that times seven, and subtract that total from the week. If you sleep eight hours per night, eight hours times seven days is 56 hours per week of sleep. Subtract that from 168, and you have 112 hours remaining in the week.

Now, how many hours do you spend each day bathing, shaving, making up, dressing, and on other ablutions? One hour? Multiply that times seven and subtract from 112. That gives us 105 hours.

And now, eating. An hour a day? More? Less? Consider an average week and see how much time you spend preparing, consuming, and cleaning up after eating. Let's say it's an hour per day, or seven hours per week. That's seven from 105, which leaves us with 98 hours.

What about other necessary personal tasks? (Include things *only* if you *actually do them* on a *consistent* basis.) Cleaning (including car and laundry)? Shopping (including groceries)? Working out? Medical appointments or activities? Church? Meditation? And so on. Calculate how much time you

> *The art of progress
> is to preserve order amid change
> and to preserve change amid order.*
>
> ALFRED NORTH WHITEHEAD

spend per week on these (don't forget transportation to and from each), and subtract that from your total.

Let's say all that came to eighteen hours per week. That leaves you with eighty hours per week. *Half* the week spent maintaining the *basics*—and thus far we haven't even considered *work!*

We are, by the way, smack dab in the middle of something most people have a *very* difficult time facing: time. Yes, it's easy to accept the *concept* that there's "only so much time to go around," but, when faced with the reality—and the *limitation*—of time *in one's own life,* that's tough.

Facing your time limitation is, however, precisely what I'm asking you to do. It may be uncomfortable, but not as uncomfortable as looking back on this coming year after it has passed and saying, "I really *meant* to do that. Where did the time go?"

Now, go through the cards that list the things you already have and would like to maintain. Calculate how much time it would take each week to maintain each of them. Write that figure on the card. Do it for what you already have in *all* categories, but keep the cards within each category (the Marriage/Family cards in the Marriage/Family pile, etc.).

Some things may require zero maintenance (that rock from Yosemite). Others may need quite a lot (children, spouse, careers, major projects). Remember, these are the things you already *have*.

Don't forget to include those things that must be *paid for* to be maintained—mortgage or rent, car payments, etc. For those, calculate the number of hours you must work per week, at your current level of income, to pay for them. For example, if you make $10 per hour, and your car payment, gas, and maintenance is $320 per month, that's $80 per week, or eight hours per week to maintain the car.

Now the truly tough choices begin.

After all these hours are calculated, go through the cards of what you have and want to maintain, and compare each with the Big Dream you selected. For each item, ask yourself, "Which is more important?"

If what you want to maintain is more important, put that in one pile. Subtract the number of hours it takes to maintain this from the remaining hours in the week. If the Big Dream is more impor-

> RULE A: *Don't.*
> RULE A1: *Rule A does not exist.*
> RULE A2: *Do not discuss
> the existence or non-existence
> of Rules A, A1 or A2.*
>
> R. D. LAING

tant, put the card of what you want to maintain back in the category pile it originally came from. For the Recreation/Fun category, you can set aside so many hours per week for various activities within the entire category. Subtract that from the hours remaining in the week.

Confused? Don't be surprised. These are difficult choices, and confusion, anger, fear, guilt, unworthiness, hurt feelings, discouragement, and all the other denizens of the comfort zone form a marching band when difficult choices present themselves. "You don't have to make these choices," they counsel, "They will make themselves," or "You need more information," or "Let's eat! We'll do this tomorrow."

I suggest, however, that you press on. Close your eyes. Take a deep breath. Get comfort and encouragement from your Master Teacher.

Now calculate the cost for *basic necessities* (food, shelter, video rentals) not covered by the things you already have that you want to keep. How many hours each week will it take to make that much money? Subtract that number from your total.

How many hours do you have left? Is this enough to fulfill your Big Dream? If you don't have *at least* fourteen hours per week—two hours per day—to spend on your Big Dream, that may not be enough. If your dream can really come true with *less* investment of time, it might be a rather small Big Dream.

Of course, you can set aside *more* than fourteen hours for your Big Dream. The more time you spend, the more quickly your Dream will come true.

Now comes the fun part. Take your Big Dream, and see how many WANTS would *automatically* (or almost automatically) be fulfilled by achieving the Big Dream. For example, if your Big Dream was to become a movie star, the smaller wants of "Live in Los Angeles," "Be famous," "Make $1,000,000," and "Meet Brooke Shields," would naturally follow. If you fulfilled the Big Dream, a great many of the smaller dreams would almost effortlessly come to pass.

It's okay to go into *any* of the piles and pull out dreams that fit within the Big Dream. But be honest, now, because with enough bending and twisting, almost *any* goal can fit behind a big enough dream. "I want to be an airline pilot, so watching

> *A musician must make music,*
> *an artist must paint,*
> *a poet must write,*
> *if he is to be ultimately*
> *at peace with himself.*
>
> ABRAHAM MASLOW

every movie that comes out will better help me tell the passengers what the movie is about on board the plane," or "I want to write a novel about being rich, so I think I'll take all my money and buy a Rolls Royce so I can get in the mood."

Now, back to the tough part. *Eliminate* all wants that are in *direct opposition* to your Big Dream. "Live in New York City" and "Experience the joys of small town life" do not belong in the same dream. One of them must go.

Be ruthless. "Oh, I can stay in Kansas and become a movie star." Uh-huh.

Please remember that simultaneously pursuing Big Dreams from two different categories is difficult. If, for example, your main area of activity is *not* Marriage/Family, please keep this in mind: if the romantic relationship you may seek *in addition to* your Big Dream does not provide you with *more time* to pursue your dream, either your Big Dream or the relationship will suffer. Usually both. I don't like this harsh reality any more than you do. It seems, however, to be the way it is.

If you still have time in your week (which is doubtful), you can add other wants to your week *providing* they are not in opposition to your Big Dream. The smart thing is to choose additional goals that somehow support or enhance the Big Dream—but as soon as you run out of hours, stop. That's it.

You can now combine the piles of The Big Dream And All That Comes With It and the pile of things already in your life you chose to maintain. Review your choices. Behold: your next year (and probably beyond).

Write at the top of each card in the new pile the following: "I am . . ." or "I have . . . ." No longer are these mere wants. They are goals.

Hold on to the WANTS *not* in the "I am . . ." or "I have . . ." pile. We'll get to them in the next chapter.

For now, review the LIMITATIONS pile. For each limitation, ask yourself how you can turn it into an *advantage*. How can it become an *ally* in fulfilling your Big Dream? We've already looked at fear becoming the energy to do your best in a new situation, guilt as the energy for personal change, unworthiness as a way of keeping on track, hurt

> *The method of the enterprising*
> *is to plan with audacity,*
> *and execute with vigor;*
> *to sketch out*
> *a map of possibilities;*
> *and then to treat them*
> *as probabilities.*
>
> BOVEE

feelings as a way of remembering the caring, anger as the energy for change, and discouragement as a reminder of our courage.

See if you can find a *positive use* for everything on your list. Impatience? Be impatient for success. Stubborn? Let it become determination. Big ego? Bravo! Put it behind your goal. Laziness? Become lazy about doing the things *not* on the way to fulfilling your Dream. Procrastinate about procrastination. And so on.

Write the positive attribute for each former limitation in larger letters on the same card. Any time you feel this limitation coming on, you can return to the card and see what the positive use for that former limitation might be. Remember: it's all *your* energy. Align it toward your goal. Be creative. If some limitations seemingly can't be turned into assets, set them aside for now.

Turn now to the QUALITIES and ABILITIES pile. Review each quality and ability. Imagine how each quality and ability can be used to fulfill your Big Dream.

Look again at the LIMITATIONS for which you have not yet seen a positive use. What QUALITIES and ABILITIES would best help you in overcoming each limitation? Let the qualities and abilities gang up—let their deck be stacked in your favor; it is, after all, *your* deck.

Review again the cards in the "I am . . ." and "I have . . ." pile—your Big Dream and its companions. Compare each dream in that pile with your purpose. See how each fulfills your purpose perfectly.

Close your eyes, find yourself in your sanctuary, thank your Master Teacher, watch the Master Teacher disappear into the white light of the people mover. As you turn to go, you notice some writing on the wall of your sanctuary—your Big Dream.

Read it, enjoy it, become it. Move to the white light of your entryway. Bathe in it, breathe it in. Leave your sanctuary, and return to the outside world to make your Dream come true.

*Take what you can use
and let the rest go by.*

KEN KESEY

Completion

You've discovered and chosen your Big Dream, your Heart's Desire. What? No cheering? No celebration?

Not quite yet.

Lying "in the ruins" are all those other heart's desires—all those deserted little 3x5 cards. The reminders of the dreams that won't immediately—and might never—come true.

Sigh.

Welcome to success.

Remember that the sadness you feel is a reminder of your caring, and the caring is *your* caring—available to place behind the Big Dream *you* have chosen to pursue.

It is important to complete each WANT that you will not—for now—be pursuing. "Complete" doesn't mean do it; complete means declare your involvement with it, for now, done. "Complete" doesn't mean to physically finish; "complete" means *you* are complete with it—that you have completed all you're going to do about it, for now.

The down side is that you must say good-bye to some valuable and desirable dreams—perhaps for good. (When we say good-bye, we never really know for how long it's going to be.)

The up side is that declaring things complete frees the mental, emotional, and physical energy we've been holding in reserve for the achievement of that goal.

> *If you don't have enough time*
> *to accomplish something,*
> *consider the work finished*
> *once it's begun.*
>
> JOHN CAGE

This can be a significant amount of energy.

For each WANT that didn't make the "I am . . ." or "I have . . ." pile and for each thing you currently have that you chose not to maintain, read it, consider it, and say, out loud, "This is complete for now." Say good-bye to it, and place it face down. Pick up another card and repeat the process.

Take your time. You may feel the sadness, or you may feel the freeing of energy. You may cry and laugh at the same time. Always have your Big Dream clearly in mind, so that you can direct the newly freed energy toward it.

With some cards you may feel that, after all, you *can* achieve this smaller dream, too. You'll just sleep less at night, or something. This is the newly freed energy (or perhaps the comfort zone) talking. Stick to your plan. Declare it complete. Direct the energy toward the Big Dream and move on.

If the dreams you are completing involve other people, let them know you will not be doing anything more about these dreams. This is only fair. The most important person to tell, however, is yourself.

Sometimes the "extra energy" is stored in material value. If you choose not to maintain certain physical posessions, sell them. Or donate them. Use that good will toward your Dream. Don't wait for the things you're not maintaining to rot. Cash them in. Convert them into energy and channel that energy toward your Dream.

The amount of power freed by telling yourself you no longer choose to put energy into something can be remarkable. Be prepared for extra energy. Be prepared, as well, to channel that newly liberated energy toward your Dream.

The way to begin that is through *commitment*.

I've been on a calendar,
but I've never been on time.

MARILYN MONROE

Committing to Your Dream —and Keeping That Commitment

Perhaps you've noticed that I haven't yet asked you to commit to your Dream. This is because, when we commit to something, *and we really mean it,* the manure hits the fan and the fan is running.

Before asking you to commit, I wanted you to understand this process, and offer some suggestions on how to use the manure as fertilizer.

Most people don't know about this process, because most people don't keep most of their agreements.

Most people add a silent, unconscious modifying phrase to all their commitments: ". . . as long as it's not uncomfortable."

What most people don't realize is that discomfort is one of the *values* of commitments, one of the reasons for making a commitment in the first place.

Within us is an automatic goal-fulfillment mechanism. When we commit to something, we are telling the goal-fulfillment mechanism, "I want this." The goal-fulfillment mechanism says, "Fine. I'll arrange for that." And it does, by performing various functions—individually or collectively:

- It looks to see what lessons we must learn in order to have our goal; then it arranges for those lessons. Sometimes, these lessons come in pleasant ways (we notice an article on what we need to know in a magazine; a conversation

> *Never take a solemn oath.*
> *People think you mean it.*
>
> NORMAN DOUGLAS

with a friend reveals information to us; a song on the radio has a line that tells us something important). At other times, the lessons are unpleasant (someone we must listen to—a boss, for example—tells us "in no uncertain terms" what we need to know; or we get sick, and the doctor tells us what we need to do "or else").

- The goal-fulfillment mechanism sees what stands in the way of our having what we want and removes it. Again, sometimes this can be pleasant (if the goal is a new car, someone offers us a great price for our old car), or unpleasant (our car is stolen, totaled, or breaks down).

There is something else the goal-fulfillment mechanism does: it gives us numerous opportunities to expand our comfort zone.

In order to have something new, we must expand our comfort zone to include the new thing. The bigger the new thing, the more the comfort zone must expand. And *comfort zones are most often expanded through discomfort.* As they say in weight training: "No pain; no gain."

Lifting weights seems like a terrible waste of time, a lot of work, and unnecessary pain, but lifting weights makes you strong enough to fulfill the goals you *do* want to achieve. The same is true with expanding the comfort zone.

When people don't understand that being uncomfortable is part of the process of achievement, they use the discomfort as a reason not to do. Then they don't get what they want. We must learn to tolerate discomfort in order to grow.

This process of growth is known as "grist for the mill." When making flour in an old stone mill, it is necessary to add gravel to the wheat before grinding it. This gravel is known as *grist*. The small stones that make up the grist rub against the grain as the mill wheel passes over them. The friction causes the wheat to be ground into a fine powder. If it weren't for the grist, the wheat would only be crushed. To grind wheat fine enough for flour requires grist. After the grinding, the grist is sifted out, and only the flour remains.

When we commit to something, the automatic goal-fulfillment mechanism throws grist in our

> *If you never want to see*
> *a man again, say,*
> *"I love you,*
> *I want to marry you.*
> *I want to have children . . ."*
> *—they leave skid marks.*
>
> RITA RUDNER

mill. It's all designed to give us our goal.

If we don't understand the process, however, we protest, "Why are you throwing gravel in with my wheat? Stop that!" The dutiful miller uses no grist, and we wind up with crushed wheat. "This isn't what I wanted. I wanted *flour.*"

When we order flour, we must be prepared for grist in our mill. We must become an "eager learner." *Whatever* comes along, look for the lesson. *Assume* it's for your good, no matter how bad it seems.

No, there's no need to run out and *invite* disaster, just as one doesn't have to bring gravel to the mill. The necessary experiences will take place. Our job is not to *seek* them, but to take part in and learn from the ones that are presented to us.

Maxwell Maltz explains the process this way:

> Your automatic creative mechanism operates
> in terms of goals and end results. Once you
> give it a definite goal to achieve, you can de-
> pend on its automatic guidance system to
> take you to that goal much better than "You"
> ever could by conscious thought. "You" sup-
> ply the goal by thinking in terms of end re-
> sults. Your automatic mechanism then sup-
> plies the means whereby.

How do we know when there's grist in our mill?
When we feel the comfort zone acting up, there's
grist in the mill. If we discard the grist (that is,
honor the comfort zone's dictates), we have
crushed wheat. If we use the grist to gain strength
and learn the lesson at hand (that is, continue on
our committed course despite the protestations of
the comfort zone), we have flour.

Keeping agreements with others is, of course,
an excellent method for getting what we want
from them. If we keep our agreements, people
learn to trust us. If we break our agreements,
they don't. It's hard to imagine people giving
something of substance to someone they don't
trust.

People may say, "Oh, that's all right," when we
make our apologies, but it is seldom truly all right
with people. "Unfaithfulness in keeping an appointment is an act of clear dishonesty," Horace Mann
explained 150 years ago. "You may as well borrow a
person's money as his time."

> *The best way*
> *to keep your word*
> *is not to give it.*
>
> NAPOLEON

Although keeping agreements is a good technique for building trust with others, the more important reason for keeping agreements is building trust with *ourselves.*

If we frequently break agreements—either with others or with ourselves—we are training ourselves to ignore our own word. Committing to something, then, means nothing. Committing to a Big Dream is about as significant as saying we will learn to fly—sounds nice, it would be fun, but it's not going to happen.

Committing to a dream is not a one-time occurrence. It must be done daily, hourly, continually. We must *choose* to commit to our *choice,* over and over.

The test of this commitment is *action*. If I say, "I commit to being a great dancer," and then don't practice, that's not a commitment; that's not dance; it's just talk. Conversely, if I'm practicing dance, I don't need to tell myself how committed I am. My action *is* my demonstrated commitment.

When we commit and act, we are confronted by the comfort zone. We are tempted to stop, encouraged to stop, *demanded* to stop. If we move ahead anyway—we expand the comfort zone, learn a necessary lesson, and the commitment becomes stronger. That causes us to come up against the comfort zone again, and the process continues.

Here are some suggestions for making and keeping commitments:

1. **Don't make commitments you don't plan to keep.** Some people are so casual about making agreements: "Talk to you tomorrow," "Let's get together next week," and, one of my favorites, "I'll have him call you back." (You *will*? What if he doesn't want to call me back?)

   Most people like to pretend that these "casual" commitments don't count. They do. Every time we give our word, it counts. For the most part, people give their word entirely too often. Our word is a precious commodity and should be treated as such.

   Imagine a commitment as a precious jewel. When you give it to someone, the other person has the jewel. When you keep the commitment, the jewel is returned to you. If you

> *The one word you'll need is no.*
>
> BETTE DAVIS
> TO
> ROBIN WILLIAMS

fail to keep the agreement, however, the jewel is gone forever. (This is true of agreements with yourself as well.)

If we remember this jewel analogy each time we give our word, we tend to be more careful. Our word *is* a precious jewel; each time we give it, we risk losing it. Don't take that risk unless you plan to "cover your assets."

2. **Learn to say no.** When we commit to a Dream, one of the great tests of our sincerity is whether we say no to things not on the way to that Dream. If we commit to moving to another city, for example, temptations from the city we have not yet left appear:

DO IT!

we're given a raise and a promotion; we hear about a larger, better, less-expensive apartment; a 24-hour gourmet restaurant (that delivers) opens nearby; and we meet Someone Wonderful.

If we're *really* committed to moving, to all of these we must say, "No." Talk about the comfort zone acting up! Wait until Someone Wonderful calls and invites you out (or, worse, *in*) on the same evening you planned to go over street maps of the city you plan to move to. Ouch.

Beyond this, we are programmed not to say no to people we know. Conversely, we are also programmed to automatically "no" all strangers. This dual programming makes for a small circle of the same friends with whom we do things we don't necessarily like. To pursue a Big Dream, we must learn to say no to both programmings.

3. **Make conditional agreements.** Doctors learn to say, "I'll be there, unless I get a call from the hospital." You can, too. If there is *potentially* something more important than the agreement you are about to make, let the other person know. "I'd love to have lunch, unless I get a call-back on my audition," "I can make it, unless Greenpeace calls," or "Yes, I'll do it, if I can find a sitter for the kids." Do not, however, use this as a substitute for saying no. That turns your Big Dream into a Big Excuse and robs it of some

> *Always do sober*
> *what you said you'd do drunk.*
> *That will teach you*
> *to keep your mouth shut.*
>
> ERNEST HEMINGWAY

power. Use the condition *only* with agreements you want to—and plan to—keep.

4. **Keep the commitments you make.** As an exercise, practice keeping *all* agreements you make—no matter how difficult, no matter how costly. This will do two things: first, it will build strength, character, and inner trust. Secondly, it will get you to reread suggestions #1, #2, and #3 and follow them more carefully.

5. **Write commitments down.** Keep a calendar and write agreements down—*including agreements you make with yourself.* Don't just say, "I'm exercising tomorrow morning," write it

down. Set a time. Arrange for it. Make it as important as an agreement you made with someone else—a *very important* someone else.

You might want to write on a sheet of paper, "All agreements with myself shall be in writing. Everything else is just a good idea." Then place the paper somewhere you will read it—often. Write it on every page in your calendar. Eventually, there will be a difference between commitments you make with yourself and those things that would be nice, would be beneficial, but are not going to happen.

6. **Renegotiate at the earliest opportunity.** As soon as a possible conflict arises, contact the person with whom you have the first agreement. Unless the original agreement was conditional, the *way* in which you renegotiate an agreement is important.

"Something more important than my agreement with you has come up," is not the best way. It's a form of breaking the agreement, just in advance. "I know I have an agreement with you, and I still plan to keep it, but something important has come up, and I wonder if we might be able to reschedule." That asks permission. If granted, you get a second chance at reclaiming your jewel. If *not* granted, see #4.

≈

¶ *Until one is committed, there is hesitancy, the chance to draw back, always ineffectiveness.* ¶ *Concerning all acts of initiative (and creation) there is one elementary truth, the ignorance of which kills countless ideas and splendid plans: that the moment one definitely commits oneself, then Providence moves too.* ¶ *All sorts of things occur to help one that would never otherwise have occurred. A whole stream of events issues from the decision, raising in one's favor all manner of unforeseen incidents and meetings and material assistance, which no man could have dreamed would have come his way.* ¶ *I have learned a deep respect for one of Goethe's couplets:*

**Whatever you can do,
or dream you can,
begin it.
Boldness has genius,
power, and magic in it.**

W. H. MURRAY
THE SCOTTISH HIMALAYAN EXPEDITION

And now you are ready to commit to your goal—your Dream.

It's important to commit to the fulfillment of the goal, not just to a certain amount of time spent pursuing the goal. Some people's commitments sound like this: "I'll spend two years pursuing this goal, and see what happens."

When we commit to *pursuing,* our goal is then *pursuing,* and we will pursue. We won't necessarily *get* what we're pursuing, because getting it is not our goal—pursuing it is.

It is fine, however, to add a time statement to your dream. "By DATE I am . . ." or "By DATE I have . . . ."

This makes it a bigger challenge, of course. We will know precisely when we have succeeded in fulfilling our Dream, because we put specific parameters on the goal (so much money, a certain credential, etc.). Adding time to our goal lets us know precisely when we have *failed,* too.

This is important. To say we want something by a certain date shows us what we must do *today, right now,* to make that happen. It gets us going. If we don't achieve it, it gives us a chance to look back, see what must be done differently in the future, correct our course, set a new date, recommit, and continue on.

So, add a time to your dream, and, if you so choose, commit.

The time to commit is now.

And now. And now. And now. And now . . .

*People hate me because
I am a multifaceted,
talented, wealthy,
internationally famous
genius.*

JERRY LEWIS

Keep Your Goals Away
from the Trolls

There is a type of crab that cannot be caught—
it is agile and clever enough to get out of any crab
trap. And yet, these crabs are caught by the thousands every day, thanks to a particularly human trait
they possess.

The trap is a wire cage with a hole at the top.
Bait is placed in the cage, and the cage is lowered
into the water. One crab comes along, enters the
cage, and begins munching on the bait. A second
crab joins him. A third. Crab Thanksgiving. Yumm.
Eventually, however, all the bait is gone.

The crabs could easily climb up the side of the
cage and through the hole, but they do not. They
stay in the cage. Other crabs come along and join
them—long after the bait is gone. And more.

Should one of the crabs realize there is no further reason to stay in the trap and attempt to leave,
the other crabs will gang up on him and stop him.
They will repeatedly pull him off the side of the
cage. If he is persistent, the others will tear off his
claws to keep him from climbing. If he persists still,
they will kill him.

The crabs—by force of the majority—stay together in the cage. The cage is hauled up, and it's
dinnertime on the pier.

The chief difference between these crabs and
humans is that these crabs live under water and humans don't.

> *These are the soul cages.*
> *These are the soul cages.*
> *Swim to the light.*
>
> STING

Anyone who has a dream—one that might get him out of what he perceives to be a trap—had best beware of the fellow-inhabitants of the trap.

The human crabs (I call them trolls) do not usually use physical force—although they're certainly not above it. They generally don't need it. They have more effective methods at hand, and in mouth—innuendo, doubt, ridicule, derision, mockery, sarcasm, scorn, sneering, belittlement, humiliation, jeering, taunting, teasing, lying, and several dozen others.

The way to handle such people is the same method used by Jonathan Joffrey Crab on *his* clan. (Remember that book about the crab who wasn't content to walk around, he wanted to learn under-water ballet?) Jonathan, knowing the dangers of attempted departure from the cage, said, "Hey! This is fun! What a gathering of crabs! I'm going to go get some more!" And he danced off to freedom.

My suggestion: keep your goals away from the trolls.

People don't like to see others pursuing their dreams—it reminds them how far from living their own dreams they are. In talking you out of your dreams, they are talking themselves back into their comfort zone. They will give you every rational lie they ever gave themselves—and add a few more. If you don't believe the lies with the same degree of devotion the trolls do, get ready for Big Time Disapproval.

Why bother? Consider your Dream a fragile seed. It's small now. It needs protection and lots of nurturing. Eventually, it will be strong—stronger than the slings and arrows of outrageously limited people.

When you've obtained your goal, *then* tell them about it. Even though faced with irrefutable evidence, the most common expression you'll hear will be, "I don't believe it!" If they can't believe reality, imagine how much difficulty they'd have believing in your Dream.

This warning, of course, does not apply to close friends and supporters who have always believed in you and offer only encouragement. If you're not sure whether to discuss your dream with someone, talk about a "friend" who has a similar Dream. If

> *Anybody who sees*
> *and paints a sky green*
> *and pastures blue*
> *ought to be sterilized.*
>
> ADOLF HILTER

the response is positive, you're in good hands. If the response is, "What a silly thing to do," it would be a silly thing, indeed, to share your goals with this person.

If some people should hear of your dream and start telling you all the reasons why you can't possibly do it, you can (a) walk away, or (b) listen to them with compassion as they describe the parameters of their own comfort zones—the limitations that may keep them firmly in the trap until it is hauled up.

Without deviation
progress is not possible.

FRANK ZAPPA

You can have
anything you want
if you want it
desperately enough.
You must want it
with an inner exuberance
that erupts through the skin
and joins the energy
that created the world.

SHEILA GRAHAM

PART FOUR

BECOMING PASSIONATE
ABOUT YOUR DREAM

I'm going to go faster. Now that you have your Dream and have committed to it, you're probably experiencing some Divine Impatience. A part of you is saying, "Let's get *on* with it!" And so we shall.

We move now from the mental realm—the world of discoveries, choices, goals, and commitments—into the emotional.

Although the mind can get the body jumping here or there, *emotion* is necessary for sustained activity. This section is about cultivating and channeling your emotional energy for consistent, persistent action.

There are a lot of different words for this emotional energy—*enthusiasm (en theos,* to be one with the energy of the divine), *desire,* and even *obsession.* The one I'm passionate about is *passion.*

The emotions are, however, controlled by the mind. What we *think about* determines how we *feel.* So, even though the goal of this section is to produce passionate emotions, much of the time I'll be discussing the uses of the mind.

To reach a dream, especially a Big Dream, we need an ally, something to counteract all the limiting emotions the comfort zone can dish out.

> *Put all your eggs in one basket and*
> *WATCH THAT BASKET!*
>
> MARK TWAIN

That ally is our passion. We must love and desire our Dream—and love and desire it *intently*—for our Dream to come true.

To paraphrase Mark Twain: "Put all your eggs in one basket—and *LOVE THAT BASKET!*"

Or, as Elbert Hubbard said, "Do your work with your whole heart, and you will succeed—there's so little competition."

*Always bear in mind
that your own resolution to success
is more important
than any other one thing.*

ABRAHAM LINCOLN

*Losers visualize
the penalties of failure.
Winners visualize
the rewards of success.*

Dr. Rob Gilbert

Visualization

To visualize is to see what is *not* there, what is *not* real—a *dream*. To visualize is, in fact, to make *visual lies*.

Visual lies, however, have a way of coming true.

As I mentioned earlier, don't let the word *visual* throw you. I'm talking about the *imagination*. Some people primarily *see* in their imagination. Others primarily *feel*. Still others primarily *hear*. Whichever sense you use to access your imagination is fine.

How do *you* visualize? What does it look, feel, or sound like? The same way you remember things, that's how the imagination looks-feels-sounds. What's the shape of an apple? What color is a carrot? ("Why is a carrot more orange than an orange?" asked the Amboy Dukes. Does anybody remember the Amboy Dukes? It was back in the sixties. You had to be there.) What is your bathroom sink like? How clean is your car? However you saw, sensed, or heard those images, that's what it's like to *visualize* the future in your imagination.

But you know all this. You already have a sanctuary built in your imagination, and probably a few taco stands, too. With such advanced readers, it must be time for a *Pop Quiz!*

POP QUIZ: Although the brain is only 2% of the total body weight, it consumes 25% of the body's oxygen. What does this mean?

(A) If you feel short of breath, stop thinking.

> *Never give in.*
> *Never. Never. Never. Never.*
>
> Sir Winston Churchill

(B) People without brains need 25% less oxygen.

(C) Our brains should be bigger.

(D) The body considers thinking an important activity.

(E) We should spend 75% of our time doing something other than thinking.

(F) You shouldn't walk, think, and chew gum at the same time.

(G) Keep breathing.

In our imagination, what we behold we can become. What we have beheld in the past has made us what we are and gotten us what we have. If we want something different—something greater—we must think greater thoughts.

We are not responsible for every thought that goes meandering through our mind. We *are*, however, responsible for the ones we *hold* there. We're *especially* responsible for the thoughts we *put* there.

It's time to plant a Dream crop of positive visions. It's time to focus on the positive; to hold an image of what we want; to see, view, play *(s'il vous plaît)* our Dream.

Or, worded for our more negatively thinking friends: Don't think about what you don't want.

No matter what else you're doing, think about your Dream *all the time.* Live your Dream in your imagination. Become obsessed by it. Fall in love with it. Court it. Seduce it. Marry it. Become passionate about it.

To paraphrase Churchill: Never lose in your imagination. Never. Never. Never. Never.

It's *your* dream. *Your* imagination. Why on earth should you lose there? Don't. If you find yourself losing, turn it around. Call in a cavalry charge. Bring on your Fairy Godmother (one of your Master Teacher's many outfits). Whatever it takes.

In your imagination, always come out on top, always be victorious. Always win.

I used to work at
The International House
of Pancakes.
It was a dream,
and I made it happen.

PAULA POUNDSTONE

Affirmations

To affirm is to make firm. An affirmation is a statement of truth you make firm by repetition.

Like goals, affirmations work best when they are worded in the present tense. *"I am* a successful orchestral conductor, making $100,000 per year" is how to state an affirmation, not "I'm going to be . . ." or "I really want to be . . ." or "If it's not too much trouble, I'd really like to be . . . ."

Your purpose and your Big Dream (Goal) are already worded as affirmations—so, affirm them. Say each, out loud, for an hour without stopping.

Before starting, you might want to ask the white light to surround you for your highest good.

When you affirm, all that is between you and fulfilling that dream surfaces—in other words, the comfort zone. Expect fear, guilt, unworthiness, hurt feelings, anger, and discouragement to do what they do to get you to stop.

Keep going.

To bring up the limitations faster, look at yourself in the mirror while repeating your affirmation. It's a powerful process.

Additionally, you can record your affirmations on an endless-loop cassette (the kind used for outgoing messages in answering machines) and have them playing softly in the background while other things are going on.

You can get an earphone and play your tape on a portable stereo wherever you go. (Talk about your

> *The thing always happens*
> *that you really believe in;*
> *and the belief in a thing*
> *makes it happen.*
>
> FRANK LLOYD WRIGHT

portable paradise!)

Some people like to make a treasure map. A treasure map is a large piece of foam core or a bulletin board that contains the keys to your inner and outer riches. Cut from magazines, newspapers, or make drawings of objects that represent portions of your Big Dream—words, pictures, people, anything.

Glue, paste, or pin them to your treasure map. (Some people use a bulletin board so that when one portion of the Dream is realized, they can take it down and replace it with another part of the Dream.)

Your treasure map becomes a colorful collage.

Put it where you'll see it often (but not where the trolls hang out). It's a visual affirmation.

Practice turning the comfort zone's chattering into instant affirmations. Anytime you catch yourself saying something negative to yourself, take charge of the thought and rescue it. Turn it around. Make the most negative thought the most positive one—just like that. Consider it a lesson in creative writing, or a new quiz show—the grand prize of which is your Dream. If stuck, you can always add, ". . . up until now, and things are changing for the better," to whatever negative nonsense the comfort zone throws at you.

Affirmations help you believe in your Dream. Belief is essential. Your Dream must become more real than your doubt. Affirmations are like lifting weights—a mechanical process that helps build strength (belief) in your Dream.

"One person with belief," John Stuart Mill wrote more than a hundred years ago, "is equal to a force of ninety-nine who have only interests."

If you want a quality,
act as if you already had it.
Try the "as if" technique.

WILLIAM JAMES

A Place to Practice Success

I bet you already know the place I'm about to suggest. Yes, your *sanctuary.*

All the tools of the sanctuary—the light at the entryway, main room, people mover, information retrieval system, video screen, ability suits, ability suit practice area, health center, playroom, sacred room, and Master Teacher—are invaluable tools in visualizing and affirming your Dream.

Think of all the experts—past, present, and future—you can invite in on the people mover. ("Mark Twain told me today, 'Courage is the mastery of fear—not absence of fear.'" Amaze your friends!)

Think of how much fun you can have wearing the ability suit of your Dream in the ability suit practice area. If that becomes too vigorous, you can sit down and *watch* yourself being successful on the video screen. The information retrieval system is the perfect place to go whenever you think, "I wish I knew about . . . ."

And, of course, there's the Master Teacher—friend, guide, supporter, champion, *bon vivant.*

All this—and so much more—is only the close of an eyelid away. Use your sanctuary. Often.

Have I ever told you
you're my hero?
You're everything
I would like to be.
I can climb higher than an eagle.
You are the wind
beneath my wings.

LARRY HENLEY & JEFF SILBAR

Find a Hero

We all need a hero, a role model—someone who had a Dream as big as ours, and lived it.

Your hero may be alive, or may "belong to the ages." Either way, he or she can live in your heart.

Kevin Kline met his hero, Sir John Gielgud. Kline was in awe. "Mr. Gielgud," he said, "Do you have any advice for a young actor about to make his first film in London?"

Gielgud stopped and pondered the question for some time. At last he spoke, "The really good restaurants are in Chelsea and the outlying regions—you want to avoid the restaurants in the big hotels."

Pianist Vladimir Horowitz asked the advice of the great conductor Arturo Toscanini. "If you want to please the critics," Toscanini told him, "don't play too loud, too soft, too fast, too slow."

"Meet the sun every morning as if it could cast a ballot," Henry Cabot Lodge, Jr., told novice political campaigner Dwight D. Eisenhower. A few years later, President Eisenhower met another of his heroes, golfer Sam Snead. When Eisenhower asked him for some advice on how to improve his golf swing, Snead coached, "Put your ass into the ball, Mr. President!"

Eisenhower himself became a hero to millions. "This must have been how Eisenhower felt just before D-Day," Larry Appleton explained to Balki Bartoukomous. "All around him the troops sleeping; not Ike! He knew that one single mistake could change the course of world history." Balki had only

The one thing I do not want
to be called is First Lady.
It sounds like a saddle horse.

JACQUELINE KENNEDY

I wish I was Donna Reed—
she'd have something wonderful to say.
Or Shirley Jones—she'd have
something wonderful to say, too,
and maybe even some fresh-baked cookies.
Or Loretta Young; of course,
she wouldn't have anything wonderful to say, but
she <u>would</u> make a stunning entrance.

JESSICA TATE

one question: "Was this before or after Ike met Tina Turner?"

A young George Gershwin came to the already famous Irving Berlin, looking for a job as piano player. After hearing some of Gershwin's music, Berlin refused to hire him. "What the hell do you want to work for somebody else for?" Berlin asked, "Work for yourself!"

A playwright asked his hero, George Bernard Shaw, if he should continue with the profession of playwrighting. "Go on writing plays, my boy," Shaw encouraged, "One of these days one of these London producers will go into his office and say to his secretary, 'Is there a play from Shaw this morning?'

and when she says, 'No,' he will say, 'Well, then we'll have a start on the rubbish.' And that's your chance, my boy."

Heroes don't have to be real. Some people find fictional characters more inspiring than real-life heroes. To this day, thousands of people write to Sherlock Holmes at 221-B Baker Street. There is currently a bank at that address. The bank dutifully responds to every letter, "Mr. Holmes thanks you for your letter. At the moment he is in retirement in Sussex, keeping bees."

One of the great things about heroes is they are *human*. There's hardly a hero you can name who doesn't have heroic flaws. (Even Holmes had his weaknesses—that seven-percent solution of cocaine, for example.) Judy Garland once said of another singer (Barbra Streisand, I think), "The first time I saw her perform she was so good I wanted to run up to the stage, put my arms around her—and wring her neck. She just has too much talent!"

That our heroes became heroes *flaws and all* gives us hope. "You mean I don't have to be perfect to fulfill my Dream, to make a contribution?" Hardly.

It takes commitment, courage, and passion to live a dream and make a contribution. Heroes had these qualities *along with* their flaws. And you have those qualities, too.

And, of course, when you find one, visit your hero often in your sanctuary.

I was going to buy a copy of
The Power of Positive Thinking,
and then I thought:
What the hell good would that do?

RONNIE SHAKES

MARY RICHARDS: I quit.
I'm going to Africa to work with Schweitzer.
LOU GRANT: Mary,
Albert Schweitzer is dead.
MARY RICHARDS: You see what I mean,
Mr. Grant? It's a lousy, lousy world.

THE MARY TYLER MOORE SHOW

Positive Focusing vs. Positive Thinking

There is a myth that in order to reach our goal we must "think positive" all the time. No, we don't have to "think positive" all the time. We don't even have to think positively *any* of the time.

To succeed—to fulfill our Dream—all we have to do is keep focused on our goal and keep moving toward it.

Let's say person A, person B, and person C all set out for the same goal. They begin at the same place at the same time. Person A is a positive thinker; person B is a positive focuser; person C is both a positive thinker *and* a positive focuser.

At the "Go," person A decides to sit down and do a little positive thinking to help prepare for the journey. Person B focuses on the goal and gets moving. Person C gets moving, too.

Person A notices an area of unpositiveness within, and remains still, working hard to remove the "darkness" before moving on the journey. Person B does not like the road, does not like the rules, does not like the weather, does not like the planned lunch, does not like not liking any of it, but keeps moving toward the goal nonetheless. Person C keeps moving, too, while enjoying the flowers, waving at passersby, singing, and thinking what good exercise all this movement is.

Guess who gets to the goal first? It's a tie between B and C. Person A hasn't left the starting

> *Keep walking
> and keep smiling.*
>
> TINY TIM

place—but is feeling much more positive now, thank you very much. Person B and person C arrived at the goal at the same time because they were equally focused on it and *moved* on it. So why bother to add the positive thinking?

Person C *enjoyed* the journey; person B did not. That's the only difference. As long as we stay focused on our goal and continue moving toward it, we can have all the negative thoughts we want.

In terms of goals, what's the difference? Well, if I were to ask C, "How would you like to go toward another goal?" C might respond, "Sure. That was fun." Person B, on the other hand, might reply, "I worked hard to get here. I want to rest for a while.

Enjoy my victory."

What's the point? There are two. First, if your thoughts are not always sweetness and light as you move toward your Dream, don't worry. If you keep moving, you'll still get to your Dream.

Second, as you move toward your goal, you might like to practice focusing on good things along the way. You don't have to "make something up"—you already have; it's called your Dream. You need only look at *what's in front of you* and *find something there to appreciate.*

Our lives are a combination of good and bad, positive and negative. It's the best of times and the worst of times, all the time. When we focus on the good *that's already present,* we feel better. If not, we don't. Either way, life goes on.

Keeping your mind on the goal and moving toward the goal are the essence of positive focusing. All the rest is fun, entertaining, enjoyable—but not essential.

*Creativity can solve
almost any problem.
The creative act,
the defeat of habit
by originality,
overcomes everything.*

GEORGE LOIS

The Energy of Achievement

In the East, the movement of energy in the human body is studied and charted as meticulously as the movement of, say, bodily fluids is studied and charted in the West.

As the merging of East and West continues, the wisdoms of each are being explored and incorporated by the other. Some Eastern health practitioners now have circulation charts on their walls, and some Western doctors have charts indicating the meridians of the body and acupressure points.

I'm going to talk about the movement of one kind of energy within the body—the energy of achievement. There are other energies, of course, just as there are fluids other than blood. I'm discussing the energy of achievement because it relates most directly to manifestation—toward making our dreams come true.

This is the energy of individual creation. It's quite powerful. It is also experienced as sexual energy (recreative or procreative) and as spiritual energy. (This is the spiritual energy as it is perceived *within* the body. What degree of spiritual energy there is *outside* the body—and how that might be organized and tapped—is a matter of speculation and belief I shall leave to The Gap.)

People experience achievement energy differently depending on what they call it. Just as a certain energy in the body can be called "fear" or called "excitement," so, too, the energy of achievement can be called creative, sexual, or spiritual.

> *Creative activity could be*
> *described as a type*
> *of learning process*
> *where teacher and pupil*
> *are located*
> *in the same individual.*
>
> ARTHUR KOESTLER

This energy is produced in the body in an area that extends from about the navel to approximately mid-thigh. It extends in a band, all the way around the body. The center of it is the area known in Western anatomy as the *perineum*. To quote *The American Heritage:* "The region between the scrotum and the anus in males, and between the posterior vulva junction and the anus in females."

Even reading a dictionary definition about this center of energy is enough to activate many people's comfort zones. As we'll see shortly, this discomfort is precisely why this energy is not available as fully as it could be. For now, allow your comfort zone to do what it does, and read on.

The energy of achievement is designed to move up, toward the brain, where the mind directs it. ("Wash the car." "Fix dinner." "Write a Pulitzer Prize–winning novel.") The mind is like the rudder of a ship—with small motions, it guides the powerful ship in the direction set by the captain (you).

Here's an ideal scene of how this energy moves within the body. The energy moves up, into the area of the stomach—a circular area with the navel at its center. Here it picks up *excitement* and more *power*—the power to make changes. It rises further, to the solar plexus. Here, the energy becomes more focused and takes on a *solid, grounded, reliable* quality. The energy travels higher, to the center of the chest, where it acquires *loving* and *caring*. This excited, powerful, focused, solid, grounded, reliable, loving, and caring energy (I call it *passion*) presents itself to the mind, asking, "What shall we do?"

The process can go the other way, too. The mind may have a direction—a task—and send down for some energy. "Coming right up!" the creative energy responds, and rises to the occasion.

With this free flow of energy, directed toward a goal, it's easy to see how seemingly effortless the fulfillment of dreams can be. It actually sounds like *fun*.

Not many people, however, experience it in this way. What happens? If we overlay the comfort zone, and the misperceptions we were programmed to have about the use of various emotions, the answer is obvious.

The energy begins to rise from the creative cen-

> *Excuse me,*
> *I have to use the toilet.*
> *Actually, I have to use*
> *the telephone,*
> *but I'm too embarrassed*
> *to say so.*
>
> DOROTHY PARKER

ter. Because it's coming from "down there," we immediately begin to wonder, "What's wrong?" Most of us were trained that any sensation from "down there" involves either elimination (when we were younger) or sexuality (a little later)—two activities that are icky at best and deadly at worst. One then feels either fearful or guilty, or—usually—both.

If the sensation is some form of elimination, for many the first thought is, "Can this be postponed?" There is a great deal of fear connected with elimination—fear of germs, fear of pain, fear of touching anything icky, fear of terrible smells. (Actually, people don't much mind their own smells, but if someone else were to smell them—disaster!) Many people are embarrassed (another word for fearful) about elimination. There are almost as many euphemisms for elimination as there are for death—going to the rest room (what are you going to rest?), the powder room (what is there to powder?), the bathroom (you're going to take a *bath?*), and so on.

If the energy is perceived as sexual, the almost automatic response of most people is, "How do I get rid of this?" It is treated as some sort of *irritation*.

For some, fear and guilt *insist* that the energy be overcome, suppressed, crushed, "put down," and subdued. If this sounds like the response of a military dictator to a people's revolt, it is not coincidental. This energy, according to some people's training, is to be neither experienced nor expressed.

Some pull God in at this point, telling themselves that fear and guilt are really Direct Messages from the Almighty. It's not "moral" to feel this energy, they tell themselves. What was a simple revolution becomes a battle for one's Immortal Soul.

For others—many who consider themselves "sexually liberated"—the desire to eliminate any sexual feelings is just as strong. They, however, attempt to use *action* rather than *suppression*.

When the creative energies begin to rise and are perceived as sexual, one is, in the popular terminology, *horny.* Horny does not mean, "Oh, I'm going to spend loving, tender, intimate moments with the one I love." Horny means, "How can I get rid of this energy?" *Satisfaction* is defined as what you feel

> *I'm at an age where I think*
> *more about food than sex.*
> *Last week I put a mirror*
> *over my dining room table.*

RODNEY DANGERFIELD

after this energy is released. Promiscuous sexual activity—with self or others—releases the energy. The feeling behind the release is *fear*—fear that the energy will increase, as though sexual feelings were some sort of curse, and if the pressure is not immediately released, we might *explode.*

Both suppression and promiscuity are based on a deeply seated cultural taboo against sex. Yes, sex is everywhere in our culture, but it's everywhere *because* of the taboo. This is especially true of humor, which is a great barometer of what is forbidden and what is accepted by a culture. Jokes about the forbidden are automatically funnier than jokes about the acceptable.

"But sex is a natural function. Wouldn't it be joked about because of that?" Moving the blood through our body is a natural function, too, but how many jokes are there circulating about blood flow? Without the sexual taboo, jokes about sex wouldn't be so titillating.

We *look* for sex jokes. We even have a special term for puns of a sexual nature—*double entendre* (borrowed from the French, of course). ("I am now going to attempt," Bette Midler told her audience as a drum roll flourished, "my world-famous *quadruple* entendre!")

The result of this sexual taboo is *guilt*. We feel something we shouldn't be feeling—that *nobody* should be feeling—and we feel guilty. Rather than explore the underlying belief and accept that having sexual energy is *not* "bad," many people suppress the feeling, or rebel *against* the guilt and act on sexual feelings promiscuously. Either action is a reaction to the guilt.

The confusion this can cause when the energy is being used creatively or spiritually is obvious. One may be involved in a creative project. The creative energy is flowing more and more. Then, for a moment, it is interpreted as sexual. "Oh, dear," the creating person says, "I'd better *do* something about this," and moves into his or her habitual response to sexual energy. Be that suppression or expression, the use of the energy in a creative way is stopped.

The same happens when people are involved in spiritual practices—prayer, meditation, contemplation—and the spiritual energy begins flowing.

> *Creativity represents*
> *a miraculous coming together*
> *of the uninhibited energy of the child*
> *with its apparent opposite and enemy,*
> *the sense of order*
> *imposed on the disciplined*
> *adult intelligence.*
>
> NORMAN PODHORETZ

When experienced for a moment as sexual, the same turmoil about "what-to-do-about-sex" takes over, and the spiritual heights to which one can ride this energy are not reached.

When this energy is needed for creative or spiritual work, to eliminate it—through suppression or expression—before it has a chance to get beyond the fear and guilt of the stomach is not productive.

I am not advocating increased sexual activity for the suppressors, nor am I advocating celibacy for the expressers. I am suggesting that the sexual energy be considered a *welcome* energy in the body. It is not bad. It does not have to be suppressed or eliminated.

Allowing it to simply *be there* forms the basis from which one can choose *how* this energy will be used. That choice may be to use it creatively, spiritually, or sexually. When we're "on automatic," we cannot choose.

Let's say the energy makes it past the stomach. It has gained excitement (rather than fear) and power to change (rather than guilt). The next hurdle is unworthiness. This is a formidable one. "Who do you think you are to have this kind of energy? And just what do you plan to do with it, anyway?"

Even if a person has pondered these questions intellectually and arrived at a satisfactory conclusion, seldom is that conclusion grounded so fully in the body that it automatically answers, "I am me, this is my energy, and I'm using it to fulfill my Dream." (If using it as spiritual energy, the body might respond, "This is God's energy, and I'm using it to do God's work.") Unworthiness's only response to this is, "Oh, all right, you may pass."

Unworthiness stands as a gatekeeper. It has an important job: let only a certain amount of energy pass for a certain task. As I discussed before, most people, unfortunately, have unworthiness programmed to allow almost *nothing* to pass—they are unworthy of *all* things, certainly all *new* things.

Visualizations, affirmations, sanctuary work, and so on, give unworthiness new instructions. "It is all right to let energy for the fulfillment of this Dream pass. In addition, you are to add *to* this energy some of your solid, grounded, reliable energy."

> *You've got to create a dream.*
> *You've got to uphold the dream.*
> *If you can't,*
> *go back to the factory*
> *or go back to the desk.*
>
> ERIC BURDON

When the energy gets above unworthiness, it comes upon the third checkpoint. There it often finds a wounded heart.

Most people, over time, have developed a definite attitude toward emotional hurt: "I'm never going to let that happen to me again." They wrongly believe that it was the *caring* that caused the hurt, "And if I never care about anything ever again, I won't be hurt."

This is the I-may-never-win-but-at-least-I'll-never-lose attitude we discussed earlier. It is a decision made in early childhood, and the limited logic and perception of a child become the "rule" many people use to govern their adult lives.

To this rule, the energy of achievement is a major threat. "This Dream you're going after—it's a *risk*. We might *fail*. That would hurt, and I can't stand being hurt anymore. You can't pass." If pressed (by now the energy is fairly powerful), the anger that often covers the hurt arises and says, "I *said* no. I *mean* no. Now leave me *alone.*"

When the heart is taught, with gentleness and affection, that risk is a part of winning, and that hurt often is a part of caring, and that hurts eventually heal, it can allow the energy to pass. The heart, of course, being the heart, automatically adds loving and caring to the energy as it moves through.

At that moment, the heart thrills. In giving, it is reborn. It comes alive. It has something—the Dream—to love again, and loving is its nature, its very life. The wounds of the past begin to heal. The wounds are forgiven, and, as importantly, forgotten.

If all this energy arrives at an unfocused mind, of course, the energy is all dissipated, scattered here and there. The power to fulfill a Dream is lost. That's why I've spent so much time in this book on the significance of the Dream—the importance of knowing the specific destination toward which the ship is to be steered.

I've described what happens when the energy begins in the creative center and rises to the mind. When the mind sends its request down for some achievement energy to fulfill a given project, it's easy to see how the mind's request might never make it through all the possible roadblocks to connect with the very energy it seeks.

> *Any activity becomes creative*
> *when the doer cares*
> *about doing it right, or better.*
>
> JOHN UPDIKE

The first challenge the mind faces is the wounded heart. "We've been hurt too many times by your bright ideas. Go away." The mind returns to its station, where yet another "best laid plan" remains unfulfilled.

This is why most people have so many wants, desires, and "good ideas" bouncing around in their heads—they never got them past the hurt (and its close friend, anger). This is why the excuses many people have for not living their dreams are so filled with *blame.* "I would have done it, except so-and-so let me down," or "so-and-so *would have* let me down."

If the idea *does* get through the heart, it gathers

the caring energy and moves on. Until it comes upon unworthiness. "You can't have this goal *just now.* You're not good enough *just yet.* Come back *later.*"

This is why so many projects we *really loved* failed. Unworthiness is subtle in its sabotage. One of its key weapons is "Later." The concept of "later" makes sense to the mind—it's logical. Not everything can be done all at once. The mind buys this, and returns to the brain to wait. (I'll talk more about *later* in a little while.)

If the mind does move through unworthiness (often with the anger of the heart saying, "Enough with the laters, already!"), it enters the land of fear and guilt. Here, one logical-sounding reason after another is given for why nothing should ever change in any way. Fear and guilt know how to cite scripture and verse—from books, movies, TV shows, newspapers, or one's own life—as *proof* that the proposed idea is unworkable, preposterous, and downright *dangerous.*

The mind, dazzled by this seemingly *factual* presentation, goes "home" to think. It tries to discover a less dangerous way. Alas, fear and guilt shoot down every idea the mind formulates with even more logic than the last time. (The fact that some of the new logic *contradicts* the previous logic is not always noticed.) And so the mind is left alone—pondering.

≈

> *The essential conditions*
> *of everything you do must be*
> *choice, love, passion.*
>
> NADIA BOULANGER

All these energies are part of our *success mechanism*. That this mechanism has been misdirected and incorrectly programmed (for adults, at least) does not in any way affect the *usefulness* of the structure. (It is, in fact, doing a very good job at what it was programmed to do.)

Please remember: the goal is not to "get rid of" any part of this mechanism. The goal is to redirect and reprogram it so that it achieves what *we* choose—not the choices made for us by parents, teachers, and society when we were too young to make choices of our own.

There's nothing to winning, really.
That is, if you happen to be
blessed with a keen eye,
an agile mind,
and no scruples whatsoever.

ALFRED HITCHCOCK

*Every creator painfully
experiences the chasm between
his inner vision
and its ultimate expression.*

ISAAC BASHEVIS SINGER

Liberating Achievement Energy

The comfort zone's blockages to the free flow of achievement energy prevent us from directing our available energy toward our Dream. The energy is "damned" up inside ("damn this," "damn that").

Each of these limitations (fear, guilt, unworthiness, hurt feelings, and anger) has two aspects—a psychological (mental) one, and a physiological (physical) one.

The psychological aspect—and how to reprogram it with visualizations, affirmations, meditations—we've explored in other chapters. In this chapter, I'm going to suggest some ways this energy can be *physiologically* freed.

As I mentioned before, each of the comfort zone's limitations has a favorite stronghold in the body—fear and guilt prefer the stomach, unworthiness the solar plexus, hurt feelings and anger the chest. It was the *mind* and its *thoughts,* of course, that created these limitations in the first place, but the limitations have been "living" in a certain part of the body for so long, that parts of the body have *physically* taken on the attributes of the limitation.

We know, for example, that mental stress ("pressure") can create tension in the neck and shoulders. In some people, however, that mental stress has been so constant and unrelenting that they have

> *Take a music bath once or twice*
> *a week for a few seasons,*
> *and you will find that*
> *it is to the soul*
> *what the water-bath is to the body.*
>
> OLIVER WENDELL HOLMES

tension in the neck and shoulders *all the time*—even when they're *not* under stress. It's known as *chronic* tension.

The same is true of fear, guilt, unworthiness, hurt feelings, and anger. We tend to have *chronic* limitations built into the structure of our body. This is why—even when everything is going great—we can feel "free floating" fear, guilt, unworthiness, hurt, or anger.

The comfort zone, then, is "built into" our body. No matter how much "mental" work we do, there is the physical tension in our body that will counteract it.

The good news is that, being physical, we can

reduce these physical tensions through *physical* means. The techniques for removing tensions in the body are varied, plentiful, and, for the most part, pleasurable. The last thirty years have seen a rebirth of these techniques in the West. These include massage, stretching, breathing, exercise—and the old standby, hot baths. Entire schools are devoted to the study of just one form of tension relief—and there are dozens of these schools.

I am not going to explore all of them in this chapter. I will, however, mention a few. Know that *any* technique that relieves physical tension can be used to reduce the chronic physical tension of fear, guilt, unworthiness, hurt feelings, and anger.

Before I suggest any techniques, there is one thing to keep in mind about physical stress release: As the stress is released, it is usually reexperienced. If you've ever had your shoulders rubbed, you probably noticed that they hurt *more* as they were being massaged. Along with this hurt was probably a good feeling—one of release. This is often referred to as, "It hurts so good."

The same is true of fear, guilt, unworthiness, hurt feelings, and anger. As each is released, the feeling itself may intensify. But along with the intensity comes the good feeling of release. Often, that good feeling is the *other* quality of the limitation—excitement for fear, the power of personal change for guilt, worthiness for unworthiness, caring for hurt feelings, and the power for external change for anger.

In all cases, know that if the feeling you want to

> *I've got to keep breathing.*
> *It'll be my worst business mistake*
> *if I don't.*
>
> SIR NATHAN MEYER ROTHSCHILD

reduce, in fact, *intensifies*—that's part of the process. To the degree you can, focus on the *good* feeling that accompanies it.

Breathing and Stretching: It's hard to tell which of the techniques for removing physical tension is the oldest, but I'd put my chips on breathing and stretching. Animals take deep breaths and stretch for the same reasons humans do—it relieves tension and it feels good.

Breathing increases the supply of oxygen to the body. Stretching moves that oxygen around (through increased blood flow to the area being stretched). Fortunately, we can consciously breathe into, and, by breathing into it, stretch each of the comfort zone's strongholds—the stomach, the solar plexus, and the chest.

Try breathing into each of these places, consciously expanding the area as you do so. If you like, as you breathe in, you can imagine a white light going to that area. As you breathe out, you can imagine any darkness (tension) that was in the area released with the exhale.

Breathing deeply into an area of tension can be done anywhere, anytime. You can practice it "formally," lying down (it's sometimes nice to place your hands over the area you're breathing into), or it can be used whenever and wherever the comfort zone wishes to remind you that "you can't have what you want."

Stretching through movement is a great way to break up the comfort zone's patterning. Leaning back—supporting yourself with your hands on your lower back—stretches all the areas at once. So does lying on the floor, face down, and arching your back by pushing the top part of your body off the floor with your hands.

You probably cannot touch your elbows together behind your back, but if you *attempt* it, it stretches the heart center. If you lean slightly back while doing that, it stretches the solar plexus and stomach as well.

Physical Exercise: Using the muscles in the area of a limitation can help break up the limitation. Does this mean people with washboard stomachs have no fear? Not necessarily. (Although they obviously have no fear of exercise.) There is, however, a

> *I like long walks,*
> *especially when they are taken*
> *by people who annoy me.*
>
> FRED ALLEN

definite zone-busting effect to increasing blood flow into an area.

Hot Baths: Is all that exercise too strenuous for you? Here's a stress-reduction technique designed in heaven—the hot bath. Alas, many of us don't take hot baths very often. We live in a "shower power" culture. Maybe if you considered hot baths *therapeutic,* you could find more time for them. There are few activities that release general physical tension better.

Touch: Simply placing your hands on the areas of limitation can have profound results. It is usually best against bare skin, but through clothing works, too. You can imagine a white light flowing through your hands, into the area, releasing the tension. This is especially useful if combined with breathing. Touching yourself is something you can do *almost* anywhere. (Some people have become experts at doing it casually in public, as though it were the most natural thing in the world—which it is. Others pretend to be doing something else, such as gently scratching an itch.) A touch can send peace to a disturbed area, or energy to a lethargic one.

Massage: Not only can we *breathe* into each of the areas favored by the comfort zone; we can also reach all of them with *both* our hands. (Is this luck, or just good design?) Physically manipulating the stomach, solar plexus, and chest is an excellent way to dissolve the patterns of limitation residing there. The process is made even more effective (and enjoyable) by using massage oil. (I like pure olive oil, myself.)

It's also good to get professionally massaged. Let the masseur or masseuse know the areas you'd like to work on. You can also tell him or her which limitations you're seeking to reduce. He or she may have some additional techniques for specific stress reduction.

Any of these techniques becomes more powerful when combined with *mental* work. Imagining a Dream while eliminating a barrier to that Dream can have profound effects. In this, you are reducing a limitation both mentally *and* physically. When a limitation is tossed out of both its thriving places often enough, it might just move back to the Midwest where it came from. (Or, perhaps, New England. As Cleveland Amory pointed out, "The New

> *An Englishman thinks he is moral*
> *when he is only uncomfortable.*
>
> GEORGE BERNARD SHAW

England conscience doesn't keep you from doing what you shouldn't—it just keeps you from enjoying it.")

All these techniques have an element of physical pleasure. In addition to enjoying it, *use* it, too. Allow yourself to *feel good*—physically—about your Dream. So often our dreams have been accompanied by physically feeling bad (thanks to the comfort zone).

More on this in the next chapter. For now, know that time spent doing body work is time well invested—reducing the comfort zone's hold, and providing more creative energy to pursue your Dream.

*We may affirm absolutely
that nothing great in the world
has been accomplished
without passion.*

Hegel

1832

Success is not the result
of spontaneous combustion.
You must set yourself on fire.

REGGIE LEACH

Redirecting Energies

Most people have their passion hard-wired (often hot-wired) in a particular direction. It might be toward a person, certain foods, a TV program, sex, money, football, macramé—whatever.

What we feel passionate about is our choice. For most of us, however, the choice was made long ago. We *know* what the choice *is*—whatever we automatically feel passionate about—but we've forgotten having made the choice.

As we free the achievement energy within ourselves, it will naturally flow toward what we already feel passionate about. We're "wired" that way. The energy takes the path of least resistance. If that's the path to your goal, great. If it is heading toward something *other* than your goal, that newly liberated energy can be redirected.

Notice I said "newly liberated." I'm not suggesting you feel any *less* passionate about the things you currently feel passionate about—unless those things are not part of your Dream.

I'm saying that most of us have a lot more passion than we currently allow ourselves to feel. As you feel this energy more, give the *overflow* to your Dream. That overflow may be ten times what you currently feel, but give it anyway. Your Dream requires—and deserves—a lot of energy.

Usually our thoughts "wire" us to a particular passion. We think about, oh, sex, we feel passion; we feel passion, we think about sex more; we think about sex more, we feel more passion. It's an ex-

> *Passion is in all great searches*
> *and is necessary*
> *to all creative endeavors.*
>
> W. Eugene Smith

panding cycle. Like the chicken and the egg, it's hard to tell which came first, the thought or the passion.

Also like the chicken-and-egg puzzlement, it doesn't matter. We have chickens, we have eggs—that's all that matters. We have passion, we have things we feel passionate about—that's what matters.

You can redirect the passion from something you currently feel passionate about to your Dream at any point in the cycle. All it takes is (a) remembering to do it, and (b) a *specific* image to feel passionate about.

Specific images are important. A general image of a Dream ("I want to be a movie star") is too vague. It doesn't have enough *fascination* to pull the passion from the current object of desire.

For someone whose dream is being a movie star, a specific image might be winning an Oscar. What *specifically* about winning an Oscar turns you on? Is it the moment you hear your name announced? Is it the moment you are being patted on the back by all those around you, and giving an obligatory kiss to your companion, whoever that may be? Maybe it's standing at the podium, bright lights shining on you, slightly out of breath, listening to the ovation, Oscar in your hand.

These are *specific* images. If some of your body work releases one of the limiting emotions, and that releases some passion, then direct that passion toward the specific image of your Big Dream. If you're thinking passionately about whatever you currently find passionating (as I said, what would a self-help book be without a coined word or two—this was number two), direct that passion toward the specific image.

As an exercise, find a specific image of your Dream. Say, winning the Oscar. Now, close your eyes and think about something—not directly related to your Dream—that you tend to feel passionate about. Let's say it's chocolate cake. Think about chocolate cake. Think about how good it tastes. In your imagination, see it, smell it, taste it—let the juices (and the passion) flow.

Then, *snap*, place in your mind the image of the Oscar. Let the passion built by and for chocolate cake be directed at Oscar. If cake comes back in

> *Many persons have*
> *a wrong idea of what*
> *constitutes true happiness.*
> *It is not attained through*
> *self-gratification but through*
> *fidelity to a worthy purpose.*
>
> HELEN KELLER

(and it will), let it. Let the passion build again, then, *snap,* switch to Oscar.

At first, you probably won't be able to hold the new image for long—the mind will go back to what it habitually feels passionate about. This is what I meant by "hard-wired." With practice, however, transferring passion from one object to another becomes easier and easier. Eventually, when you feel passion stirring in your body, it will *automatically* move toward your Dream.

As an advanced exercise, switch the thought from The Passion-Arousing Thing to the specific image *while doing the passion-arousing thing.* No, this is not an excuse to go have some chocolate cake. ("I ate an entire chocolate cake last night—it's an exercise in a book I'm reading.") Although I couldn't imagine any suggestion that would sell more copies of this book, I must advise you don't do The Passion-Arousing Thing just for the purposes of this exercise.

The next time you *are* doing The Passion-Arousing Thing, however, from time to time, mentally switch to your new image. (If another person is involved, *do* be discreet. "What are you doing?" "I'm sorry, dear, I was thinking about an Oscar." "Oscar who?!")

Sometimes I sits and thinks
and sometimes I just sits.

S<small>ATCHEL</small> P<small>AIGE</small>

Meditate, Contemplate, or "Just Sits"

In addition to visualization and affirmations, you might like to try any number of meditative and contemplative techniques available—or you might want just to sit quietly and relax.

Whenever you meditate, contemplate, pray, do spiritual exercises, or "just sits," it's good to ask the white light to surround, fill, and protect you, knowing only that which is for your highest good and the highest good of all concerned will take place during your quiet time. You may want to do your meditation in your sanctuary.

Before starting, prepare your physical environment. Arrange not to be disturbed. Unplug the phone. Put a note on the door. Wear ear plugs if noises might distract you. (I like the soft foam-rubber kind sold under such trade names as E.A.R., HUSHER, and DECIDAMP.) Take care of your bodily needs. Have some water nearby if you get thirsty, and maybe some tissues, too.

Contemplation is thinking *about* something, often something uplifting. You could contemplate any of the hundreds of quotes or ideas in this book. Often, when we hear a new and potentially useful idea, we say, "I'll have to think about that." Contemplation is a good time to "think about that," to consider the truth of it, to imagine the changes and improvements it might make in your life.

Or, you could contemplate a nonverbal object,

> *How beautiful it is*
> *to do nothing,*
> *and then rest afterward.*
>
> SPANISH PROVERB

such as a flower, or a concept, such as God. The idea of contemplation is to set aside a certain amount of quiet time to think about just *that,* whatever you decide "that" will be.

Meditation. There are so many techniques of meditation, taught by so many books and organizations, that it's hard to define the word properly.

You might want to try various meditations to see what they're like. With meditation, please keep in mind that *you'll never know until you do it.* We may like to think we know what the effects of a given meditation will be by just reading the description, but I suggest you try it and *then* decide.

Breathing Meditation. Sit comfortably, close

your eyes, and simply be aware of your breath. Follow it in and out. Don't "try" to breathe; don't consciously alter your rhythm of breathing; just follow the breath as it naturally flows in and out. If you get lost in thoughts, return to your breath.

Mantras. Some people like to add a word or sound to help the mind focus as the breath goes in and out. Some people use *one* or *God* or *AUM* (*OHM*) or *love.* These—or any others—are fine. As you breathe in, say to yourself, mentally, "love." As you breathe out, "love." If you don't like synchronizing sounds to breath, don't. It doesn't matter.

It's not so much the *sound,* but the *meaning you assign* to the sound. You may use a mantra such as "Ummmm" just because it sounds good—satisfying and relaxing. Or you may say "Ahhhh" represents the pure sound of God. Because you *say* it does, it will.

Affirmations. Brief affirmations can be used in meditation. My favorites include "God is within me" and "I love myself."

Some people think meditation takes time *away* from physical accomplishment. Taken to extremes, of course, that's true. Most people, however, find that meditation *creates* more time than it *takes.* Meditation is for rest, healing, balance, and information. All these are helpful to attain a goal.

One of the primary complaints people have about meditating is, "My thoughts won't leave me alone." Well *naturally*—that's what the mind does; it *thinks.* Rather than fight the thoughts (good luck), you might listen to the thoughts for nuggets of

> *True silence*
> *is the rest of the mind;*
> *it is to the spirit*
> *what sleep is to the body,*
> *nourishment and refreshment.*
>
> WILLIAM PENN

information. If a thought reminds you of something to do, write it down (or record it on a tape recorder). Then return to the meditation.

As the "to do" list fills, the mind empties. If the thought, "Call the bank," reappears, you need only tell yourself, "It's on the list. I can let that one go." And you will. It is important, however, to *do* the things on the list—or at least in a nonmeditative state to consider doing them. If you don't, you will continue to think about them, again and again.

When finished meditating, not only will you have had a better meditation; you will also have a "to do" list that can be very useful. One insight gleaned during a few minutes of meditation might save *hours*, perhaps *days* of unnecessary work. That's what I mean when I say—from a purely practical point of view—meditation can make more time than it takes.

Be bold—
and mighty forces will
come to your aid.

BASIL KING

The Willingness to Do
Creates the Ability to Do

When looking at all that must be done to fulfill your Dream, it's easy to wonder, "How am I going to *do* all this?" Don't worry about *how* you'll do the work; just be *willing* to do it.

Be *willing* to get off your buts.

You can start by using your *buts* to your benefit. When the comfort zone creates a limiting thought, you can add, ". . . but I'm willing to _____." "I don't know how to do this . . . but I'm willing to know." "I'm too tired to do this . . . but I'm willing to have the energy." "I'm not worthy of this . . . but I'm willing to be worthy."

The willingness opens the doors to knowledge, direction, and achievement. Be willing to know, be willing to do, be willing to create.

Be willing to follow your Dream.

If you have built castles in the air,
your work need not be lost;
that is where they should be.
Now put the foundations under them.

HENRY DAVID THOREAU

Just Do It!

ADVERTISEMENT FOR
RUNNING SHOES

PART FIVE

DOING IT

The mind and emotions (your passion) are now in alignment behind your Dream (or moving in that direction more and more).

Now it's time for *action*—to *DO IT!*

Laziness is nothing more than the habit of resting before you get tired.

JULES RENARD

The Biggest Lie in Action

The biggest lie we tell ourselves in the area of action is, "I'll do it later." As C. Northcote Parkinson said, "Delay is the deadliest form of denial."

Putting things off is known, of course, as procrastination. I know that "pro" means *for*, but I don't know what "crastination" means. Maybe it means *laziness*. Maybe it means *don't go after your Dream, but kid yourself into thinking that someday you will*. Whatever crastination means, I'm against it.

You could say I'm pro anticrastination.

(I looked it up: *crastination* comes from *crastinus*, Latin for pertaining to *tomorrow*. *Procrastinus* is "putting things off till tomorrow." "Never put off till tomorrow," Mark Twain said, "what you can do the day after tomorrow." *Procrastinus-crastinus?*)

The interesting thing about "later" is that a statement containing it can never be proven false. One can never reproach us for not doing something. If confronted, we can always say, "I said I'd do it later. It's not later yet."

In this way, we can put off and put off and put off *indefinitely*. We only run out of laters when we run out of breath. Death is nature's way of saying, "No more laters left."

We know how many laters we have stockpiled from the past. We know that adding another later to that pile is like adding a grain of sand to a beach. Somehow, we know we're probably never going to get back to that particular grain of sand.

> *If you trap the moment before it's ripe,*
> *The tears of repentance*
> *you'll certainly wipe;*
> *But if once you let the ripe moment go*
> *You can never wipe off the tears of woe.*
>
> WILLIAM BLAKE
> 1791
>
>
>
> *He who hesitates is poor.*
>
> ZERO MOSTEL
> *THE PRODUCERS*

We know "later" is a lie.

If you can do something now, do it. If it can't be done now, (a) decide if it is going to get done. If yes, (b) choose *when* it will get done.

If something doesn't get done, and you decide you will still do it, reschedule a *specific date and time*. Write it in your appointment book. If it's not worth the amount of time it takes to schedule it *now*, it's probably not going to get done "later."

When we put necessary activities off until some mythical Laterland, we drag the past into the future. The burden of yesterday's incompletions is a heavy load to carry. *Don't carry it.*

A Dream is an ephemeral thing. In traveling to

it, you have to travel light. "I travel light;" Christopher Fry wrote, "as light, that is, as a man can travel who will still carry his body around because of its sentimental value."

Getting in the habit of doing what needs to be done as it presents itself to be done—whether it *needs* to be done in that moment or not—creates an inner freedom for the next moment, the next activity.

Such as pursuing your Dream.

*Have no fear
of perfection—
you'll never reach it.*

<small>SALVADOR DALI</small>

We're Not Perfect—
We're Human

How do we learn? By doing. As Aristotle said, "For the things we have to learn before we can do them, we learn by doing them." Yes, *everything* is best learned by doing.

A primary reason people don't do new things is because they want to do them perfectly—first time. It's irrational, impractical, unworkable—and yet, it's how most people run their lives. It's called the Perfection Syndrome.

Whoever said we had to do it perfect?

Our parents. And if not our parents, there were those bastions of perfection—school teachers. (The ones who would point out that the last paragraph should read, "Whoever said we had to do it per-*fectly?*" They would also point out that paragraphs should be more than one sentence long.)

For the most part, we weren't taught to set our own goals and to achieve them. In addition, we had to achieve someone else's goal in "the right way." Merely *reaching* the goal was not enough. The goal had to be attained the way someone else (whoever was teaching us) thought was the "best way" (that is, *their* way).

I say, don't worry—just DO IT!

Don't worry about "right way"; don't even worry about doing it "my way." DO IT! When it's all said and done—when you've reached your goal—you can look back and discover what *your*

> *When in doubt,*
> *make a fool of yourself.*
> *There is a microscopically*
> *thin line between being*
> *brilliantly creative and acting*
> *like the most gigantic idiot on earth.*
> *So what the hell, leap.*
>
> CYNTHIA HEIMEL

way really was. As Margaret Mead said, "The best way to do field work is not to come up for air until you're done." Amen.

Most people have an ideal image of themselves. If they can't perform according to their own imaginary standards of perfection, they "take their ball and go home." As Cardinal Newman observed, "Nothing would be done at all if a man waited until he could do it so well that no one could find fault with it."

"Men would like to learn to love themselves, but they usually find they cannot," Gerald Brenan explained. "That is because they have built an ideal image of themselves which puts their real self in the shade."

This "ideal image" of ourselves—the one that's "perfect" and won't let anyone see us as other than perfect—we must send on a long field trip somewhere. Maybe Alpha Centauri.

The only way to even *approach* doing something perfectly is through experience, and experience, as Oscar Wilde observed, "is the name everyone gives to their mistakes."

Mistakes are excellent teachers. Sir Humphrey Davy wrote, "I have learned more from my mistakes than from my successes." Make as many mistakes as you can, as quickly as you can. "Show me a guy who's afraid to look bad," said Rene Auberjonois, "and I'll show you a guy you can beat every time." Set out each day to look foolish, stupid, blundering, awkward—anything you consider the perfect representation of *im*perfect.

In this way, you shatter the false image of a "perfect self," and get used to being a stumble-through-it, catch-as-catch-can, make-do, seat-of-the-pants, mistake-making human being—just like every other successful dreamer.

After all, it's not perfect being perfect.

The superior man thinks
always of virtue;
the common man thinks
of comfort.

CONFUCIUS

Be Prepared to Be Scared

When we put ourselves on the path of expansion by committing to a goal that's outside our comfort zone, we're going to be given a lot of opportunities to expand. We are *not* going to be able to choose all those opportunities for expansion.

Our choice is either "expand" or "contract." If we choose "expand," we will expand—and we'll *always* wish there were more comfortable ways of doing it.

Let's say someone's goal is to get her body in shape. The *way* this would happen, she imagines, is in a sparkling health club with chrome-plated barbells and Tom Cruise holding her feet while she does sit-ups. How, she wonders, will the money "materialize" so she can pay the queen's ransom of a membership?

Meanwhile, in the first week after committing to her goal, her car runs out of gas, and she has to walk five miles to the nearest phone; an emergency happens at work and she is asked to fill in, packing boxes in the warehouse; her freezer is accidentally unplugged and all her ice cream melts; and, on the weekend, she goes on a spiritual retreat, hoping to get some rest. All weekend, however, is devoted to what they call "dharma yoga," which sounds nice *in principle,* but in reality is digging ditches, cutting down trees, and helping a pair of not-so-busy beavers build a dam.

At the end of the first week, she has lost two pounds, taken an inch off her waist, and looks

> *Minds, like bodies,*
> *will often fall into a pimpled,*
> *ill-conditioned state*
> *from mere excess of comfort.*
>
> CHARLES DICKENS

better—but feels sorer—than she has in years.

This is how it happens. We get the Dream, but we don't get to dictate every step toward the Dream.

We can, of course, refuse to do an uncomfortable activity placed before us. When we know something *might* move us a step closer to our goal and we choose not to do it "because it's uncomfortable," we are also choosing not to pursue our goal. It's that simple.

This refusal has two results. First, we are not one step closer to our goal. Second, the opportunities to expand—to reach the goal—will, in the future, be presented less frequently.

When we *un*commit through inaction (honoring the comfort zone), the goal-fulfillment mechanism backs off, too. Our goal-fulfillment mechanism is not there to *hurt* us; it's there to *help* us. If we indicate—through nonaction—that we aren't ready to take the steps necessary to reach the goal, it says, "Fine. Let me know when you're ready."

It's as though we went to a friend's house for the evening. After asking three or four times in the first hour if we wanted anything to drink, and receiving a "No, thank you" each time, our host would, naturally, ask less frequently, and, eventually, stop.

Whatever you find *most* uncomfortable in getting to your goal, be willing to do it. You may not *have* to do it, but be *willing* to. Your willingness will be tested. If you say, "I'm willing!" and the opportunity arises and you're *not,* then you're not being honest with yourself.

When a portion of the comfort zone is being expanded, it always *seems* as though expansion of *any other part* would be more tolerable, more acceptable. We want to put it off, postpone, and do it later, so some *other* part of the comfort zone can be challenged.

In fact, when that *other* part is challenged, it will seem as though *this* is the worst part of the comfort zone to expand, and *any other* area would be better than *this.* Discomfort always seems more tolerable anywhere other than the place in which it's being felt.

The solution? *Plan* to be uncomfortable. Understand that it's a necessary part of success. Learn to

> *One of the best ways to properly evaluate and adapt to the many environmental stresses of life is to simply view them as normal. The adversity and failures in our lives, if adapted to and viewed as normal corrective feedback to use to get back on target, serve to develop in us an immunity against anxiety, depression, and the adverse responses to stress. Instead of tackling the most important priorities that would make us successful and effective in life, we prefer the path of least resistance and do things simply that will relieve our tension, such as shuffling papers and majoring in minors.*
>
> DENIS WAITLEY

be comfortable with discomfort. Have compassion for the part of you that's growing. The first step is a *willingness* to be uncomfortable.

The next step is to realize *which* emotion from the comfort zone you're feeling each time you feel "uncomfortable." Fear? Guilt? Unworthiness? Hurt feelings? Anger? Observe it. See if you can locate it in the body.

As I mentioned earlier, fear is probably the most frequently felt of the comfort zone's emotions. Not only do we feel fear, we also tend to fear every other comfort-zone emotion. Unworthiness, for example, seldom has to make an appearance. The *fear* of unworthiness is enough to keep most people in check. If you feel fear, ask yourself if you're fearing *something,* or if you're afraid of feeling some other *emotion.*

The final step is turning your *perception* of each "negative" emotion into its positive counterpart. Learn to see fear as excitement, guilt as the energy for personal change, unworthiness as the discipline to live your Dream, hurt feelings as caring, and anger as the energy for outer change.

This reprogramming can take some time. Do not, however, wait until you have the "conversion technique" mastered before moving—steadily and persistently—toward your Dream. Some people are past their first Dream and well on the way to their second before they can even locate the comfort zone's feelings in the body.

For now, be willing to be uncomfortable. Be comfortable being uncomfortable. It may get tough, but it's a small price to pay for living your Dream.

Guilt is never a rational thing;
it distorts all the faculties
of the human mind,
it perverts them,
it leaves a man no longer
in the free use of his reason,
it puts him into confusion.

EDMUND BURKE

Guilt (again)

Guilt is probably the most insidious resident of the comfort zone. Most people think the worst one is fear. It's probably true that fear is the most *noticeable* limiting emotion. Guilt, however, is often more powerful because it can be so *hidden*.

Fear increases as we come closer and closer to actually *doing* the thing we're afraid to do. Let's say we're afraid of walking up to a stranger in a supermarket and saying, "Hello." We have decided that meeting strangers is a necessary part of reaching our Dream (a Marriage/Family dream, for example). So, the next "perfect stranger" we see in a public place—we *committed* to walk up and say, "Hello, I'd like to meet you."

There's the stranger and here we are, with nothing between us but the canned peas. Emotion: fear. No, it's *not* excitement—no matter how many times we've read the chapter, "Fear is the Energy to Do Your Best in a New Situation." This is a new situation, and this is *fear—panic*.

We know, however, that we must do this. We have gone over it and over it in our mind and with supportive friends. This may or may not be *our* perfect stranger, but this *is* the perfect opportunity to "move through fear," to "feel the fear and do it anyway."

No matter *what* happens, at least we will have learned to meet new people, so that some enchanted evening, if we see a stranger across a crowded room, we can fly to his side and make him

> *Guilt is the source of sorrows,*
> *the avenging fiend*
> *that follows us behind*
> *with whips and stings.*
>
> NICHOLAS ROWE

our own, so that all through our life we won't dream all alone.

We take one step in the direction of the stranger. The stranger's head moves—maybe to *look* at us! We grab a can of peas and begin studying the label intensely.

This is *silly*, we tell ourselves. We are an *adult*. We are *committed*. The blood courses in our ears. Our heart is pounding. We take charge of the situation, and we *act*.

"Do you think these peas are as good as the ones on sale?" we ask the stranger.

"Gee, I don't know," the stranger replies. "I only buy fresh peas myself." We notice the stranger is wearing a wedding ring. Hmmm. *Not* the perfect stranger after all.

"Oh, of course," we smile. "Thank you."

That's a fairly typical move-through-fear situation. Before it, we can pep-talk ourselves, and we can rah-rah our way through it. We can physically *feel* the comfort zone becoming more and more dense as we begin doing the thing we're afraid to do. That's all fear.

Guilt is all the rest we live with after.

Guilt berates us for moving through the fear. We are reminded of a story on the news about someone meeting another person in a supermarket and the terrible result of that meeting *that could have happened to us.* Guilt projects an endless succession of "What-ifs" across our inner nightmare gallery.

If we don't give in to the chatterings that we *shouldn't* have done it in the first place—if we hold firmly to the idea that walking up to strangers and meeting them is part of our Dream, and that we're going to continue doing it no matter *what* guilt says—then the guilt changes its tack.

"Why didn't you see that the stranger was wearing a wedding ring?" guilt asks. "Why aren't you more observant? You went through all that for *nothing.* Besides, your commitment was to say, 'Hello, I'd like to meet you,' not to discuss canned vegetables. You can't even do *that* right."

And on and on.

If the guilt gets us and we agree to abide by the limitation "next time," guilt floods us with positive

> *If you're going*
> *to do something wrong,*
> *at least enjoy it.*
>
> LEO ROSTEN

feelings. We feel a sense of freedom and joy that parallels enlightenment. Euphoric feelings reign.

"Of course," we say, "this restriction is *me*. I *choose* to have it. It's part of *who I am*." With each statement of limitation, we soar higher and higher.

Guilt cannot only make us feel terrible; it can also make us feel wonderful.

Guilt is a trainer with both sugar cubes and a cattle prod. When we toe the mark—the confines of the comfort zone—we get sweetness. When we "overstep our bounds," we get punished.

The next time we *don't* walk up to a stranger, we are rewarded with a good feeling and a pep talk. We are *proud* of our limitation. This is the booby prize of life—complacency tinged with self-righteousness.

So, how do we use guilt *for* ourselves? As the old Hindu saying goes, "It takes a thorn to remove a thorn," or, as we say in the West, "Fight fire with fire." Start feeling guilty when you *don't* take steps toward your Dream. Feel all those guilt-things when you *honor* the comfort zone.

Yes, for a while, this will put you in a lot of dammed-if-I-do-and-dammed-if-I-don't situations—you're going to feel guilty no matter *how* you act. Eventually, however, guilt will be as staunch an ally to your Dream as it currently is to your comfort zone.

While you're reprogramming your guilt, *external support* comes in handy—a friend, counselor, therapist, or support group—to encourage you to continue taking risks, to continue moving toward your Dream.

*My philosophy is that
not only are you responsible
for your life,
but doing the best
at this moment
puts you in the best place
for the next moment.*

OPRAH WINFREY

Response Ability

Responsibility is a misunderstood word. Most people use it to mean *blame*. "Who's responsible for this?" means "Who's to blame for this? Whom can I punish?"

We are experts at finding blame. We blame others for not making us happy, for letting us down, for not fulfilling our dreams. If people become involved in personal growth or therapy of some kind, they often don't become more responsible—they just find new things to blame. Childhood! Parents! Heredity! Environment!

Let's blame our parents for programming us to blame others, shall we?

Enough! It's time to grow up. If we want to play adult games—like living our Dream—we must play by adult rules. One of the primary adult rules: We are individually responsible for our own lives.

Responsibility simply means, "the ability to respond." In any of life's challenges, opportunities, or disasters, we can *respond* in whatever way we choose. Our response dictates what life hands us next. Our response is either a workable response (it takes us one step closer to our goal) or an unworkable response (it does *not* take us one step closer to our goal).

It's not a matter of right/wrong, good/bad. It's a matter of *practical analysis* of the situation. From *that* situation, we have the ability to respond again. When the outcome of that is known, we will either be closer to, or farther from, our goal. Then we have the ability to respond to *that*.

> *If you are distressed*
> *by anything external,*
> *the pain is not due to the thing itself,*
> *but to your estimate of it;*
> *and this you have the power*
> *to revoke at any moment.*

MARCUS AURELIUS

121–180

And so it goes. The one common denominator in our lives, as adults, is *us*. In everything we experience, there is *one person* who is *always there*. It's not Mommy and it's not Daddy—it's *us*.

In addition to what we can do *physically* about a situation, we also have the ability to choose what our *inner* response to that situation is.

This is a big one. It sounds like a radical new idea, but it's not. It's centuries old. The idea is this: We control our emotional *reaction* to the external environment—the external environment doesn't.

Dr. Albert Ellis has been a major proponent of this theory in our time. The title *alone* of one of his books activates comfort zones: *How to Stubbornly*

DO IT!

*Refuse to Make Yourself Miserable About Anything—
Yes, Anything!* *

I'm not talking here about significant losses. I'm talking about the daily slings-and-arrows for which we feel quite justified in blaming someone or something outside ourselves. Yes, it was the milkman's *fault* the milk wasn't delivered, but our negative inner *reaction* to that situation is our own.

Are we going to cry over undelivered milk? If we really want the milk, we're going to have to make alternate arrangements, and those arrangements are going to have to be made *regardless* of how miserable we make ourselves.

This is a big concept. It challenges us in a fundamental way. To reeducate ourselves is not easy. Our culture *supports* and *encourages* our deeply rooted programming that what happens "out there" is directly connected to what happens "in here." (See? I just blamed the *culture* for making it *difficult.*)

Please remember: it is okay to feel good when things go bad. Being content, satisfied, and joyful no matter *what* happens is a radical concept—but it's also a basic rule of adult life.

Without this rule—to at least *try* to follow—we live in a land of Victims and Victors, of endless finger-pointing and name-calling. Even if we *can* affix blame, so what? If we need to get the milk, *we need to get the milk.* If you want to fulfill your

*Dr. Ellis's Rational-Emotive Institute can be reached at 45 East 65th Street, New York, NY 10021. (212) 535–0822.

> **BLANCHE:** *I'm reading this Spock book on baby care, and he says it's very important for a young child to have a male role model around during its formative years. Now what are we gonna do? . . .*
> **ROSE:** *Oh, Blanche, we don't have anything to worry about. If we give that baby love and attention and understanding, it'll turn out fine.*
> **DOROTHY:** *That's beautiful.*
> **ROSE:** *Besides, what does Spock know about raising babies? On Vulcan, all the kids are born in pods.*
>
> THE GOLDEN GIRLS

Dream, look more for "What's next?" than "Who's wrong?"

Our inner life reflects our outer, and our outer life reflects our inner. I suggest making changes in *both*. When a situation arises, ask yourself, "What response can I make—inner, outer, or both—that would get me closer to my goal?" These are more useful questions than, "Whom can I punish?" (Most often, the answer to "Whom can I punish?" is *ourselves*. It's guilt's favorite question.)

Start by forgiving your parents. They didn't have a manual on raising kids—not a complete one, anyway. Besides, *they* didn't raise us; *we* raised us. We chose from all that happened to us to sink or swim, rise or fall. Many great people—however you'd like to define the word great—had childhoods more miserable than ours, and somehow they managed to be great.

We have the same opportunities for greatness. They happen every day, every minute. Do we learn a lesson, or blame the teacher? The teacher could be a flat tire, a broken agreement, or undelivered milk. Do we look into the mirror and change ourselves, or do we break it? Do we pursue our Dream, or have all the reasonable reasons why not?

It's important, however, not to become a victim of never seeing yourself as a victim. If a company cheats you out of a large sum of money, *get your money back*. Certainly learn the lesson about how not to be cheated in the future, but *get your money back*.

As with all ideas in this book: balance.

Next week there can't be any crisis.
My schedule is already full.

HENRY A. KISSINGER

Most modern calendars mar the sweet
simplicity of our lives by reminding us
that each day that passes is the
anniversary of some perfectly
uninteresting event.

OSCAR WILDE

We Don't Plan to Fail,
We Just Fail to Plan

It's a well-known fact: long-range planning never works. We almost always get to our goal through means *other* than the ones we put on our schedule. So why plan? Because people who *don't* make long-range plans seldom get to where they want to be.

In short, a plan will get you to your goal, but not in the way that's on the plan.

So, plan. And, be prepared not just to change *horses* in midstream, but to change to a *boat* in midstream. Keep your goal, your Dream. Stay firm and fixed on that. Be prepared, however, for whatever methods come along to get you there. *Especially* methods not on your plan. Plan on it.

How to plan? Simple. Take a segment of time, take a goal, and divide up the latter into the former. Keep dividing it up until you have a *next action step*—something you can do *right now* to move toward your goal.

Let's say you want to produce a play within the next year. Get some kind of calendar. Twelve months from now, write, "Play opens." You have the goal (the play), and you have the time (twelve months). Now, chop up the goal.

What needs to happen before the play opens? Make a list. One item per 3x5 card is good, or list them on a sheet of paper. This list doesn't need to be in any particular order. Brainstorm. Free-associate.

> *The journey of ten thousand miles*
> *begins with a single phone call.*
>
> CONFUCIUS BELL

When the list is complete, put the steps in order, according to time. What needs to happen first, second, third, etc. "Find a play," for example, would probably come before, "Design the posters." If something is a toss-up ("Do I find the play first or the director?"), choose the way you would *like* it to go and schedule that.

Now, start laying these steps out *backwards* in time. How many weeks of rehearsal? Six weeks? Put those in. That means casting will have to be completed by six weeks before a year from now. How much time do you want to work with the director before casting? Put that time in. Continue.

When everything is roughly laid out, you can

ask yourself, "Is a year enough time? Is a year too much time?" Let's say a year is a good period of time—not too ambitious, not too lethargic.

Continue breaking the plan down until you know what you must do *next*—something specific you can actually, physically *do*. "Find a play," is too vague. "Call this list of twelve people and let them know I'm looking for a play," is a workable next action step. This might be followed by, "Read plays submitted." That's a do-able action step.

When the plays *are* submitted, the action steps become more precise. "Read *DO IT! The Musical!*" would be a next do-able action step. (And an excellent one, too, I might add. The musical has this great opening number, called "Let's Get Off Our Buts," featuring a dancing comfort zone—like the plant in *Little Shop of Horrors*—and, well, a word to the wise producer is sufficient.)

Now, start *scheduling* the next action steps. *When* will you call the twelve people on the list? "Next week" is not good enough for that one. *When* next week? What *day*? What *time*? Schedule it in.

When you plan your Big Dream, do *something* on it every day. Remember when I suggested that if you don't plan to devote at least fourteen hours per week—two hours per day—to your Dream, maybe it's not a big enough Dream, or maybe you don't really want it? Here's where that Dream begins to manifest—in the fourteen (or more) hours you schedule it into your calendar *this week*. The two (or more) hours you schedule in *tomorrow.*

You can schedule general tasks—completing

> *The writer's only responsibility*
> *is to his art.*
> *He will be completely ruthless*
> *if he is a good one.*
> *He has a dream.*
> *Everything goes by the board:*
> *honor, pride, decency, security, happiness,*
> *all, to get the book written.*
> *If a writer has to rob his mother,*
> *he will not hesitate;*
> *the "Ode on a Grecian Urn"*
> *is worth any number of old ladies.*
>
> WILLIAM FAULKNER

this book, for example, or making some exploratory phone calls, or, if you *are* a producer, finding out if there really *is* a musical version of *DO IT!* Your Dream may have some very specific action steps that can be scheduled today—or tomorrow, at the latest. "I will write from 6:00 to 8:00 a.m. tomorrow."

The output may be one word or one thousand. For writing (meditating, phone calling, or any number of things), getting off our *buts* means getting *on* our *butt*—putting it into a chair and *not moving from the chair* for a set period of time.

Don't plan specific events too far in advance, especially early in a project. One exploratory phone call might change the entire course of your project—a method may appear that's far better than any you considered yourself. Expect that. *Do* plan specific *amounts* of time doing *something* on your Dream *every day.* Those segments of time will fill as the project rolls (and flies) along.

Someone once said, "A blank sheet of paper is God's way of letting you know what it feels like to be God." So is a blank calendar. A calendar for the next year represents your *time,* one of the most precious commodities you have. Use it well. Choosing what you want to do, and when to do it, is an act of creation.

You are creating your Dream.

Writing is easy.
All you do is stare at a blank
sheet of paper until drops of blood
form on your forehead.

GENE FOWLER

If you want to be a writer—
stop talking about it
and sit down and write!

JACKIE COLLINS

The multitude of books
is a great evil.
There is no limit
to this fever for writing.

MARTIN LUTHER

It took me fifteen years to discover
that I had no talent for writing,
but I couldn't give it up
because by then I was too famous.

ROBERT BENCHLEY

God is love, but get it in writing.

GYPSY ROSE LEE

Write Things Down

Everyone is a professional writer. You may not get paid for writing *per se*,* but you will be well paid for what you write down.

Make lists of things to do, people to call, letters to write. In fulfilling your Dream, you're in business for yourself. Pursue your Dream with all the tools of the business world. One of the basic tools is listmaking.

People who want to appear clever rely on memory. People who want to get things done make lists. Even if you're good at remembering things, write them down. That way, you don't have to remember them. Your mind is free for more creative pursuits.

The two enemies of memory are *time* and *volume*. Over time, we tend to forget. (Who sat two rows behind you in third grade?) And, when there's too much to remember, we forget. Write it all down.

Make notes of phone conversations. Most of these notes you'll never look at again, but when they come in handy, *they come in handy*.

Send letters to people confirming things, and cards thanking people for the gift of their time, advice, or direction. (You'll be receiving lots of favors as you move toward your Dream.)

---

*The first rule of writing is never use the phrase *per se*. The *New Yorker* once had a cartoon of a street sign that read, "No parking, *per se*."

Every man has the right
to risk his own life
in order to save it.

JEAN-JACQUES ROUSSEAU

Taking Risks

As often as successful people counsel us to "take risks," that's about how often we ignore such counsel. For the vast, vast majority of people, taking risks is just too *risky.*

If we don't take risks, however, it's doubtful we'll ever get to our Dream. "A lot of successful people are risk-takers," Phillip Adams wrote. "Unless you're willing to do that, to have a go, to fail miserably, and have another go, success won't happen."

There must be *something* risky between you and your Dream; otherwise, you'd be living it. Attaining dreams requires new behavior, and trying new behavior is taking a risk.

"Be daring, be different, be impractical," Sir Cecil Beaton advised; "be anything that will assert integrity of purpose and imaginative vision against the play-it-safers, the creatures of the commonplace, the slaves of the ordinary."

"There are risks and costs to a program of action," John F. Kennedy said, "but they are far less than the long-range risks and costs of comfortable inaction."

Of course, there are limits. Andy Warhol had a suggestion for Kennedy and his kind: "The president has so much good publicity potential that hasn't been exploited. He should just sit down one day and make a list of all the things that people are embarrassed to do that they shouldn't be embarrassed to do, and then do them all on television."

> *Don't play for safety—*
> *it's the most dangerous thing*
> *in the world.*
>
> HUGH WALPOLE

A great idea from Mr. Warhol. Unfortunately, none of our presidents has taken him up on it—not *intentionally,* at any rate.

The irony is that the person *not* taking risks feels the same amount of fear as the person who *regularly* takes risks. The non-risk-taker simply feels the *same* amount of fear over *trivial* things.

People not taking calculated risks in pursuing their Dream sometimes take foolish risks in general. They drive too fast, drink too much, abuse drugs, or engage in other reckless behavior. "Take calculated risks," George Patton advised. "That is quite different from being rash."

Maybe the risk-taking mechanism in these rash

individuals needs to be exercised—or maybe they want to prove (to themselves as much as to others) that they're not so cowardly after all. I maintain that if they *really* want to display their courage, all they have to do is pursue their dreams.

The reverse of that is more often true. Having given up on their dreams, many give up on life and die a little more each day. As Benjamin Franklin wrote, "Some people die at twenty-five and aren't buried until they are seventy-five." Or, to quote Auntie Mame's famous line, "Life is a banquet, and some poor sons-of-bitches are starving to death."

All you have to do with what you fear is walk right up and confront it. It's among the hardest things to do, but it's the only thing to be done. The farther you run from confronting your fears, the farther you run from your Dream. "Do the thing you fear," wrote Emerson, "and the death of fear is certain."

"Often the difference between a successful man and a failure is not one's better abilities or ideas," Maxwell Maltz observed, "but the courage that one has to bet on his ideas, to take a calculated risk—and to act."

*The greatest obstacle to discovery
is not ignorance—
it is the illusion of knowledge.*

Daniel J. Boorstin

Don't Say No till You Know What You're Saying No to

As I mentioned before, when we commit to a goal, the methods to achieve that goal will appear. When the methods do appear, they may not be (and seldom are) dressed in familiar garb.

Many people habitually say "no" to all new experiences. Behind this habit, of course, is the comfort zone—"It's new, so don't do it."

Many people say no because they don't want to know. "The mind of a bigot is like the pupil of an eye," wrote Oliver Wendell Holmes, Jr.; "the more light you pour upon it, the more it will contract." I, of course, recommend becoming a pupil *of* light; a pupil of life.

"My mind is made up," the old saying goes, "don't try and confuse me with the facts." The retort comes from Aldous Huxley: "Facts do not cease to exist because they are ignored." William S. Burroughs said, "A paranoid is a man who knows *a little* of what's going on."

If something new presents itself to you and you don't know enough about it to decide if it might help you achieve your goal, don't say no—find out more. How do we find out more? By asking, doing, listening—by getting involved.

As you may have gathered, my advice on each new opportunity is: if it's not going to *physically* harm you, and it *might* be helpful on the path to your Dream—try it. Other than the comfort zone's

> *Try everything once*
> *except incest and folk dancing.*
>
> SIR THOMAS BEECHAM

control of your life, what have you got to lose?

Another reason people don't even want to hear about new opportunities is that they are afraid to say no—especially after they've "gotten to know" someone. It's the old don't-say-no-to-people-you-know-but-do-say-no-to-people-you-don't-know rule. This is a rule perpetrated by the people we know— for obvious reasons. ("Why are you giving your money to this charity to save *eagles* when *your own brother* needs new carpeting?")

This phenomenon was described by the great philosopher Gypsy Rose Lee: "She's descended from a long line her mother listened to." It's easier for most people to say no while the person offering the new experience is still a stranger.

I'm not suggesting you listen to the spiel of *every* person who tries to sell you a flower at the airport. It is safe to assume that one besuited flower-seller will supply you with roughly the same information as any other. I am suggesting, however, that you listen to one flower-seller spiel *once*.

You might try activities that are more clearly on your path more than once. As Virgil Thomson—who thrived until his death at ninety-three—once said, "Try a thing you haven't done three times. Once, to get over the fear of doing it. Twice, to learn how to do it. And a third time to figure out whether you like it or not." The *other* famous Virgil (the one who lived 70–19 B.C.) seemed to agree: "Fortune sides with him who dares."

Doing something *once* will get us over the *fear* of doing it. That's fine, but if it was a significant challenge to our comfort zone, doing it once is not enough to really feel *free* about it—there's still *guilt* to reckon with. Doing something *three times* usually works through the fear of doing it, reduces the fear of feeling guilty about doing it, and takes a good slice out of the guilt about doing it.

We are not free to *choose* to do a thing or not until it's fully *within* our comfort zone.

The person who has never been to New York City—but has heard nasty things about it—is not free regarding New York City. The person who's visited New York City often enough to feel comfortable there is completely free to choose to travel to New York or not.

> *All men should try to learn*
> *before they die*
> *what they are running from,*
> *and to, and why.*
>
> JAMES THURBER

After listening to people present whatever it is they have to present to you, then you can say no. You are not obligated to say yes just because you *listened*. You are only obligated if you *committed* to a certain course of action. Listening to information is not an agreement to do anything *with* the information. You may decide that the information is all very interesting, but it doesn't help you fulfill *your* Dream. Say no, and be on your way. You may also do some things that turn out to be a complete waste of time. Oh, well. As someone once said, "Don't be afraid to go on an occasional wild goose chase. That's what wild geese are for." Or, to quote Flip Wilson, "You can't expect to hit the jackpot if you don't put a few nickels in the machine."

Your goal-fulfillment system is working all the time—pulling experiences, lessons, information, and people to you to help you fulfill your Dream. "Let your hook always be cast," Ovid said two thousand years ago. "In the pool where you least expect it, will be a fish."

*There is the greatest
practical benefit in making
a few failures early in life.*

T. H. HUXLEY

The Value of Action

There are two primary benefits to action.

The first is obvious: if we don't *do* something, we're not going to *get* anything except "what comes our way," which may or may not be what we want.

The second benefit: *we make mistakes.* Mistakes show us what we need to learn.

Many people read about the value of mistakes, say, "That makes sense," and then continue living their lives in the same avoid-mistakes-at-all-costs manner as before. They continue to play it safe, don't learn what they need to know, and then wonder why they're not much closer to their Dream.

"Men stumble over the truth from time to time," Winston Churchill wrote, "but most pick themselves up and hurry off as if nothing happened."

Mistakes indicate what we must study in order to have success. This "study" might be finding out more information, or it might mean more practice of what we already know. Either way, when we make a mistake, it's a golden arrow indicating, "Study this if you want success."

"From error to error," Freud said, "one discovers the entire truth."

People who aren't ready to welcome mistakes as the great aids to education they are, simply deny them. Instead of *looking for* mistakes so that they can learn more and do better, people ignore, filter, and flat-out *deny* mistakes.

> *The higher up you go,*
> *the more mistakes*
> *you're allowed.*
> *Right at the top,*
> *if you make enough of them,*
> *it's considered to be your style.*
>
> FRED ASTAIRE

All great people review their actions—even those actions that led to success—and ask themselves, "How could I have done this better?" It's known as critical thinking. We *criticize* our behavior so that we can do *better* next time.

Most people, however, improperly use their critical ability—they use it to find reasons for giving up. "I did so many things *wrong*. Why should I bother trying? I quit."

Of course we're going to do things wrong. We should be grateful that we have the ability to recognize wrong when we do it. The mediocre are satisfied with any old thing—and that's precisely what they wind up with.

You'll do better next time. As long as you're actively involved in pursuing your goal, there will always be a next time. If you're moving toward your Dream, opportunity doesn't just knock once—it will knock you down.

The process of learning can be summarized in four steps:

1. ACT.

2. LOOK FOR THE MISTAKES (CRITICIZE, EVALUATE).

3. LEARN HOW TO DO IT BETTER NEXT TIME.

4. GO TO 1.

First we form habits,
then they form us.
Conquer your bad habits,
or they'll eventually
conquer you.

DR. ROB GILBERT

Let Go of Distractions

Distractions do not bring satisfaction. A distraction is anything not on the way to our goal that consumes our time, thoughts, or energy.

There are the obvious distractions—the physical bad habits and addictions people know are bad for them. There are the more subtle distractions—channel surfing, hanging out, aimlessly chatting on the phone. Then there are the distractions that *appear* to be wonderful—virtues, even—but are distractions, nonetheless.

This latter category is tricky. These actions are indisputably good for you and/or are good for others, but are *not* directly on the path to your goal. You could win a Nobel Prize for your charitable work, and, if your Dream were to be a pro golfer, all the charity work would, in fact, be a distraction.

Imagine that you are walking along a path. At the end of the path is your Dream. The way is clear, the goal is in sight. All you have to do is keep walking on your path till you reach your Dream.

Along the way, lining the path on either side, however, are distractions. It's their job to test you—to see if your goal is *really* the goal you want; to see if you are worthy of your Dream. The distractions can do *anything they want* to tempt you off your path: offer sex, food, fame, power, success in an area not part of your Dream, recognition, easy money—*anything*. What they *cannot* do is get *on* your path and *stop you*. Leaving the path is always *your choice*.

Pursue your Dream. Follow your path.

*The sun will set
without thy assistance.*

THE TALMUD

Follow Your Dream

Your job is to fulfill your Dream.

It is *not* your job to right all the wrongs of the world, to teach everyone everything you know so that *they* will be able to right all the wrongs of the world, to become involved in any way with the struggle that always has been and probably always will be part of this planet, or anything else.

Your job is to fulfill your Dream.

If your Dream involves social or individual change, fine. Then saving *part* of the world is your business—but only part. If, for example, cleaner air is your passion, let someone else save the whales.

Areas of your concern—but not of your Dream—*are* the Dreams of others. Let them fulfill their Dreams. You fulfill yours. "Nature arms each man with some faculty which enables him to do easily some feat impossible to any other," wrote Emerson. If we each bring our separate dish (our Dream) to the table—even if it's "just" dessert—we can all enjoy the banquet.

We don't have to *react* to news or information that doesn't apply to our Dream. If we react to everything—including all the things other people think we *should* react to—we will have less mental and emotional energy to focus on our Dream.

If it's not on our path, *it doesn't apply to us.* Someone just died somewhere in Russia. Does that *profoundly* sadden you? Why not? Because it doesn't really apply to your life. It's a tragedy for someone, but not for you. The same is true of all the other

> *Drawing on my fine command*
> *of the English language,*
> *I said nothing.*
>
> ROBERT BENCHLEY

events and incidents delivered by the media. This "news" is designed to keep those *not* on their path in a state of constant distraction.

Follow your Dream.

You need not give—or have—an opinion on every subject under the sun. "One of the lessons of history," wrote historian Will Durant, "is that nothing is often a good thing to do, and always a clever thing to say."

For those who prefer the scientific formula rather than the historical perspective, Albert Einstein: "If A is success in life, then A equals X plus Y plus Z. Work is X, Y is play, and Z is keeping your mouth shut."

Even with something you *do* know about, something you have very definite opinions about, something you have every right to feel passionate about (I'm talking about your Dream, of course), it's good to be quiet about that with others, too.

"It is a mistake for a sculptor or a painter to speak or write very often about his job," said Henry Moore. "It releases tension needed for his work." Keep the tension—the passion—within. Express it in deeds—in *actions*—not in words.

Keep attainments to yourself. ("Be smart, but never show it," advised Louis B. Mayer.) Keep problems to yourself as well. ("You can't tell your friend if you've been cuckolded." wrote Montaigne. "Even if he doesn't laugh at you, he may put the information to personal use.")

Pursue your dream. Follow your path.

*The term clinical depression
finds its way into too many
conversations these days.
One has a sense that
a catastrophe has occurred
in the psychic landscape.*

LEONARD COHEN

Depression

Are you depressed because you're not living your Dream, or maybe you are not living your Dream because you are depressed.

The word *depression* is used to describe two distinct maladies. One use is to express *disappointment:* "They didn't return my phone calls. I'm depressed." "How depressing—the coffee machine is out of *cafe olé.*" We also feel this mild kind of depression in the normal cycle of life's ups and downs.*

The other use of the word *depression* is medical—it describes a physical illness caused by a biological (yes, usually genetic) imbalance in the body.

The simple solution for disappointment depression: Get up and get moving. *Physically* move. Do. Act. Get going.

Depression is often caused by a sense of not having accomplished enough. We question the usefulness of what we've achieved in the past, and doubt our ability to achieve anything useful in the future. Self-doubt robs us of our energy. We feel depressed.

We look at all we want to do. It seems overwhelming. We tell ourselves, "I can't do all this," and instantly fulfill our own prophecy by not even

---

*A severe loss can trigger a form of depression that is a natural part of the healing process. (Please see the book *How to Survive the Loss of a Love,* at bookstores, or call 1-800-LIFE-101.)

> *We should be taught not to wait*
> *for inspiration*
> *to start a thing.*
> *Action always*
> *generates inspiration.*
> *Inspiration seldom*
> *generates action.*
>
> FRANK TIBOLT

trying. The energy drops even more, and the depression deepens.

When we eventually feel we *must* do something, there seems to be so much left undone from our previous inertia that we become confused. The confusion leads to indecision. The indecision leads to, "Oh, what's the use," and more inaction, which leads to . . . you guessed it.

At some point, the cycle must be broken by action. Do something—*anything*—physical. If the house is a mess, pick up *one thing*—*any* one thing— and *do* something with it: put it away, throw it out, send it to your brother, donate it to charity, something, *anything*. Pick up one more thing. Continue.

Eventually, you will have a clean house. Before "eventually," however, the depression will begin to lift.

Yes, disappointment depression is a Master Teacher. Its message is, "Get moving. The energy is here. Use it." When you start to move, the energy will meet your movement. But first, you must move.

Medical ("clinical") depression is not caused by disappointment or lack of action, but by a biological imbalance in the chemistry of the brain. This form of depression takes a bit more explaining—there are *so many* misconceptions about it. Here's my story.

Over an almost-thirty-year period, I had attended more personal growth workshops, visited more healers, meditated more hours, taken more vitamins, and not only read but written more self-help books than almost anyone I knew. Nevertheless, I was not happy. I wasn't even satisfied. I wasn't even simply bored.

I was miserable.

By mid-1993, I was ready to try anything—even psychiatry. I called Harold H. Bloomfield, M.D., one of my co-authors on *How to Survive the Loss of a Love,* told him I wanted to make a professional appointment, and met him at his office. We spoke for an hour. Finally, he said, "Peter, you've been suffering!"

Yeah. That's what I was doing—although I had never applied the word *suffering* to myself. His official diagnosis: depression.

> *I am now the most*
> *miserable man living.*
> *If what I feel*
> *were equally distributed*
> *to the whole human family*
> *there would be not one*
> *cheerful face on earth.*
> *Whether I shall ever be better,*
> *I cannot tell.*
> *I awfully forebode I shall not.*
> *To remain as I am is impossible.*
> *I must die or be better*
> *it appears to me.*
>
> ABRAHAM LINCOLN
> WHO SUFFERED FROM DEPRESSION
> MOST OF HIS ADULT LIFE

Like many people, I had some serious misconceptions about depression. I didn't *like* depression. I didn't *want* depression. But then, I guess you don't get to pick your disease.

To my surprise, I learned that depression is a physical illness, a biochemical imbalance in the brain most likely caused by certain neurotransmitters (the fluid the brain uses to communicate with itself) being pumped away too soon. When there are too few of certain neurotransmitters, brain function becomes inharmonious, and the complex mental, emotional, and physical manifestations of depression result.

These manifestations can include a "down" feeling, fatigue, sleep disorders, physical aches and pains, eating irregularities, listening to Julio Iglesias, irritability, difficulty concentrating, feeling worthless, guilt, addictions (attempts to self-medicate the pain away), suicidal thoughts, and my favorite, anhedonia.

Anhedonia means "the inability to experience pleasure." The original title for Woody Allen's movie *Annie Hall* was *Anne Hedonia*—the perfect description of Woody Allen's character. It was also the description of my life. Although I had spikes of happiness, nothing gave me pleasure for any length of time. The concept of "just being" was entirely foreign to me. My intensive self-help seeking since 1965 had been my attempt to obtain the simple enjoyment of living that many people seemed to have naturally.

All my attempts had been unsuccessful—I had a *physical illness* that prevented even the best-built self-esteem structure from standing very long. In the book Harold and I later wrote, *How to Heal Depression,* the chapter explaining this phenomenon is entitled, "The Power of Positive Thinking Crashes and Burns in the Face of Depression." You can plant all the personal growth seeds you want, but they become like the seeds that fell on the rock in Jesus' parable (Matthew 13:5–6):

Guilt is the mafia of the mind

BOB MANDEL

> Some [seed] fell on rocky places, where it did
> not have much soil. It sprang up quickly, be-
> cause the soil was shallow. But when the sun
> came up, the plants were scorched, and they
> withered because they had no root.

That's what depression had wrought inside me:
one, vast, barren rock garden—without the garden.

I also learned that most depression is inherited. I
realized that if I looked around my family tree and
saw a lot of nuts, there was a very good chance I
was not a passion fruit (which is *just* what I thought
I was). Since depression is a genetic biological illness, like diabetes or low thyroid, it wasn't lack of
character, laziness, or something I could "snap out

of"—it would be like trying to snap out of a tooth-ache. This meant the dozens of other causes for depression given to me by John-Roger and other quacks in his cult were invalid, too.*

I was ready to consider what the good Doctor Bloomfield recommended I do about my depression.

He explained several options, which included two short-term "talk" therapies (Cognitive Therapy and Interpersonal Therapy) and antidepressants—as in Prozac. I, who had been programmed by John-Roger to think drugs were the devil's own tool, thought—as many people did—that Prozac was the devil itself.

The Church of Scientology had done a brilliant job programming the media and, hence, the general public, into believing that not only was Prozac unsafe, but *astonishingly* unsafe. They accomplished this (for whatever reason) by finding a handful of people who had done some aberrant things. Scientology then presented the aberrant behavior of these people as typical side effects of Prozac. It was a thoroughly imbalanced and unscientific presentation. More than five million people take Prozac in this country every day—ten million worldwide. Millions more have used Prozac since its introduc-

*For the story of my fifteen years of cult life—and its aftermath—please read *LIFE 102: What to Do When Your Guru Sues You*. Available at bookstores or by calling 1-800-LIFE-101.

> *I have bad reflexes.*
> *I was once run over by a car*
> *being pushed by two guys.*
>
> WOODY ALLEN

tion in 1987. It is among the safest of all prescribed medications. (No one has ever died from taking Prozac—although hundreds die each year from allergic reactions to penicillin, or from internal bleeding caused by aspirin.)

Still, I didn't like the idea of taking a pill that would—as *Newsweek* pointed out on its cover—give me a different personality. I didn't necessarily like the personality I had, but I also didn't want to become a *Stepford* writer.

Harold explained that antidepressant medications do not give one a new personality. There is no "high" connected to them. They're not tranquilizers, pep pills, or mood elevators. All antidepressants do is keep the brain from pumping away certain neurotransmitters too quickly. This allows the neurotransmitters to rise to appropriate levels, which lets the brain function harmoniously again.

An analogy might be that antidepressants plug a hole in a rain barrel so the barrel can fill. The depression lifts because the brain's naturally produced neurotransmitters are allowed to rise to natural levels. Antidepressant medications, then, don't add a synthetic chemical to the brain that alters the brain's function; they merely keep the brain from pumping away its own naturally produced neurotransmitters too quickly.

Further, if you take antidepressants and feel better, it's *because you are depressed*. If you take an antidepressant and are not depressed, you won't feel much of anything. In this, antidepressants are like aspirin: if you have a headache and take an aspirin, your headache goes away and you feel better. If you don't have a headache and take an aspirin, you won't feel much different. The good feelings touted so enthusiastically by people taking antidepressants are not *caused* by the antidepressant medication, but by the lifting of the depression—when a pain you've grown accustomed to goes away, the feeling of just plain "ordinary" can seem like euphoria.

Okay. I was ready. Lay on the Prozac.

Within a week of beginning the medication, I felt not exactly better, but as though the bottom of my emotional pit had been raised. In the past, small setbacks had caused a toboggan ride all the way down to an emotional state best described as

> *It's surprising*
> *how many persons*
> *go through life*
> *without ever recognizing that*
> *their feelings toward other people*
> *are largely determined*
> *by their feelings toward themselves,*
> *and if you're not*
> *comfortable within yourself,*
> *you can't be*
> *comfortable with others.*
>
> SYDNEY J. HARRIS

"What's the point of living?" In the choice between life and death, I would reluctantly choose life (with about the same enthusiasm as Michelangelo's Adam on the Sistine Chapel receiving the spark of life from God), and crawl back up to "normal" again.

Normal for me, however, *was* depression. As it turns out, I've had a long-term, low-grade depression since I was three. This depressed state was my benchmark for "normal." On top of this, I would have, from time to time, major depressive episodes—lasting from six months to more than a year. When the two of these played together (that is, played havoc together on me), I had what is known in psychiatric circles as a *double depression* (a fate I would not wish upon my worst enemy).

After I'd taken Prozac for two weeks, I felt the floor of my dungeon had risen even higher. By the third week, I felt I had—for the first time—some level ground on which to build my life. I still was concerned how firm it was, so I walked across it lightly, as one does across a piece of land that was once quicksand.

That was the image I had: any good deed, any positive project, any accomplishment, I placed on the quicksand where—like Janet Leigh's car in *Psycho*—it would slowly, painfully, inexorably sink.

Now I inched a little farther toward the center of my land, seeing how *firma* the *terra* really was. It was a great victory when I could jump up and down in what was once my pool of emotional quicksand and know it was finally safe to build there.

What I built, of course, was up to me: if I built depressing things, my life would still be depressing. But now I had a chance to build something stable, something reliable, something good.

I also began feeling *spiritual* for the first time. I felt connected to God in a solid, unpretentious way. The discovery of this connection was no great "hooray, hooray, I found God," but a slow clarification—like watching a Polaroid picture develop. It all seemed so natural—and simple. It had nothing to do with John-Roger's intricate cosmology I had so carefully memorized.

> *The future may teach us*
> *how to exercise a direct*
> *influence by means of*
> *particular chemical substances,*
> *upon the amount of energy*
> *and their distribution*
> *in the apparatus of the mind.*
> *It may be that there are other*
> *undreamed of possibilities*
> *of therapy.*
>
> SIGMUND FREUD

And—just as so many other great teachers had said—the kingdom of God was within.

I also found myself simply *enjoying* things: ordinary, everyday, no-big-deal activities were *pleasurable*. I remember sitting in a chair, waiting for a table at a restaurant, and I was enjoying just sitting there. I felt so contented, all alone, sitting there, it was almost like being in love.

In fact, it seemed that I *was* falling in love—with myself.

Are *you* depressed? Well, here's a checklist from the National Institutes of Health. On this checklist they also give symptoms of *mania,* which is the irrational, unpredictable upperswing of manic depression. (I never had mania, but I *did* overachieve as a compensation for the depression—I was trying to "prove" my worthiness by outward achievement. Doesn't work.)

According to the National Institutes of Health:

> A thorough diagnosis is needed if four or more of the symptoms of depression or mania persist for more than two weeks or are interfering with work or family life.

> With available treatment, eighty percent of the people with serious depression—even those with the most severe forms—can improve significantly. Symptoms can be relieved, usually in a matter of weeks.

Symptoms of Depression Can Include

❑ Persistent sad or "empty" mood

❑ Loss of interest or pleasure in ordinary activities, including sex

❑ Decreased energy, fatigue, being "slowed down"

❑ Sleep disturbances (insomnia, early-morning waking, or oversleeping)

❑ Eating disturbances (loss of appetite and weight, or weight gain)

❑ Difficulty concentrating, remembering, making decisions

❑ Feelings of guilt, worthlessness, helplessness

❑ Thoughts of death or suicide, suicide attempts

❑ Irritability

❑ Excessive crying

❑ Chronic aches and pains that don't respond to treatment

Nobody grows old by merely
living a number of years.
People grow old
only by deserting their ideals.
Years wrinkle the face,
but to give up enthusiasm
wrinkles the soul.
Worry, doubt, self-interest,
fear, despair—
these are the long, long years
that bow the head and turn
the growing spirit back to dust.

WATTERSON LOWE

In the Workplace, Symptoms of Depression Often May Be Recognized by

- ❏ Decreased productivity
- ❏ Morale problems
- ❏ Lack of cooperation
- ❏ Safety problems, accidents
- ❏ Absenteeism
- ❏ Frequent complaints of being tired all the time
- ❏ Complaints of unexplained aches and pains
- ❏ Alcohol and drug abuse

Symptoms of Mania Can Include

- ☐ Excessively "high" mood
- ☐ Irritability
- ☐ Decreased need for sleep
- ☐ Increased energy and activity
- ☐ Increased talking, moving, and sexual activity
- ☐ Racing thoughts
- ☐ Disturbed ability to make decisions
- ☐ Grandiose notions
- ☐ Being easily distracted

These symptoms are not "just life." If you've had four or more of them for more than two weeks, or *any* of them is interfering with your work or relationships (including with yourself), a diagnosis is in order.

Even if you checked every box (as I must have—I could have been depression's poster boy), you are not *necessarily* depressed. This is simply a checklist to see if a diagnosis from a physician (an M.D., D.O., or psychiatrist) is in order. Your physician may say you're not depressed, but you do (for example) have low thyroid (which mimics depression symptoms in about twenty percent of the cases). This is why a *physician* should be consulted for diagnosis.

On the other hand, emotional support and the administration of short-term "talk" therapies—such as Cognitive or Interpersonal Therapy—is often best given by psychologists (Ph.D.s or MFCCs).

*Opportunity is missed by most people
because it is dressed in overalls
and looks like work.*

THOMAS EDISON

*You can't build a reputation
on what you're GOING to do.*

HENRY FORD

Do the Work

Pursuing your Dream requires work—mental, emotional, and physical. Work is what we don't want to do, but we do anyway to get something else. To reach your Dream, you'll you'll have to do a lot of things you don't want to do.

Some people live in a fairy-tale fantasy about the attainment of their Dream. They think that every step on the way to their Dream should be effortless—a private jet picks them up on their front lawn and transports them to Paradise. Not only that, they are *carried* to the private jet, and fed peeled grapes along the way.

Dismiss any simliar fantasies you entertain. While you're at it, dismiss the fantasy that the work *ever* stops. Some people like to include a completely work-free life as part of their Dream. They tend to agree with Charlie McCarthy, who said, "Hard work never killed anybody, but why take the chance?" Alas, the work continues even *after* we have our Dream.

If we're alive, there's still work to do.

The work may change form, but it remains as irksome as work always is. Actors work to find an agent. Once an agent is found, they work to get a part. Once they get enough parts to be a star, they work to find the right script. The work never ends.

"It is a rough road that leads to the heights of greatness," Seneca said. Part of the roughness is doing all the mundane things you know you'll hire somebody *else* to do once you achieve your Dream. "Our main business is not to see what lies dimly in

> *The hand*
> *is the cutting edge of the mind.*
>
> JACOB BRONOWSKI

the distance," wrote Thomas Carlyle, "but to do what lies clearly at hand." Is stuffing envelopes with your resume "at hand"? Stuff.

There are some things we can *never* hire someone else to do. If our Dream requires a personal physical ability or skill, we have to work to develop and maintain that. "Nothing I do can't be done by a ten-year-old—with fifteen years of practice," said magician Harry Blackstone, Jr. You can't hire someone to practice for you.

Sometimes we have an opportunity, but it requires extra work. Do it. "If an unusual necessity forces us onward, a surprising thing occurs," observed William James:

> The fatigue gets worse up to a certain point,

when, gradually or suddenly, it passes away and we are fresher than before!

We have evidently tapped a new level of energy. There may be layer after layer of this experience, a third and fourth "wind." We find amounts of ease and power that we never dreamed ourselves to own, sources of strength habitually not taxed, because habitually we never push through the obstruction of fatigue.

The French proverb sums it up: "One may go a long way after one is tired."

Some people say they would like "more luck." What they usually need is more *work.* "The harder you work," the saying goes, "the luckier you get." Luck itself is fairly evenly distributed. "Breaks balance out," said Darrell Royal. "The sun don't shine on the same ol' dog's ass every day."

A lot of people miss valuable opportunities—or flatly refuse to partake of them—due to their unwillingness to work. "Problems are only opportunities in work clothes," observed Henry J. Kaiser (sounding a lot like Edison).

Do the *necessary* work. A lot of people decide how much is necessary before they really know how much it will be. They say, "I've done enough work," and give up. They were wrong. It wasn't enough.

When we have what we want, it was enough. Until then, it wasn't. Do the work until it's enough—until you have your Dream.

It's a lot of work pursuing your Dream. Be prepared for it.

*I prefer Hostess fruit pies
to pop-up toaster tarts
because they don't require
as much cooking.*

CARRIE SNOW

In Training for Success

Consider the pursuit of your dream a major athletic event. Train for it. What we exercise gets stronger. That's true mentally, emotionally, and physically.

Physically: Keep fit. Exercise. Eat a good diet. Precisely *what* constitutes a good diet, however, is so controversial, that we might open a special chamber of The Gap just to accommodate the many beliefs about nutrition. I can, nonetheless, offer with confidence this diet by Joel Weldon, found on the bulletin board of Dr. William Hellman:

BREAKFAST:
1/2 Grapefruit
1 piece Whole Wheat Toast
8 Oz. Skim Milk

LUNCH:
4 Oz. Lean Breast of Chicken
1 Cup Steamed Zucchini
1 Oreo Cookie
1 Cup Herb Tea

MID-AFTERNOON SNACK:
Rest of Package of Oreo Cookies
1 Quart Rocky Road Ice Cream
1 Jar Hot Fudge

DINNER:
2 Loaves Banana Bread
1 Large Pepperoni Pizza
1 Large Pitcher of Beer
5 Milky Way Bars
1 Entire Frozen Cheesecake—
    eaten directly from the freezer

> *My grandmother started walking*
> *five miles a day*
> *when she was sixty.*
> *She's ninety-five now,*
> *and we don't know*
> *where the hell she is.*
>
> ELLEN DeGENERES

"I went on a diet," said Joe E. Lewis, "swore off drinking and heavy eating, and in fourteen days I lost two weeks."

"Only Irish coffee provides in a single glass all four essential food groups," Alex Levine tells us: "alcohol, caffeine, sugar, and fat."

Exercising the Emotions: Keep them flexible by practicing *unexpected* emotional reactions to life's challenges. For example, be friendly even if you *don't* get your way, smile and wave at the person who cuts you off in traffic, *enjoy* being stood up.

Exercising the Mind: Keep it open. Eagerly consider new ideas, thoughts, suggestions, information, insights, perceptions, and intuitions.

Stretching the Comfort Zone: Keep expanding it. Each day, do at least *one* thing you don't want to do that has absolutely no practical benefit whatsoever. This keeps the comfort zone growing. For example, walking up and talking to people whom you *don't* want to meet will expand the comfort zone. Eventually, walking up and meeting strangers will be easy—comfortable. Then, when you see someone you *want* to meet, saying "Hello" will be easy.

"Do something every day that you don't want to do." Mark Twain advised. "This is the golden rule for acquiring the habit of doing your duty without pain."

Your duty is fulfilling your Dream.

I am in earnest;
I will not equivocate;
I will not excuse;
I will not retreat a single inch;
and I will be heard.

WILLIAM LLOYD GARRISON

If It's Written in Stone, Bring Your Hammer and Chisel

Nothing is impossible. "The one unchangeable certainty," said John F. Kennedy, "is that nothing is unchangeable or certain." The more *improbable* something is, however, the more work it takes to achieve.

If there's something "impossible" about your Dream, do it anyway. "The greatest pleasure in life," says Walter Bagehot, "is doing what people say you cannot do." Benjamin Jowett adds, "Never retreat. Never explain. Get it done and let them howl."

Waiting around does not do it. *You* do it. "Things may come to those who wait," wrote Abraham Lincoln, "but only the things left by those who hustle." Thomas Edison (sounding a lot like Lincoln) said, "Everything comes to him who hustles while he waits."

Be daring. "Even God lends a hand to honest boldness," Menander wrote. "If you have an important point to make, don't try to be subtle or clever," Winston Churchill said. "Use a pile driver. Hit the point once. Then come back and hit it again. Then a third time—a tremendous whack!"

Not only does boldness get us closer to what we want; it also has an important secondary benefit. "To know oneself," Camus wrote, "one should assert oneself."

> *You will make all kinds of mistakes;*
> *but as long as you are*
> *generous and true,*
> *and also fierce,*
> *you cannot hurt the world*
> *or even seriously distress her.*
>
> SIR WINSTON CHURCHILL

How do we help guarantee success? Dorothea Brande suggested, "Act as if it were impossible to fail."

If you want to win anything
—a race, your self, your life—
you have to go
a little berserk.

GEORGE SHEEHAN

They always say that
time changes things,
but you actually have to
change them yourself.

ANDY WARHOL

If It's Written on the Wind, Bring Your Camera

Keep track of your successes—the achievement of the interim goals on the way to the Big One.

At the end of the day, list all your accomplishments for that day. This is more than checking off what you did on various "to-do" lists. We usually accomplish more than we set out to do. Listing *all* accomplishments at the end of the day—those planned, those spontaneous, and those serendipitous—gives a more accurate picture of progress.

As this list grows, it becomes a testament to your power, your creativity, your achievement. Soon, the evidence becomes overwhelming: you *will* achieve your Dream. It's a logical outcome of the direction you are obviously heading.

It's also a good idea to *document* certain victories—with photos, video, mementos, newspaper clippings, or paperwork. This helps show your direction and relative invincibility to others who may need some persuading along the way.

Besides, in the years to come, your many biographers will appreciate all the help you can give them.

It is a good idea to obey
all the rules when you're young
just so you'll have the strength
to break them when you're old.

MARK TWAIN

Shortcuts to Success

People, books, tapes, videos, magazines, etc. are all shortcuts to success. Learn from the accumulated wisdom of the ages. That's what it's been accumulating for.

A doctor, for example, is a shortcut to health. A teacher, a shortcut to learning. Any expert is a shortcut to success.

A picture may be worth 10,000 words, but a bit of advice from someone who has achieved a goal similar to yours is worth 10,000 pictures.

Sometimes you learn how to do something by following advice. Other times, you learn to do precisely the *opposite* of what is recommended. Knowing a source of consistently *bad* advice is a godsend. Consult it regularly, then do the contrary. As the churchgoer once said, "Father, your sermons are like water to a drowning man."

When others give advice, they do you a favor. When you put that advice to good use, the favor is returned.

In the last analysis,
our only freedom
is the freedom
to discipline ourselves.

BERNARD BARUCH

Freedom Is Found in Discipline, Not Rebellion

When young, we are asked to follow rules that often lead us someplace we do not care to go. No wonder so many people learn to rebel against rules.

In following *your* Dream, however, you will probably notice that you have more rules than ever before. What's going on? Isn't your Dream supposed to bring *freedom*?

Yes, and freedom is found in discipline. Discipline comes from the word *disciple*—being a devoted student. Think of discipline as a container. Once a container is constructed—and maintained—it can envelop your Dream.

A rule is a tool, as a drinking glass is a tool. Using the drinking glass, we can hold, carry, and consume water. Rules are restrictions, just as a drinking glass is a restriction. If we say, "I don't want any rules, because I don't want any restrictions," then we might as well say, "I don't want any restrictions on my water, either." Then it's a lot harder to drink.

There are rules—*lots* of rules—that we use daily for pursuing our Dream: walking, talking, reading, writing, and so many others. When we accept the rules of a given discipline and make them our own, we are no longer the disciple—we take a step toward mastery.

*If your parents
didn't have any children,
there is a good chance
that you won't have any.*

CLARENCE DAY

What Have You Learned?

You've been fulfilling dreams for quite some time. They may have been your dreams, or they may have been the dreams of others. Either way, the *process* of dream fulfillment remains the same.

Review your list of accomplishments—the list you made about twenty years ago in the chapter "What Have You Accomplished?" For each achievement, ask yourself, "How did I do this? What did it take for me to fulfill that dream? What worked? What didn't?"

Begin to formulate your own set of "rules" on how *you* best achieve dreams. To fulfill our Dream, we need only examine our life, and do two things:

1. MORE OF WHAT WORKS.

2. LESS OF WHAT DOESN'T.

*Leisure time is the five or six hours
when you sleep at night.*

GEORGE ALLEN

Nurture Yourself

It's important to nurture yourself while you're nurturing your Dream. In the large sense, of course, pursuing your dream *is* nurturing yourself. Along the way to your Dream, however, take time to be good to yourself.

Self-nurturing is not the same as self-indulgence. One of the most misused statements I've heard lately is, "I'm doing this to take care of myself." Usually, when people say this, they're running their old limitations under a new banner.

Succumbing to the comfort zone's demands is *not* "taking care of yourself."

Nurturing yourself means taking care of yourself *while you do what needs to be done.* This might mean working twenty hours on a project you *could* complete in fifteen. It does *not* mean not doing the project.

Learn to take the pressure off while you do what you do. When you think of *recreation,* think of re-creating your *attitude* toward the work at hand.

Rehabilitate your attitude toward words such as *work, vacation,* and *time off.* The idea that we need "time off" comes from working for another to fulfill another's dreams. Now your life is directed toward fulfilling *your* Dream. Why would you want to take "time off" from that?

Some activities on your path are more enjoyable than others. Alternate these more pleasant activities with the more bothersome ones.

> **INTERVIEWER:** *Your Holiness,*
> *how many people work in the Vatican?*
>
> **POPE JOHN XXIII:** *About half.*

Learn to seek *satisfaction* in a job well done, rather than seek diversion in activities designed to distract you from the "harsh reality of work." That sort of diversion may be necessary for those who work for others. Remember, however: you're working for yourself now.

True nurturing is learning to enjoy the path, the process, the journey toward your Dream.

Self-respect
is a question of recognizing
that anything worth having
has a price.

JOAN DIDION

Many of life's failures
are people who did not realize
how close they were to success
when they gave up.

THOMAS EDISON

Persistence

Nothing succeeds like persistence. The common denominator of *all* successful people is their persistence.

Said Calvin Coolidge,

> Nothing in the world can take the place of persistence. Talent will not; nothing is more common than unsuccessful men with talent. Genius will not; unrewarded genius is almost a proverb. Education alone will not; the world is full of educated derelicts. Persistence and determination alone are omnipotent.

Coolidge could be a role model for those who think one needs a sparkling personality to fulfill a Dream. "Silent Cal," as he was known, was so *laid back* that Dorothy Parker, when told of his death, asked, "How could they tell?"

"Let me tell you the secret that has led to my goal," wrote Louis Pasteur. "My strength lies solely in my tenacity."

This same message rings throughout history—to win: persevere. The ancients knew it. "He who labors diligently need never despair," wrote Menander, "for all things are accomplished by diligence and labor." "The drops of rain make a hole in the stone," said Lucretius, "not by violence, but by oft falling."

Goethe: "Austere perseverance, harsh and continuous, may be employed by the least of us and rarely fails of its purpose, for its silent power grows irreversibly greater with time." Longfellow: "Perse-

> *Fall seven times,*
> *stand up eight.*
>
> Japanese Proverb

verance is a great element of success. If you only knock long enough and loud enough at the gate, you are sure to wake up somebody."

A persistence rhyme from Edmund Cooke:

> You are beaten to earth?
> Well, well, what's that?
> Come up with a smiling face,
> It's nothing against you to fall down flat
> But to lie there—that's disgrace.

I will spare you what Napoleon, George Gobel, Churchill, Lincoln, Socrates, Orson Welles, Richard Nixon, and the Lennon sisters had to say about persistence. It's the same theme: "Keep going and you will win."

Persistence is a simple process:

1. WHAT'S THE NEXT STEP?

2. WHAT'S IN THE WAY OF TAKING THAT STEP?

3. REMOVE* THE OBSTACLE.

4. TAKE THE STEP.

5. GO TO 1.

Without persistence, we may end up doing our Marlon Brando imitation: "I coulda had class. I coulda been a contender. I coulda been somebody. Instead of a bum, which is what I am."

---

*In many cases, the word *Remove* can be replaced by *Disregard* or *Ignore*.

*The real secret of success
is enthusiasm.*

WALTER CHRYSLER

Enthusiasm and Joy

Rather than comfort and joy, try enthusiasm and joy. Enthusiasm and joy are Siamese twins—it's hard to find one without the other.

Enthusiasm comes from the Latin *en theos*—one with the energy of the divine.

"Nothing great was ever achieved without enthusiasm," wrote Emerson.

"I rate enthusiasm even above professional skill," said Sir Edward Appleton.

"Every production of genius," wrote Benjamin Disraeli, "must be the production of enthusiasm."

Joy is a feeling we can feel no matter what else is going on. The way to create joy is to do things joyfully. It's one of the easiest feelings to create. We need only remember to create it.

When you get there,
there is no there there.
But there will be a pool.

DAVID ZUCKER

PART SIX

LIVING YOUR DREAMS

This section will make more sense when you've had a chance to live the first five sections for a while. In following the suggestions in those parts, you either have achieved your Dream, or are well on the way to achieving it.

The question arises, "What next?"

That's what this section is about. "There are two things to aim at in life: first, to get what you want; and after that, to enjoy it," wrote Logan Pearsall Smith.

"Only the wisest of mankind achieve the second."

As Miss America,
my goal is to bring peace
to the entire world and then
to get my own apartment.

JAY LENO

Choose New Goals

When your Dream is *almost* realized—but not quite—it's time to choose another goal.

The goal may remain the same, but the quantifying factors are raised. The goal to conduct an orchestra remains intact, for example, but the yearly salary increases from $100,000 to $200,000.

Or, the goal may change entirely.

"Life affords no higher pleasure than that of surmounting difficulties," wrote Samuel Johnson, "passing from one step of success to another, forming new wishes and seeing them gratified."

Just as the comfort zone knows no limits in keeping you from fulfilling your Dreams, it also has no limits on how much it can expand.

Our goals may move from one area of life to another, or they may stay in the same area.

In 1980, Sting said, "Given the choice of friendship or success, I'd probably choose success." He got it. In 1990, he chose again: "Friendship's much more important to me [now] than what I thought success was."

Now that you know that all the techniques in this book work, you can be *truly* bold in following your Dreams. Reread the book from the beginning. It will make a lot more sense. Do the exercises. Choose another Dream.

Dream on.

*A man is rich in proportion
to the number of things
which he can afford
to let alone.*

THOREAU

Wealth Is What You
Can Live Without

When you tell most people, "Nothing outside yourself is going to make you happy; *you* must make yourself happy," they nod approvingly, and more often than not think, "I'll make myself happy when I have a new house, lover, job, meditation blanket, etc."

The shock that takes place when someone realizes, "I have my Dream and I'm still not happy," can be either depressing or enlightening. Depressing, if one thinks, "This was the *wrong dream*. I need to find the *right dream—then* I'll be happy." Enlightening, if someone says, "Maybe my happiness *does* depend on me," and begins the journey.

"Not the fruit of experience," wrote Walter Pater, "but experience itself, is the end." Robert Townsend said it for our generation: "Getting there isn't half the fun—it's all the fun."

Elizabeth Taylor has a needlepoint pillow in her living room. It reads: "It's not the having, it's the getting."

What's the true value of setting a goal and achieving it? It's not obtaining the goal, but what we learn about ourselves along the way. To get to our Dream we must be focused, disciplined, persevering, caring, worthy, excited, enthusiastic, and passionate.

What do we learn about ourselves? How to be more focused, disciplined, persevering, caring, worthy, excited, enthusiastic, and passionate. Goals

> *There is only one success—*
> *to be able to spend your life*
> *in your own way.*
>
> CHRISTOPHER MORLEY

come and go, dreams fade, but these qualities travel with us wherever we go.

"There is no end. There is no beginning," said Federico Fellini. "There is only the infinite passion of life."

This is our true wealth—the riches we take with us, the joy we carry inside, the support we learn to give ourselves, and the self-loving that flows as a natural by-product of that support.

To the degree we can live without the things of this world, we are wealthy. The key word in that sentence is "live." I'm not talking about austerity or sacrifice. I'm talking about *living*.

When we know how easy it is to fulfill a Dream

(easy compared to how *impossible* most people be-lieve it to be), we know we *can* take it. Once we are free to take it, we are also free to leave it. "You never know what is enough," wrote Blake, "until you know what is more than enough."

Do not, however, turn the idea that you can live without many things into just another wonderful-sounding excuse for not pursuing your Dream. "The comfort zone hath power to assume a pleasing shape."

Go fulfill a few Dreams. *Know* you can do it. Have fun. *Then* decide what you can live without.

Is this madness? Sure. "You have everything but one thing," Zorba the Greek told his young friend, "madness. A man needs a little madness or else—he never dares cut the rope and be free."

Concerns for man and his fate
must always form
the chief interest
of all technical endeavors.
Never forget this in the midst
of your diagrams
and equations.

ALBERT EINSTEIN

Give Others
What You Know

On the way to your Dream, others helped you—others whom you couldn't possibly repay. The old saying comes to mind, "Don't repay a kindness; pass it on."

After fulfilling a Dream or two (or twenty), we will be called to pass on some of what we have learned to others. Just as, "When the student is ready, the teacher appears," so, too, "When the teacher is ready, the student appears."

Go out and *do*, learn from the doing, then teach from the knowing. If you just read a lot of books on a subject, memorize a lot of platitudes, and set yourself up as guru, that's not teaching; that's deception.

When you know from experience, others will recognize it, and they will know to ask the right questions. And, as busy as you might be, you will stop and give them the right answers. Why? Their intention pulls it from you.

Also, you'll be an even nicer person.

"The common idea that success spoils people by making them vain, egotistic, and self-complacent is erroneous," wrote Somerset Maugham. "On the contrary, it makes them, for the most part, humble, tolerant and kind. Failure makes people bitter and cruel."

Cast not ye pearls before swine—but it's noble to pass on a few gems to properly eager pearl divers.

> *We are here on earth*
> *to do good to others.*
> *What the others are here for,*
> *I don't know.*
>
> W. H. AUDEN

When people give to themselves—when they fulfill their own Dreams—they are filled to overflowing. The overflow has two interesting characteristics: (1) it is abundant, and (2) it can't be stored. What can one do with the overflow?

There's only one thing to do with it—give it away.

"Giving it away" is not standing on a street corner dispensing hugs. One gives of what one has. Whatever ability one has developed—in whatever area one has developed it—that's what is given.

Robert Ingersoll wrote at the end of the last century:

My creed is that:
Happiness is the only good.
The place to be happy is here.
The time to be happy is now.
The way to be happy is to make others so.

And there we have one of the great open secrets of life: giving to others gives us more than we give away. When people discover this, there's no stopping them. The idea that doing for others is a duty to be done reluctantly—like paying taxes, or picking seeds out of a watermelon—vanishes.

Giving—like fear, guilt, unworthiness, and all the rest—was put here for our upliftment.

Doing for others feels good.

Don't take my word for it. See what you think.

DO IT!

There is more to life
than increasing its speed.

GANDHI

The Tools for Achieving Material Goals Can Be Used for Achieving Non-Material Goals

The inner reflects the outer; the outer reflects the inner. What we learn from fulfilling Dreams in the outer world can be used for pursuing Dreams within ourselves.

After obtaining several material Dreams, you may wonder, "Where are these Dreams coming from?"

Important question. Seeking the answer to that question may begin an important inner quest.

"Try not to become a man of success," wrote Albert Einstein, "but rather try to become a man of value."

Life is short. Live it up.

NIKITA KHRUSHCHEV

Humor and Fun

Life is a game. Like all games, it's only fun when we "take it all seriously"—when we get lost in the illusion, when it seems devastatingly real.

If some butinsky stood over us while we were playing Monopoly, reminding us, "That's only paper; it's not real money. That's just plastic; those aren't real hotels. It's not a real jail they're going to send you to; it's just a square on a board," we'd throw him out of the room.

We want to believe the illusion is real, or else it wouldn't be any fun.

It wouldn't be any fun, either, if the competition weren't very good and the score weren't very close. Without challenges, life would be like playing tennis with a three-year-old. Lots of "victories," but little fun. George Leonard explains,

> In terms of the game theory, we might say the universe is so constituted as to maximize the play.
>
> The best games are not those in which all goes smoothly and steadily toward a certain conclusion, but those in which the outcome is always in doubt.
>
> Similarly, the geometry of life is designed to keep us at the point of maximum tension between certainty and uncertainty, order and chaos. Every important call is a close one. We survive and evolve by the skin of our teeth.
>
> We really wouldn't want it any other way.

> *He deserves Paradise*
> *who makes his companions laugh.*
>
> THE KORAN

> *Among those whom I like or admire,*
> *I can find no common denominator,*
> *but among those whom I love, I can:*
> *all of them make me laugh.*
>
> W. H. AUDEN

As we're playing this game of life, something occasionally reminds us not to take it all too seriously. "Enjoy yourself," it says, "you'll never get out of this alive."

It's called humor.

"Humor is something that thrives between man's aspirations and his limitations," explained Victor Borge. "There is more logic in humor than in anything else. Because, you see, humor is truth."

Alice-Leone Moats described Philadelphia society in this way: "The parties all reminded me of the Gay Nineties—all the men are gay and the women are in their nineties."

Humor is truth, truth is humor.

Humor is probably most refreshing when we use it to look at ourselves.

"You grow up," said Ethel Barrymore, "the day you have your first good laugh—at yourself." Friederich Nietzsche wrote: "One is healthy when one can laugh at the earnestness and zeal with which one has been hypnotized by any single detail in one's life." (What other book in the *world* would have Ethel Barrymore and Friederich Nietzsche agreeing on something in the same paragraph?)

When things are going awful, terrible, horrible—it helps to remember that, in six months, you'll be telling this "tragedy" as an anecdote. You'll have your friends laughing hysterically about it. If it'll be funny then, it's funny now. By remembering that truth in the middle of the chaos, you can take a deep breath and say to yourself, "This is funny."

"Humor is emotional chaos," James Thurber explained, "remembered in emotional tranquility."

"Humor is an affirmation of dignity," said Romain Gary, "a declaration of man's superiority to all that befalls him."

We're all in this alone.

LILY TOMLIN

The End

And so we come to the end of *DO IT!* But not really. Come back often—review the tools of achieving Dreams. Renew your passion.

Allow me to close with this from Guillaume Apollinaire—

"Come to the edge," he said.

They said, "We are afraid."

"Come to the edge," he said.

They came.

He pushed them . . .

And they flew.

'Tis God gives skill,
But not without
men's hands:
He could not make
Antonio Stradivari's violins
Without Antonio.

S<small>TRADIVARIUS</small>

A New Edition—
Completely Revised

LIFE 101

Everything We Wish We Had Learned About Life In School — But Didn't

Peter McWilliams

FABULOUS!
—Liz Smith

A GUIDE TO BUILDING SELF-ESTEEM
—Entertainment Weekly

PRACTICAL AND WITTY
—Detroit News

INTRODUCTION TO LIFE

Welcome to life.

I call this book *LIFE 101* because it contains all the things I wish I had learned about life in school but, for the most part, did not.

After twelve (or more) years of schooling, we know how to figure the square root of an isosceles triangle (invaluable in daily life), but we might not know how to forgive ourselves and others.

We know what direction migrating birds fly in autumn, but we're not sure which way we want to go.

We have dissected a frog, but perhaps have never explored the dynamics of human relationships.

We know who wrote "To be or not to be, that is the question," but we don't know the answer.

We know what pi is, but we're not sure who we are.

We may know how to diagram a sentence, but we may not know how to love ourselves.

That our educational system is not designed to teach us the "secrets of life" is no secret. In school, we learn how to do everything—except how to live.

Maybe that's the way it should be. Unraveling life's "mysteries" and discovering life's "secrets" (which are, in fact, neither mysterious nor secretive) may take the courage and determination found only in a self-motivated pursuit.

> *Only the curious will learn and*
> *only the resolute overcome*
> *the obstacles to learning.*
> *The quest quotient has*
> *always excited me more*
> *than the intelligence quotient.*

EUGENE S. WILSON

You probably already know there's more to life than reading, 'riting, and 'rithmetic. I'm glad you learned reading, of course, or you wouldn't be able to read this book. I'm also glad I learned 'riting (such as it is).

And 'rithmetic? Well, as Mae West once said, "One and one is two, two and two are four, and five'll get you ten if you know how to work it." That's what this book is about: knowing how to work it, and having fun along the way.

Although a lot can be learned from adversity, most of the same lessons can be learned through enjoyment and laughter. If you're like me, you've probably had more than enough adversity. (After graduating from the School of Hard Knocks, I automatically enrolled in the University of Adversity.)

I agree with Alan Watts, who said, "I am *sincere* about life, but I'm not *serious* about it." If you're looking for serious, pedantic, didactic instruction, you will not find it here. I will—with a light heart—present hundreds of techniques and suggestions, and for each of them I make the same suggestion:

Give it a try.

If it works for you, fine—use it; it's yours. If it doesn't work for you, let it go and try other things that may. When you find things that *do* work for you, I advise you to follow Shakespeare's advice: "Grapple them to thy soul with hoops of steel."

Naturally, not everything in *LIFE 101* will be for you. If I say something you find not "true," please don't discount everything else in the book. It may be "true" for someone else. That same someone else might say, "What nonsense," about something which has you knowingly muttering, "How true." It's a big world; we are all at different points on our personal journeys. Life has many truths; take what you can use and leave the rest.

If you take from this book ten percent—any ten percent—and use it as your own, I'll consider my job well done.

Which brings me to the question: Who is the *real* teacher of *LIFE 101?* I'll get to that shortly. (Hint: It's certainly not me—or *I,* as the grammatically correct among us would say.) (Second hint: It is *definitely* not me.)

> **Fred Sanford:** *Didn't you
> learn anything being my son?
> Who do you think I'm
> doing this all for?*
>
> **Lamont Sanford:** *Yourself.*
>
> **Fred:** *Yeah, you
> learned something.*

For now, welcome to *LIFE 101*. When you were born, you probably had quite a welcome, although you may have been too young to remember it. So, as you begin this "life," please feel welcome.

Although it may be "just a book," it's a book of ideas from my mind to yours; a book of best wishes from my heart to yours. As James Burke observed, "When you read a book, you hold another's mind in your hands." (So be careful!) Here's to our time together being intimate, enjoyable, and loving.

Welcome.

We don't receive wisdom;
we must discover it
for ourselves after a journey
that no one can take for us
or spare us.

MARCEL PROUST

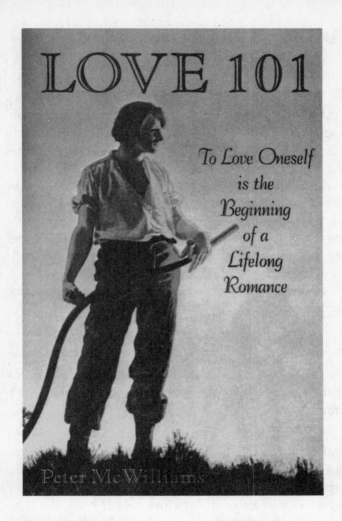

LOVE 101

To Love Oneself
is the
Beginning
of a
Lifelong
Romance

Peter McWilliams

TRADE PAPERBACK
5x8, 448 pages, $11.95
ISBN: 0-931580-70-6

AUDIO TAPES
*Presented by the author
with old songs and lots of fun!*
Eight tapes
Unabridged, $24.95
ISBN: 0-931580-71-4

*Definitely NOT
just "your basic
book-on-tape"*

Author's Notes

In the early 1970s, I went to the American Booksellers Association annual convention, where publishers rent booths at exorbitant rates and show their recent wares to the booksellers of America. At the Penguin booth, I saw a book entitled *Self Love*. It had an introduction by Alan Watts, who was then and is still my favorite philosopher. I was excited to discover a book about the love of oneself endorsed by him and published by such a distinguished house as Penguin—then known primarily for its reprints of the classics. As was the custom at ABA, complimentary copies were available. I took my copy and thanked the salesperson, a dignified British man who nodded his acceptance of my appreciation.

"I can really use this book," I said. "I'm very bad at self-love."

The sales representative smiled one of those smiles that doesn't go up at the edges, but merely makes one's mouth wider while perfectly horizontal.

"In fact, of all the things I need to work on," I continued, "I think self-love is the most essential." I was twenty-something at the time, and determined to be "open about my process." I could see, however, that saying I didn't know how to love myself made the Penguin sales representative a bit uncomfortable, so I said my good-bye.

"Thank you again," I said, extending my hand. As he shook it, I said, "In fact, I'm going up to my hotel room right now and read this." He dropped my hand.

The Penguin book on self-love was about the joys of masturbation.

> *The last time I saw him*
> *he was walking down Lover's Lane*
> *holding his own hand.*

FRED ALLEN

My seeking self-love in the early 1970s was sincere. Like many people, I had inhaled the book *How to Be Your Own Best Friend*. I read it clandestinely—it seemed to be as taboo a subject as that *other* form of self-love. In 1971, the idea that one could be one's own friend, much less *best* friend, was radical.

Today, the notion that one can be the most significant love object in one's own life, is just as radical.

I certainly do not present myself as a pillar of self-loving, nor put myself on a pedestal labeled AN IDEAL SPECIMEN OF A SELF-LOVING PERSON. I'm just a person who has been struggling with the notion of loving himself since 1967. Twenty-eight years later, I finally feel as though I have *something* worth sharing; that I know enough about the subject to write a book on it; and, since there's something more to learn about everything, "The best way to learn about a subject," Benjamin Disraeli once said, "is to write a book about it."

Although your path and discoveries on the road to greater self-love will differ from mine, allow me to offer three personal observations:

1. God* is within you.**

2. You are lovable, *just as you are now.*

3. You *can* learn to love yourself, more and more each day.

In this book I will not be spending a great deal of time on point #1. The discovery of, defining of, relating to, and praise for God I will leave to you, God, and any number of excellent source materials on the subject. *LOVE 101* can be read by anyone, from devout fundamentalist to confirmed atheist, and he or she can learn enough about self-loving to proclaim, "Glory, hallelujah! I'm glad I read this book."

In the end, of course, we must all write our own book on how to love ourselves. Thanks for reading my

---

*As you perceive him, her, or it to be, from God the Father, to Mother Nature, to Universal Mind, to the "illimitable superior spirit who reveals himself in the slight details we are able to perceive with our frail and feeble mind" (Einstein).

**For those who find this an anti-Christian statement, please consider this from Jesus: "The kingdom of God is within you" (Luke 17:21).

> *Style is knowing who you are,*
> *what you want to say,*
> *and not giving a damn.*
>
> GORE VIDAL

book. My best and warmest wishes to you as you write your own.

Take good care,

> Peter McWilliams
> Los Angeles, California
> January 3, 1995

P.S. *LOVE 101: To Love Oneself Is the Beginning of a Life-long Romance* was completed on January 3, 1995. Precisely one hundred years earlier—to the day—the curtain rose at London's Theatre Royal on Oscar Wilde's latest play, *An Ideal Husband*. As the third act opens, we find this stage direction:

Enter LORD GORING *in evening dress with a button hole [flower in his lapel]. He is wearing a silk hat and Inverness cape. White-gloved, he carries a Louis Seize cane. His are all the delicate fopperies of fashion. One sees that he stands in immediate relation to modern life, makes it, indeed, and so masters it. He is the first well-dressed philosopher in the history of thought.*

Could Wilde possibly be describing himself? But of course. Goring addresses his butler:

LORD GORING: You see, Phipps, fashion is what one wears oneself. Whereas unfashionable is what other people wear.

PHIPPS: Yes, my lord.

LORD GORING: Just as vulgarity is simply the conduct of other people.

PHIPPS: Yes, my lord.

LORD GORING [putting in new button hole]: And falsehoods the truths of other people.

PHIPPS: Yes, my lord.

LORD GORING: To love oneself is the beginning of a lifelong romance.

PHIPPS: Yes, my lord.

And from that bit of typical Wilde dialogue comes the subtitle for this book.

*To fall in love
with yourself
is the first secret
of happiness.*

*I did so at the age
of four-and-a-half.*

*Then if you're not
a good mixer
you can always
fall back on
your own company.*

Robert Morley

INTRODUCTION:
You Are Already Living
with the Love of Your Life

This is a book about a myth and a taboo.

THE MYTH: In order to be complete and fulfilled, you must find one "significant other" to love. This significant other must consider you his or her significant other and love you back with equal devotion till death do you part.

THE TABOO: It is somehow unwholesome to love yourself.

In *LOVE 101* I'll be challenging both the myth and the taboo. If you're not ready to have these challenged, it would be best if you stop reading now—this book will only upset you.

If, on the other hand, you have been gradually coming to the seemingly forbidden conclusion that before we can truly love another, or allow another to properly love us, we must first learn to love ourselves—then this book is for you.

The taboo that we shouldn't love ourselves is one of the silliest in modern culture. Who else is more qualified to love you than you? Who else knows what you want, precisely when you want it, and is always around to supply it?

Who do you go to bed with, sleep with, dream with, shower with, eat with, work with, play with, pray with, go to the movies with, and watch TV with?

> *The continued propinquity*
> *of another human being*
> *cramps your style after a time*
> *unless that person*
> *is somebody you think you love.*
>
> *Then the burden*
> *becomes intolerable at once.*
>
> QUENTIN CRISP

Who else knows where it itches, and just how hard to scratch it?

Who are you reading this book with?

Who have you always lived with, and whom will you eventually die with?

And, who will be the only person to accompany you on that ultimate adventure (just think of death as a theme park with a high admission cost), while all your *other* loved ones are consoling each other by saying how happy you must be with God and how natural you look?

Spiritually, who is the only person who can join you in your relationship with God, Jesus, Buddha, Mohammed, Moses, Mother Nature, The Force, Creative

Intelligence, or whomever or whatever you consider to be the moving force of existence?

And, who has been there every time you've had sex?*

So, from the sacred to the profane (and all points in between), your ideal lover is *you*.

Then why is loving ourselves such a taboo? Why is the notion that we *need* another to love (who will love us back) such an enormous myth?

In a word, control.

The self-contained, emotionally autonomous, intellectually free individual is the greatest threat to the institutions that want to control us. Those of us who refuse to act like sheep—who question authority and want genuine answers, not just knee-jerk clichés—are a pain in the *gluteus maximus* (and regions nearby) to those who want to rule by *power* rather than by providing *leadership*.

We see attempts to manipulate almost everywhere—in politics, religion, advertising, entertainment.

When we are programmed to "fall" for the hunk or the honey of a certain aesthetic type, and to believe that these images of sex and beauty mean "true love," then these images can be used to sell us anything from cigarettes to movie tickets. And they are, they are.

*Yes, from time to time others may have been nearby doing what they could to help, but whatever pleasure you felt was inside yourself, experienced in those inner electrochemical, physiological pleasure places that are entirely your own. This is true for *anything* pleasurable we see, feel, hear, touch, or taste: without *our senses* nothing "out there"—from movies to pepperoni pizza—would be in the least enjoyable.

Excerpt from *LOVE 101*

> *Conformity*
> *is the jailer of freedom*
> *and the enemy of growth.*
>
> JOHN F. KENNEDY

Further, when the only "moral" outcome of a romantic relationship is a till-death-do-us-part, state-licensed, church-blessed marriage, we see the fundamental forces of conformity at work. If we're all the *same,* we are much easier to *serve*—also sell to, also control.

If we're all the same—and marriage is one of the best homogenizers around—then we only need one religion, one political party: the Family Values Party. In fact, why not combine religion and government in one?

That's been the history of the world—church and state hand-in-hand, slavish conformity, and those troublemakers (ungodly and unpatriotic) who fail to shape up . . . well, there have always been ways of dealing with *them.*

But this book is not a political diatribe. It's a book about personal freedom—the freedom to choose the life you want, even though the powers that be think you should not do so. They know best.

Except they don't. More than half the people in this country live outside the "traditional" mama-papa-children household. It hasn't worked.

Please understand that I am not against family, marriage, children, or even romance. I am merely against the idea that we should *all* be herded into that mode of relating when there are viable, satisfying alternatives (which we'll explore later in this book).

There will always be people who want to get married and raise children. More power to them. The trouble arises when people who want to do something *else* (write, pray, save the dolphins) get married and have children because they think they *should,* not because they *want to.*

This clutters up the marriage market with unqualified players—those who would rather be training for a decathlon just don't have the same *commitment* to child-rearing. So, they drop out of the marriage—emotionally or entirely—and the other partner, who still *wants* a marriage, wonders, "What happened?"

What happened is what happens every time we are all programmed to do the same thing—those who don't really want to be there muck it up for those who do.

If a group of people were all taken to an opera one night, a rock concert the second night, the latest Woody Allen movie the third night, and an Englebert Humperdink concert the fourth, chances are that on at least one

> *Mass democracy, mass morality*
> *and the mass media thrive*
> *independently of the individual,*
> *who joins them only at the cost*
> *of at least a partial perversion*
> *of his instinct and insights.*
>
> *He pays for his social ease*
> *with what used to be called his soul,*
> *his discriminations, his uniqueness,*
> *his psychic energy, his self.*
>
> AL ALVAREZ

of those nights, some of the audience would be, to paraphrase S. J. Pearlman, if not disgruntled, certainly not fully gruntled.

If, on the other hand, each individual in the group had a choice to go to any, all, or none of the four, then self-selection would lead to far more gruntled audiences at *all* the events.

This book is about you getting more gruntled in *all* your relationships—especially your relationship with yourself.

You'll note I've only talked about the failure of marriage. Imagine how much more unsuccessful romance is. There are two million divorces in the United States each year. Is it fair to estimate that for every divorce there are at least ten break-ups between nonmarried romantics? If so, there are, counting the newly divorced, twenty-two million broken hearts littering the emotional landscape. There are also twenty-two million (the ones who did the dumping) who are proclaiming "Free at last!"

And yet the majority of those millions, who now have already had first-hand experience that a romantic relationship doesn't necessarily lead to a lifelong happy marriage, will *again* be jumping into the next acceptable pair of eyes, or thighs, that come along. "The *person* was the problem," they tell themselves. "If only I find the right *person*." Maybe it's the *type of relationship* that's not working. Maybe.

What does it cost us to fall for this myth that we must find another to love, and must (in the same person) find someone to love us? It costs us the loving, laughing, emotionally stable, intellectually stimulating, and physically satisfying relationship with the person perfectly qualified to be our best friend in this lifetime—ourselves.

We trade the ongoing, here-and-now, potentially vibrant, fun-filled, nurturing relationship with ourselves for some future promise of Prince Charming or Cinderella riding in on a white charger or a refurbished pumpkin, transforming our lives with True Love. That's like not eating your home-cooked food because you have been convinced that any day now (real soon), a gourmet (not just any gourmet, mind you, but your own personal star-crossed gourmet) will appear—pots, pans, leeks, and all.

Am I saying you should turn the gourmet away?

> *Love, love, love—all the wretched cant*
> *of it, masking egotism, lust, maso-*
> *chism, fantasy under a mythology of*
> *sentimental postures, a welter of self*
> *induced miseries and joys, blinding*
> *and masking the essential personalities*
> *in the frozen gestures of courtship, in*
> *the kissing and the dating and the*
> *desire, the compliments and the*
> *quarrels which vivify its barrenness.*
>
> GERMAINE GREER

Not *at all*. Being with others, sharing with others, supporting and being supported by others are among the most fulfilling activities we can enjoy. I'm simply saying that loving oneself *while* loving others makes *all* interactions more enjoyable.

Some even say that loving oneself is a *prerequisite* to loving others. I won't take it quite that far, but I do know loving oneself is an *important* part of loving others (and allowing others to love you).

When we are already loving and loved by ourselves, our desire to love and be loved by others is just that—a desire. We no longer have the burning, aching *need* to love and be loved. Back in my desperately seeking-another-to-love-who-will-love-me-back days, I wrote a poem:

My needs destroy
the paths
through which
those needs
could be
fulfilled.

I had on my wall in letters a foot tall, the needy proclamation taken from Peter Townsend's *Tommy:*

SEE ME

FEEL ME

TOUCH ME

HEAL ME

Talk about an *intimidating* message to present to the newly met.

At seventeen, my muse gave me the answer. I was sitting in a coffee shop as the sun was coming up and wrote on a paper napkin (as all poets do from time to time):

I must conquer my loneliness
alone.

I must be happy with myself
or I have
nothing
to offer.

Two halves have
little choice
but to
join,
and yes,
they do
make a
whole.

> *I am two fools, I know,*
> *For loving, and for saying so*
> *In whining poetry*
>
> JOHN DONNE
> 1572–1631

But two
wholes,
when they coincide . . .

that is
beauty.

That is
love.

It took me some time—with any number of false
starts, dead ends, and dashed hopes*—to get the wisdom of this edict off the napkin and into my life.

LOVE 101 is what I learned along the way. You may
have a different way with different learnings, but I pray

*But I did sell a large pile of poetry books along the way!
When life gives you lemons, write *The Lemon Cookbook.*

that some of my musings you'll find useful, inspiring, or amusing.

I wrote this book for myself—a collection of what I have learned about self-loving so that if I fall into a pit of self-loathing (an inevitability—what lovers don't have quarrels?), I will have these reminders to help me de-pit myself.

I hope you'll read along in my "manual on loving me" and make as much of it your own as you care to.

THE **LIFE 101** SERIES

YOU CAN'T AFFORD THE LUXURY OF A NEGATIVE THOUGHT

A NEW EDITION COMPLETELY REVISED

A Book for People with Any Life-Threatening Illness— Including Life

PETER McWILLIAMS

PAPERBACK
4x7, 622 pages, $5.95
ISBN: 0-931580-24-2

AUDIO TAPES
*Presented by the author
with old songs and lots of fun*
Eight cassettes, $24.95
ISBN: 0-931580-13-7
Available October 1995

WORKBOOK
Focus on the Positive
7x10, 200 pages, $11.95
ISBN: 0-931580-23-4

WRISTWATCH
Paul LeBus design
$35.00
Mail order only

Introduction

This is not just a book for people with life-threatening illnesses. It's a book for anyone afflicted with one of the primary diseases of our time: negative thinking.

I come before you a certified expert on the subject: I'm a confirmed negaholic. I don't just see a glass that's half-full and call it half-empty; I see a glass that's completely full and worry that someone's going to tip it over.

Negative thinking is always expensive—dragging us down mentally, emotionally, and physically—hence, I refer to any indulgence in it as a *luxury*. When, however, we have the symptoms of a life-threatening illness—be it AIDS, heart trouble, cancer, high blood pressure, or any of the others—negative thinking is a *luxury* we can no longer afford.

I remember a bumper sticker from the 1960s—"Death Is Nature's Way of Telling You to Slow Down." Well, the signs of a life-threatening illness are nature's way of telling us to—as we say in California—lighten up.

Be easier on yourself. Think better of yourself. Learn to forgive yourself and others.

This is a book about getting behind on your worrying. Way, way behind. The further behind on your worrying you get, the further ahead you'll be.

My favorite quote on worry: "Worrying is a form of atheism." Second favorite: "Worrying is the interest paid on a debt you may not owe."

Excerpt from *You Can't Afford the Luxury of a Negative Thought*

> *We are, perhaps,*
> *unique among the*
> *earth's creatures,*
> *the worrying animal.*
> *We worry away our lives,*
> *fearing the future,*
> *discontent with the present,*
> *unable to take in*
> *the idea of dying,*
> *unable to sit still.*
>
> LEWIS THOMAS

This is not so much a book to be read as it is a book to be *used*. It doesn't have to be read cover to cover. I like to think you can flip it open at any time to any page and get something of value from it. This is especially true of the second—and longest—section of the book.

This book has two sections: **The Disease** and **The Cure.**

The disease is not any specific illness, but what I believe to be a precursor of all life-threatening illnesses—negative thinking.

The cure is not a wonder drug or a vaccination or The Magic Bullet. The cure is simple: (1) spend more time focusing on the positive things in your life *(Accentuate the Positive);* (2) spend less time thinking negatively *(Eliminate the Negative);* and (3) enjoy each moment *(Latch on to the Affirmative).*

That's it. Simple, but far from easy.

It's the aim of this book to make the process simple and, if not easy, at least easier.

Please don't use anything in this book against yourself. Don't interpret anything I say in **The Disease** as blame. When I use the word *responsibility,* for example, I simply mean you have the *ability* to *respond.* (And you *are* responding or you wouldn't be reading this book.)

And please don't take any of the suggestions in **The Cure** as "musts," "shoulds," or "have-tos." Think of them as joyful activity, creative play, curious exploration—not as additional burdens in an already burdensome life.

This book is not designed to replace proper medical care. Please use this book *in conjunction with* whatever course of treatment your doctor or health-care provider prescribes.

You are far more powerful than you ever dreamed. As you discover and learn how to use your power, use it only for your upliftment and the upliftment of others.

You are a marvelous, wonderful, worthwhile person—just because you are. That's the point of view I'll be taking. Please join me for a while—an hour, a week, a lifetime—at that viewing point.

Excerpt from *You Can't Afford the Luxury of a Negative Thought*

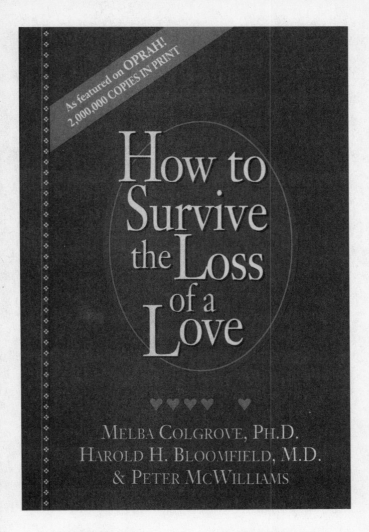

As featured on OPRAH!
2,000,000 COPIES IN PRINT

How to Survive the Loss of a Love

♥♥♥♥ ♥

MELBA COLGROVE, PH.D.
HAROLD H. BLOOMFIELD, M.D.
& PETER MCWILLIAMS

When an emotional injury takes place,
the body begins a process
as natural as the healing
of a physical wound.

Let the process happen.
Trust the process.
Surrender to it.

Trust that nature will do the healing.
Know that the pain will pass,
and, when it passes,
you will be stronger,
happier, more sensitive and aware.

Excerpt from *How to Survive the Loss of a Love*

THE STAGES OF RECOVERY

- Recovering from a loss takes place in three distinct—yet overlapping—stages.

- They are:

    —shock/denial/numbness
    —fear/anger/depression
    —understanding/acceptance/moving on

- Each stage of recovery is:

    —necessary
    —natural
    —a part of the healing process

the fear that I would
come home one day and
find you gone has turned
into the pain of the
reality.

"What will I do if it happens?"
I would ask myself.

What will I do
now that it
has?

Excerpt from *How to Survive the Loss of a Love*

One:
You Will Survive

- You *will* get better.

- No doubt about it.

- The healing process has a beginning, a middle, and an end.

- Keep in mind, at the beginning, that there *is* an end. It's not that far off. You *will* heal.

- Nature is on your side, and nature is a powerful ally.

- Tell yourself, often, "I am alive. I will survive."

- You are alive.

- You will survive.

in my sleep
I dreamed
you called. you said
you were moving back
with your old lover.
you said you thought a
phone call would be the
cleanest way to handle it,
"it" being that we could
never see each other
again, and that I should
understand why.
I moved to wake
myself and found I wasn't
sleeping after all.
my life became
a nightmare.

　　　　Excerpt from *How to Survive the Loss of a Love*

Five:
It's OK to Feel

- It's OK to feel numb. Expect to be in shock for awhile. This emotional numbness may be frightening.

- It's OK to fear. "Will I make it?" "Will I ever love again?" "Will I ever feel good about anything again?" These are familiar fears following a loss. It's OK to *feel* them, but, to the degree you can, don't *believe* them.

- It's OK to feel nothing. There are times when you'll have no feelings of any kind. That's fine.

- It's OK to feel anything. You may feel grief-stricken, angry, like a failure, exhausted, muddled, lost, beaten, indecisive, relieved, overwhelmed, inferior, melancholy, giddy, silly, loathful, full of self-hatred, envious, suicidal (feelings OK, actions not), disgusted, happy, outraged, in rage or *anything* else.

- *All* feelings are a part of the healing process.

- Let yourself heal. Let yourself feel.

Spring:
leaves grow.
love grows.

Summer:
love dies.
I drive away,
tears in my eyes.

Bugs commit suicide on my windshield.

Autumn:
leaves fall.
I fall.

Winter:
I die.
I drive away,
nothing in my eyes.

Snowflakes commit suicide on my windshield.

Excerpt from *How to Survive the Loss of a Love*

Seven:
You're Great!

- You are a good, whole, worthwhile human being.

- You are OK. You're more than OK, you're great.

- Your self-esteem may have suffered a jolt. Your thoughts may reflect some guilt, worry, condemnation or self-deprecation. These thoughts are just symptoms of the stress you are going through.

- There is no need to give negative thoughts about yourself the center of attention.

- Don't punish yourself with "if only's." (*"If only* I had [or hadn't] done this or that I wouldn't be in this emotional mess."*) Disregard any thought that begins "If only . . ."

- You are much more than the emotional wound you are currently suffering. Don't lose sight of that.

- Beneath the surface turmoil:

    —you are good
    —you are whole
    —you are beautiful

    just because you are

I am Joy.
I am everything.
I can do all things but two:

1. forget that I love you.

2. forget that you no longer love me.

Twenty-five:
The Question of Suicide

- You may be having suicidal thoughts. They may or may not be as eloquent as *"to be or not to be,"* but they may arise.

- Know they are a natural symptom of the pain, and that there is no need to act on them.

- If you fear these impulses are getting out of hand, seek professional help *at once.* Call directory assistance and ask for the number of your local Suicide Prevention Hotline. Then call it. The people (almost entirely volunteers) are there to help. They *want* to help. Give them the gift of allowing them to do so.

- Don't turn the rage against yourself. (Although feeling rage is perfectly alright—after all, an utterly outrageous thing has happened to you.) Find a safe way to release it. Beat a pillow, cry, scream, stomp up and down, yell.

- Above all, suicide is silly. It's leaving the world series ten minutes into the first inning just because your favorite hitter struck out. It's walking out of the opera during the overture just because the conductor dropped his baton. It's . . . well, you get the picture. In this play called life, aren't you even a little curious about what might happen next?

- The feeling *will pass.* You can count on that. You *will* get better. *Much* better.

- We do promise you a rose garden. We just can't promise you it will be totally without thorns.

THE QUESTION OF SUICIDE:

Keep it a question.
it's not really an answer.

Ninety-three:
Your Happiness Is Up to You

- Happiness depends on your *attitude* toward what happens to you, not on what happens to you.

- It may sound revolutionary, but problems don't have to make you unhappy.

- This runs counter to our cultural programming—which tells us we *must* react in certain negative ways to certain "negative" events.

- Nonetheless, happiness is always our choice. That is a reality of life.

- Stop waiting for Prince Charming, Cinderella, more money, the right job, total health *or anything else* before you're happy.

- Stop waiting.

- Choose satisfaction.

- Be happy.

- Now.

I am worthy.

*I am worthy of my life and
all the good that is in it.*

*I am worthy of
my friends and their friendship.*

*I am worthy of spacious skies, amber waves
of grain and purple mountain majesties
above the fruited plain. (I am worthy, too,
of the fruited plain.)*

*I am worthy of a degree of happiness
that could only be referred to as
"sinful" in less enlightened times.*

*I am worthy of creativity,
sensitivity and appreciation.*

*I am worthy of peace of mind, peace on Earth,
peace in the valley and a piece of the action.*

I am worthy of God's presence in my life.

*I am worthy
of my love.*

"If you can't remember the last time
you felt genuinely good,
please read this book."
Larry King

How to
Heal
Depression

By the co-authors of
How to Survive the Loss of a Love

Harold H. Bloomfield, M.D.
& Peter McWilliams

HARDCOVER
5½x8¼, 240 pages
$14.95
ISBN: 0-931580-34-0

PAPERBACK
4x7, 240 pages
$5.95
ISBN: 0-931580-61-7

AUDIO TAPES
Read by the authors
(with lots of classic blues songs)
Six cassettes, $19.95
ISBN: 0-931580-37-4

Authors' Notes

Welcome.

Our goal is to make this book brief, practical, and to-the-point.

The *last* thing a person with depression wants is an intricate tome, heavy with footnotes, citations, Latin words, and sentences such as "Depression is a biopsychosocial disorder, sometimes treated with monoamine oxidase inhibitors."

We have also included quotes from people, some well known and some not, across many cultures and centuries, to show that depression—and the desire to heal it—is a deeply human and universal experience.

Our approach to the treatment of depression is twofold. Each part is equally important.

- One is healing the brain, as current medical research points to biochemical imbalances in the brain as the seat of depression.

- The other is healing the mind—overcoming negative habits of thought and action which may cause, or be caused by, depression.

Treating the brain *and* the mind is the most effective way to heal depression. Recent medical and psychological breakthroughs make depression among the most successfully treatable of all serious illnesses.

Harold H. Bloomfield, M.D.
Peter McWilliams

Excerpt from *How to Heal Depression*

As a confirmed melancholic,
I can testify that the best
and maybe the only antidote
for melancholia is action.
However, like most melancholics,
I also suffer from sloth.

EDWARD ABBEY

About This Book

Our book is divided into four parts.

In Part I, **"Understanding Depression,"** we discuss what depression is (and is not); how you can be depressed without "feeling depressed"; and the possible causes of depression. There's even a short self-evaluation for depression, compliments of the National Institutes of Health (page 22).

In Part II, **"Healing the Brain,"** we look at the biological causes of depression and its medical treatment. This includes antidepressant medication, nutrition, exercise, and such strenuous activities as hot baths and massage. This is the domain of the psychiatrist, family doctor, and other healthcare specialists.

Part III we call **"Healing the Mind."** We explore unlearning mental habits either caused by or contributing to depression, while learning new mental patterns that tend to enhance effectiveness, well-being, and emotional freedom. We discuss exciting new short-term therapies (usually only ten to twenty sessions) that have proven to be highly successful in healing depression. This is the domain of the psychologist, psychiatrist, clinical social worker, and mental health professional.

The final section, Part IV, is **"As Healing Continues . . . ."** Although most people treated for depression find remarkable results within a short time, the complete healing of depression often continues for a while. There are ups and downs, lessons to be learned, new pathways to be explored.

Thank you for joining us on this healing journey.

Excerpt from *How to Heal Depression*

One:
You Are Not Alone

- If you or someone you know is depressed, you are not alone.

- *That's* something of an understatement.

- One in twenty Americans currently suffers from a depression severe enough to require medical treatment.

- One person in five will have a depression at some time in his or her life.

- Depression in its various forms (insomnia, fatigue, anxiety, stress, vague aches and pains, etc.) is the most common complaint heard in doctors' offices.

- Two percent of all children and five percent of all adolescents suffer from depression.

- More than twice as many women are currently being treated for depression than men. (It is not known whether this is because women are more likely to be depressed, or whether men tend to deny their depression.)

- People over sixty-five are four times more likely to suffer depression than the rest of the population.

- Depression is the #1 public health problem in this country. Depression is an epidemic—an epidemic on the rise.

I am now experiencing myself
all the things that
as a third party
I have witnessed going on
in my patients—
days when I slink about
depressed.

S<small>IGMUND</small> F<small>REUD</small>

Three:
There Is No Need to Suffer

- More than eighty percent of the people with depression can be successfully treated.

- Long-term, expensive treatments are seldom necessary.

- Modern treatment for most depression is antidepressant medication and short-term "talk" therapy—usually just ten to twenty sessions.

- Treatment for depression is relatively inexpensive—but whatever the cost, it is more than made up for in increased productivity, efficiency, physical health, improved relationships, and enjoyment of life.

- Yes, life will always have its "slings and arrows of outrageous fortune," and, yes, they will hurt. But there's no need to suffer from depression as well.

Pain is inevitable.
Suffering is optional.

M. KATHLEEN CASEY

Excerpt from *How to Heal Depression*

Ten:
The Symptoms of Depression

After careful evaluation, the National Institutes of Health developed the following checklist:

Symptoms of Depression Can Include

- ☐ Persistent sad or "empty" mood
- ☐ Loss of interest or pleasure in ordinary activities, including sex
- ☐ Decreased energy, fatigue, being "slowed down"
- ☐ Sleep disturbances (insomnia, early-morning waking, or oversleeping)
- ☐ Eating disturbances (loss of appetite and weight, or weight gain)
- ☐ Difficulty concentrating, remembering, making decisions
- ☐ Feelings of guilt, worthlessness, helplessness
- ☐ Thoughts of death or suicide, suicide attempts
- ☐ Irritability
- ☐ Excessive crying
- ☐ Chronic aches and pains that don't respond to treatment

In the Workplace, Symptoms of Depression Often May Be Recognized by

- ☐ Decreased productivity
- ☐ Morale problems
- ☐ Lack of cooperation
- ☐ Safety problems, accidents
- ☐ Absenteeism
- ☐ Frequent complaints of being tired all the time
- ☐ Complaints of unexplained aches and pains
- ☐ Alcohol and drug abuse

Symptoms of Mania Can Include

- ☐ Excessively "high" mood
- ☐ Irritability
- ☐ Decreased need for sleep
- ☐ Increased energy and activity
- ☐ Increased talking, moving, and sexual activity
- ☐ Racing thoughts
- ☐ Disturbed ability to make decisions
- ☐ Grandiose notions
- ☐ Being easily distracted

Eleven:
Are You Depressed?

- *"A thorough diagnosis is needed if four or more of the symptoms of depression or mania persist for more than two weeks,"* say the National Institutes of Health, *"or are interfering with work or family life."*

- The symptoms on the facing page are *not* "just life." If four or more of the symptoms have been a regular part of your life for more than two weeks or regularly tend to interfere with your life, a consultation with a physician experienced in diagnosing and treating depression is in order.

- You need not suffer any longer. Treatment is readily available.

- *"With available treatment, eighty percent of the people with serious depression—even those with the most severe forms—can improve significantly,"* say the National Institutes of Health. *"Symptoms can be relieved, usually in a matter of weeks."*

- Please talk to your doctor. (And read on!)

ABOUT THE AUTHOR

PETER MCWILLIAMS has been writing about his passions since 1967. In that year, he became passionate about what most seventeen-year-olds are passionate about—love—and wrote *Come Love With Me & Be My Life*. This began a series of poetry books which have sold nearly four million copies.

Along with love, of course, comes loss, so Peter became passionate about emotional survival. In 1971 he wrote *Surviving the Loss of a Love*, which was expanded in 1976 and again in 1991 (with co-authors Melba Colgrove, Ph.D., and Harold Bloomfield, M.D.) into *How to Survive the Loss of a Love*. It has sold more than two million copies.

He also became interested in meditation, and a book he wrote on meditation was a *New York Times* bestseller, knocking the impregnable *Joy of Sex* off the #1 spot. As one newspaper headline proclaimed, MEDITATION MORE POPULAR THAN SEX AT THE *NEW YORK TIMES*.

His passion for computers (or, more accurately, for what computers could do) led to *The Personal Computer Book*, which *TIME* proclaimed "a beacon of simplicity, sanity and humor," and the *Wall Street Journal* called "genuinely funny." (Now, really, how many people has the *Wall Street Journal* called "genuinely funny"?)

His passion for personal growth continues in the ongoing LIFE 101 SERIES. Thus far, the books in this series include *You Can't Afford the Luxury of a Negative Thought: A Book for People with Any Life-Threatening Illness—Including Life*; *LIFE 101: Everything We Wish We Had Learned About Life In School—But Didn't* (a *New York Times* bestseller in both hardcover and paperback); *DO IT! Let's Get Off Our Buts* (a #1 *New York Times* hardcover bestseller); *WEALTH 101: Wealth Is Much More Than Money*, and *We Give To Love: Giving Is Such a Selfish Thing*.

His passion for visual beauty led him to publish, in 1992, his first book of photography, *PORTRAITS*, a twenty-two-year anthology of his photographic work.

Personal freedom, individual expression, and the right to live one's own life, as long as one does not harm the person or property of another, have long been his passions. He wrote about them in *Ain't Nobody's Business If You Do: The Absurdity of Consensual Crimes in a Free Society*.

After successfully being treated for depression, he wrote with Harold H. Bloomfield, M.D., *How to Heal Depression*.

His fifteen-year sojourn through John-Roger's destructive cult, the Church of the Movement of Spiritual Inner Awareness (MSIA), is documented (with a surprising degree of humor) in *LIFE 102: What to Do When Your Guru Sues You*.

All of the above-mentioned books were self-published and are still in print.

Peter McWilliams has appeared on *The Oprah Winfrey Show*, *Larry King* (radio and television), *Donahue*, *Sally Jessy Raphael*, and, a long time ago, the *Regis Philbin Show* (before Regis met Kathie Lee—probably before Kathie Lee was *born*).

Other Books by Peter McWilliams

DO IT! Audio Tapes
The unabridged text of this book, read by the author. **Eight cassettes.** $24.95.

The Portable DO IT!
A collection of reminders and quotes to encourage you to continue getting off your buts. The perfect pocket companion on the road to fulfilling your dreams. 208 pages. **Trade paperback,** $5.95.

LIFE 101 Everything We Wish We Had Learned About Life In School—But Didn't
The overview book of the LIFE 101 SERIES. The idea behind *LIFE 101* is that everything in life is for our upliftment, learning and growth—including (and, perhaps especially) the "bad" stuff. "The title jolly well says it all," said the *Los Angeles Times*—jolly well saying it all. 480 pages. **Trade paperback,** $5.95. **Audio tapes** (unabridged, five cassettes), $22.95. **Wristwatch,** $35.00.

The Portable LIFE 101
179 essential excerpts plus 177 quotations from the *New York Times* bestseller *LIFE 101*. Think of it as the Cliff Notes to life. **Trade paperback,** $5.95.

LOVE 101 Loving Oneself is the Beginning of a Lifelong Romance
If you were arrested for being kind to yourself, would there be enough evidence to convict you? If not, this book (or audio tape set) is a must. It explores improving the most important relationship in your life—your relationship with yourself. After all, you're the only person you'll be eating with, watching TV with, bathing with, and sleeping with for the rest of your life. 400 pages **Trade paperback,** $11.95. **Audio tapes** (unabridged, eight cassettes, includes Meditation tape),** $24.95.

How to Heal Depression
by Harold H. Bloomfield, M.D.,
and Peter McWilliams

The first companion book of the eighteen-year bestseller, *How to Survive the Loss of a Love*. In simple, clear, direct prose (with quotes on every other page) it explains what depression is, what causes it, and what the most effective treatments are. **Hardcover,** $14.95. **Audio tapes** (unabridged, six cassettes, read by the authors), $19.95.

You Can't Afford the Luxury of a Negative Thought
A Book for People with Any Life-Threatening illness including Life

This is a book for anyone afflicted with one of the primary diseases of our time: negative thinking. 622 pages. **Paperback,** $5.95. **Audio tapes** (unabridged, eight cassettes), $24.95. **Wristwatch,** $35.00.

Focus on the Positive

Exercises, processes, journal space, drawing room, and more—all designed to complement the material in the preceding book. 200 pages. **Trade paperback,** $11.95.

How to Survive the Loss of a Love
by Melba Colgrove, Ph.D., Harold H. Bloomfield, M.D., and
Peter McWilliams

A directly helpful guide to recovering from any loss or major change in life. 212 pages. **Hardcover,** $12.95 **Trade paperback** (rack size), $5.95. **Audio tapes** (unabridged, two cassettes, read by the authors), $11.95.

Surviving, Healing and Growing
The How to Survive the Loss of a Love Workbook

Exercises, processes, and suggestions designed to supplement *How to Survive the Loss of a Love*. Lots of room to write, draw, doodle, survive, heal & grow. 200 pages. **Trade paperback,** $11.95.

Ain't Nobody's Business If You Do
The Absurdity of Consensual Crimes in a Free Society

The idea behind this book is simple: As an adult, you should be allowed to do with your person and property whatever you choose, as long as you don't physically harm the person or property of another. 818 pages. **Hardcover,** $11.47. **Paperback,** $5.95.

LIFE 102:
What to Do When Your Guru Sues You
This book is presented as a moral tale—the journey of a New Age Candide—exploring the dangers of uninvited programming. It even includes lessons on how to counter-program and reprogram destructive programming, be it from a cult leader, a relative, the Tobacco Institute, or yourself. Peter McWilliams explains what we can do to obtain and maintain our personal freedom—a difficult but rewarding task. 424 pages. **Hardcover,** $19.95.

Come Love With Me & Be My Life
The Complete Romantic Poetry of Peter McWilliams
Touching, direct, emotional, often funny, this is the best of Peter McWilliams's romantic poetry. 250 pages. **Hardcover,** $12.95. **Audio tapes** (unabridged, two cassettes, read by the author), $12.95.

I Marry You Because . . .
Poetry and quotations on love and marriage. 192 pages. **Trade paperback,** $5.95.

PORTRAITS: A Book of Photographs
The first published collection of Peter McWilliams's photographs, focuses on portraits of people. The book is a large format (9x12) and features more than 200 black & white and color photographs, exquisitely printed. 252 pages. **Hardcover,** $34.95.

To order any of these books,
please check your local bookstore, or call

1–800–LIFE–101

or write to

Prelude Press
8159 Santa Monica Boulevard
Los Angeles, California 90046

Please write or call for our free catalog!

Index

A

M

VICAR: *You know, Life—Life, is rather like opening a tin of sardines. We are all of us looking for the key. Some of us—some of us think we've found the key, don't we? We roll back the lid of the sardine tin of Life, we reveal the sardines, the riches of Life, therein and we get them out, we enjoy them. But, you know, there's always a little piece in the corner you can't get out. I wonder— I wonder, is there a little piece in the corner of your life? I know there is in mine.*